MAN'S ULTIMATE COMMITMENT

BOOKS BY THE SAME AUTHOR

Religious Experience and Scientific Method

The Wrestle of Religion with Truth

Methods of Private Religious Living

The Source of Human Good

The Directive in History

MAN'S ULTIMATE COMMITMENT

Henry Nelson Wieman

SOUTHERN ILLINOIS UNIVERSITY PRESS

CARBONDALE

To

L. M. W.

ACKNOWLEDGMENTS

Ideas developing for fifty years and more are derived from many sources. Hence my indebtedness to former teachers, to students and friends and colleagues and authors is too manifold to be specified here. But two persons have been most immediately helpful in the writing of this book. Professor Daniel Day Williams read with great care and detailed criticism a late version of the manuscript. Parts of the book I have rewritten under the stimulus of his suggestions. He stated the points on which he disagrees with me and matters which I have neglected. Doubtless these disagreements still stand. But his criticisms enabled me to correct statements and to develop some neglected themes. For the time and care he gave to the manuscript I am deeply grateful.

Mr. Raymond P. Fassel, editor on the staff of Southern Illinois University Press, has been indefatigable in the final preparation of the manuscript and in making constructive suggestions. He and Mr. Vernon A. Sternberg, director of the Press, have given such attention and consideration to the book that I want to express my gratitude to them.

H. N. W.

CONTENTS

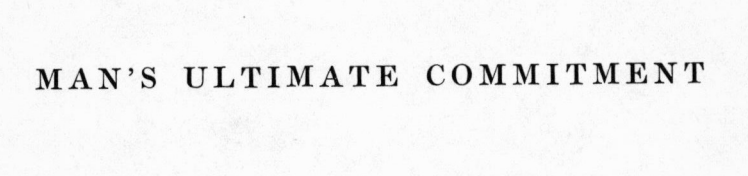

MAN'S ULTIMATE COMMITMENT

INTRODUCTION

CREATIVITY is the central theme of this book. Like every word in common usage, it has many meanings. Hence, to avoid confusion and misunderstanding I must specify here at the beginning the particular meaning which I attach to "creativity." First of all a negative statement is required to clear away a common meaning which I do not intend. By creativity I do not mean creative work whether in art or science or technology or social organization or in any other area of human achievement. To be sure, creative work may accompany the kind of creativity which I shall discuss. But I shall be examining not creative work but the creative transformation of the individual in the whole-ness of his being. Not the activity by which the individual pro-duces innovations, but the transformation of the individual him-self when this change is of the kind here called creative is what I mean by creativity.

Creative transformation of the individual is distinguished from every other kind of change by four characteristics. These four are not the only features pertaining to it, for creativity is very complex and in its depth fades into mystery. In the course of the writing which follows some of these other components of cre-ativity will be noted. But the four here to be mentioned will serve to distinguish this kind of transformation from other kinds.

Creativity is an expanding of the range and diversity of what the individual can know, evaluate, and control. Creativity is an increasing of his ability to understand appreciatively other persons and peoples across greater barriers of estrangement and hostility. Creativity is an increasing of the freedom of the individual when freedom means one's ability to absorb any cause acting on oneself in such a way that the consequences resulting from it express the character and fulfil the purpose of the individual himself. The way Socrates died is an example. His death expressed the character and fulfilled the purpose of Socrates much more than the character and the purpose of those who caused his death. The fourth component of the transformation here called creative can be described thus: Increasing the capacity of the individual to integrate into the uniqueness of his own individuality a greater diversity of experiences so that more of all that he encounters becomes a source of enrichment and strength rather than impoverishing and weakening him.

Examination of these four components of creativity will reveal that they involve one another and cannot be separated.

Creativity occurs when individuals engage in a kind of interchange with one another which is distinguished from every other interpersonal and social process by two features: [1] This kind of interchange creates appreciative understanding of the unique individuality of the other; [2] each individual who attains this appreciative understanding integrates into his own individuality what he thus acquires from others. What he thus acquires from others is not only knowledge; it is also all the values characterizing the individuality of the other so far as these are understood appreciatively and so far as they can be modified to develop the individuality of him who has attained this appreciative understanding of the other person. One who attains appreciative understanding of the errors and wrong valuings of the other has gained as much wisdom, strength, and resourcefulness for dealing with the exigencies of life as when he learns the truth and right valuings activating the lives of others. Right valuings are those which do not obstruct creative transformation.

Creativity and creative interchange should not be equated

with Christian love until this love has been purged of the evils commonly embodied in it. One loves those who help him uphold the false picture of himself into which his self-esteem has been tied. One loves those who strengthen the social bias by which one misjudges and practices injustice toward people belonging to alien cultures. One loves those who share his highest ideals and goals and thus help him to freeze these ends of life in their present limited form. This prevents the correction of error and evil in these goals and obstructs creative transformation. Even when one claims to love all men or every man or those who need his help, such love imposes judgments on others which are corrupted by the false basis of one's own self-esteem and by the cultural bias of his own tradition. Therefore love is here rejected as the highest standard unless "love" is identical with creativity and creative interchange. To quote Bruno Bettelheim, "Love is not enough."

I have tried to guard against two misunderstandings: one, that creativity refers to creative work; two, that creative interchange is identical with Christian love as Christian love is commonly understood and commonly practiced.

The title of this book reveals my conviction concerning the difference between philosophy and religion. Philosophy is ultimate concern. Religion is ultimate commitment and nothing less.

PART ONE

The Call to Commitment

Chapter 1

THE PROBLEM OF
RELIGIOUS FAITH

Religion like every other persistent and important concern in human life should be defined by the problem which it tries to solve. Also, like every other human undertaking which reaches into the basic issues of our existence, the beliefs and practices of religion are very far from being a complete and finished solution of this problem. In still another respect religion is like other essential and institutionalized interests of man. Most people who practice religion quite sincerely, like most people who practice the education, government, the family, and industry, are quite unaware of the basic problems of human existence which these beliefs and practices try to solve. Very often the beliefs and practices which are accepted as though they were solutions contain monstrous errors and evils.

The problem which religion tries to solve is exposed when we note two features which are characteristic of the human level of existence.

The first of these features generating the problem for religious inquiry is man's capacity for undergoing radical transformation. He can be transformed to the depths of cruelty and misery and to the heights of saintly virtue and blessedness. He can experience horror and boredom on the one hand; he can also experience ecstasy and a sense of glory which is faintly suggested by great music and other forms of high art.

The religious problem which is exposed when we look at this capacity of man for radical transformation can be stated thus: What can transform man in such a way as to save him from the depths of evil and bring him to the greatest good which human life can ever attain? This problem has its moral and its religious aspects and the two should not be confused. The moral aspect includes all which man can do to transform himself. The religious aspect is the self-giving of ultimate commitment to what the individual believes has the power to transform him as he cannot transform himself. It must not be forgotten, however, that this belief and the consequent commitment may be tragically mistaken. Often men commit themselves in religious faith to what they think will save from evil when in truth it does the opposite.

A second feature of human existence reveals the religious problem from another angle. It is man's awareness of his own original experience which is his own true self. This original experience stands in contrast to the superimposed patterns which are common to all members of the society and distinctive of none. Perhaps most people most of the time conceal from themselves the qualities of their own original experience. In place of these the conscious mind is occupied with the routine experiences of social adjustment which conceal the individuality of original experience beneath the demands of the social mechanism. By original experience is meant every experience which the individual can have when he does not conceal and overlay it with the drab qualities of conventional experience. The artist, when faithful to his true vocation, struggles to cast off these common patterns which conceal original experience. The parable of the child who alone could see that the king wore no clothes points to this contrast between original and conventional experience. In the parable about king and child the social conventions were so strong that people saw only what the conventions prescribed. The child alone was not blinded in this way.

This original experience is the individual as he truly is. It is his true self in contrast to the uniformities adopted by everyone in his society to facilitate the routine adjustments of everyday life. The dull and pallid qualities of conventionalized experience conceal the vivid qualities of original experience.

The religious problem arising out of this predicament can be stated thus: What shall I do to be saved from the death of my own true self under the suffocating imposition of this automatic and trivial existence? How must I live to realize my own potentialities? What ultimate commitment will bring forth to full flowering the original experience which is my genuine and total self? When one awakens to the reality of his original experience and its potentialities, the conventional patterns of social adjustment appear to be unreal, like shadows of that reality which original experience alone can apprehend. These conventional patterns are trivial and unheroic, without the greatness in living which one craves when original experience breaks through the crust of social convention. This suppression of original experience beneath trivial conventions has been given a name in the current discussions of our time. It is called meaninglessness. So the religious question emerges: What ultimate commitment will deliver me from the false and superficial level of life and enable me to live myself out to the full with whatsoever struggle and suffering and courage and ecstasy this may involve?

Two features of our existence have been mentioned which reveal two aspects of the religious problem. The one feature is man's capacity to undergo radical transformation and the other is his awareness of an original experience underlying conventional experience. The problem having these two aspects can now be stated: What operates in human life with such character and power that it will transform man as he cannot transform himself, to save him from the depths of evil and endow him with the greatest good, provided that he give himself over to it with whatsoever completeness of self-giving is possible for him?

This problem which is the primary concern of religion is very commonly misconceived. For example, religion is often presented in such a way as to make it appear that its chief concern is to believe in God. On this assumption people discuss such questions as these: Is it possible to believe in God by way of evidence or

authority or on some other basis? Is there a Being properly called
God? Such discussions miss the basic religious problem completely. The word "God" is irrelevant to the religious problem
unless the word is used to refer to *whatever in truth* operates to
save man from evil and to the greater good *no matter how much
this operating reality may differ from all traditional ideas about
it.* But this is not the common way of conceiving the problem.
Rather the question as commonly conceived is this: Is there anything in reality corresponding to some conventional idea of God?
When undertaken in this way, the discussion is as remote from
the basic problem in religion as one can get. The basic problem
is to find and commit oneself to what does in truth save from
evil and to the good even though it be different from the belief
about it which happens to possess the mind at the time, or happens to prevail in the tradition I inherit. The word "God" should
refer to what actually operates to save and not merely to some
belief *about* what operates in this way. But in current usage the
word frequently refers to pictures in the mind and not to the
actuality. This raises the question whether one should use the
word at all since a word becomes very misleading when it has
acquired a conventional meaning contrary to what one wishes to
discuss. On the other hand, there is no other word in our language
which conveys the meaning of central concern in the religious
problem. Hence the dilemma in which anyone is placed who attempts to discuss the problem which religion tries to solve.

There is another common attitude which conceals the true
significance of the religious problem. It is the assumption that
the solution of this problem can be found by searching that body
of religious tradition which happens to prevail in one's religious
fellowship. This procedure may be modified by searching all the
great religious traditions of the world. This certainly should be
done; but it leads to dangerous falsehoods if it springs from the
mistaken notion that this problem has been already solved so
perfectly that no further inquiry is needed except to understand
the truth already established in one or in all religious traditions.
That notion is as foolish in religion as it would be in education

or government or family. None of these problems has been so completely and finally solved that we need only to recover the truth already discovered in some ancient time.

The religious problem involves other questions additional to the one which has been stated, although these other questions are subsidiary to the central one. Three of these subsidiary questions are: What is the evil from which man needs to be saved? What is the good to which he can be saved? What are the conditions which must be met before this saving power can operate effectively? All these will be discussed in the following pages but something more needs to be said at this point concerning the evil from which salvation is sought.

In one aspect this evil is the inner conflict by which the self is divided into parts which war against one another. When one of these warring parts of the total self is dominant I seek with avid passion what is rejected with contempt or horror or disgust when some other part of the total self possesses the conscious mind. One classic expression of this inner conflict is often quoted: What I would not, that I do.

This conflict within the total self may drive a man to acts of cruelty or to self-destructive passions. These cruelties and passions can become compulsive under the stress of keeping down within oneself the rebellion against them from some other part of the total self. Or again this inner conflict may torment one to the point of despair or produce an apathy akin to death or a frenzy of wild dissipation.

A second aspect of this evil from which one needs to be saved is the sense of triviality, futility, and unendurable boredom already mentioned which possesses the mind when one awakens to the contrast between his original experience with its potentialities and its freedom over against the mechanisms of adjustment demanded by an impersonal social order. Awareness of this contrast can drive to all the excesses which inner conflict engenders. Perhaps most men most of the time keep this contrast between original experience and conventional experience out of consciousness by concentrated preoccupation with the mechanisms of adjustment;

but this can lead to spiritual death when spiritual death means the dying out of original experience and the resolving of the self into a system of mechanized adjustments.

Another aspect of this same evil appears when we examine the guilt which accumulates and multiplies from an initial guilt. The initial guilt is the refusal of responsibility for the preservation and development of the true self in the form of original experience.

This initial guilt can be stated in various ways. It is the guilt of refusing to decide what one shall live for. It is the guilt of ignoring the question: What should be the ruling aim of my existence? It is refusal to make ultimate commitment to what can both unify the self and develop all its constructive potentialities. It is refusal to assume responsibility for the conduct of one's life. It is to drift with circumstance instead of uniting all one's resources to achieve what one is best fitted to accomplish.

This evasion of responsibility leads to self-deception, futilities, failures, blindness to opportunity for greatness and nobility. It can bring forth all the other evils which we are examining. In this way the initial guilt can multiply itself into a mountain of guilt.

The fourth aspect of this evil from which man needs to be saved is loneliness. Harry Stack Sullivan in consequence of his work in psychiatry claims that this evil of loneliness is more unendurable than any other.[1] Therefore people try to conceal it from consciousness by every possible device and sacrifice. One becomes aware of this loneliness when he awakens to the fact that people recognize in him only the conventional patterns of adjustment to society and not the original experience which is himself. These conventional patterns conceal his true self. Hence the individual in his true character is ignored. He is a blank nothing so far as concerns the other person if the other recognizes in him only the conventional forms.

We have looked at four aspects of the evil from which men need to be saved. They are not four evils but four ways of looking at the same evil. Summarized they are: inner conflict, futility or meaninglessness, guilt, and loneliness. The concentration camps of the Nazis and other evils of like sort occurring throughout the expanse of human history are the outward manifestations of this inner condition "of the human heart." These horrors are what men do when they are driven by inner conflicts, when they strive to escape from the futility and boredom of social conventions which suppress the freedom and power of original experience; when guilt begins to multiply itself, when loneliness leads to desperate efforts to liberate the hidden self and make it recognized by others.

The problem of religion is to discover what will deliver man from this evil deep laid within the human personality or, if it cannot be cast out, then somehow to bring it under control and, if possible, make it the servant of the good. In religion men seek to commit themselves to what has the power to master the evil within them which they cannot master themselves.

A baffling part of this religious problem emerges after the initial steps have been taken toward its solution. This further difficulty is encountered when men discover that they cannot commit themselves completely and perfectly to what might deliver them from evil. They cannot free themselves from all inner resistances to the commitment. Always to some degree they are unfaithful in the depths and complexities of the total self. In the language of the Christian tradition, this unfaithfulness to the ultimate commitment is called sin. In this case the problem is not to get rid of this sin, since that is impossible, but to treat it so that it will not be an insuperable barrier to what can save and transform. The overcoming of this barrier is called the forgiveness of sin.

These two words, "sin" and "forgiveness," carry many meanings which I do not wish to defend. Here again we encounter the difficulty of language in using ancient words which have acquired many grotesque meanings but which yet seem to be the only words established in current usage for dealing with profound and inescapable problems. I must make plain the meaning I attach to these terms.

The forgiving of sin refers to what causes that change in the sinner which enables him to confess freely and fully his guilt and unfaithfulness, condemning them as evil, and doing it in such a way that this repentance intensifies his devotion and the completeness of his commitment. His unfaithfulness and hence his sin continue; but his confession of it and his condemnation of it serve to make his commitment more complete. Not his sin, but his confession and repudiation of his sin, become positive factors in bringing his total self more completely under the control of what saves and transforms. In this manner his unfaithfulness ceases to be a barrier between himself and what commands his ultimate commitment. By the ardor and sincerity of his confession and repentance he has nullified its power to separate him from what saves.

This raises the question: What can cause this change in the sinner whereby his sin is no longer a barrier to his salvation? On this point I disagree with many traditional answers to this question. The answer must be found by empirical inquiry into what actually does bring about such a change. I can find no evidence for the claim that a declaration of forgiveness by a supernatural person can bring about such a change, whether that declaration is granted freely or must be purchased by the blood and suffering and death of Christ or by any of the other kinds of sacrifice practiced in the various religions.

I shall try to show that the change enabling an individual to recognize, confess, and repent of his sin is brought about by what I shall later describe as creative interchange. It occurs when the individual finds one or more persons with whom he can engage in that kind of interchange which creates in each an awareness of the original experience of the other person and at the same time a recognition of the exceeding preciousness of this original experience even though it includes all the sin and evil we have been describing. When individuals engage in the kind of interchange which creates in each this recognition and understanding of the unique individuality of one another, including both the good and the evil, and when this interchange is sufficiently penetrating and persistent, each becomes able to recognize, confess, and repent of his own sin because he sees himself as the other sees him.

This claim that forgiveness is brought about by creative interchange is based on the reports of psychological studies made in the field of clinical psychology and the various branches of psychotherapy. It is also based upon studies which have been made of cases of religious conversion. When members of the Salvation Army or of a church receive a sinner with this appreciative recognition of his individuality, not condoning the evil in him, rather recognizing it in its true character, but accepting him nevertheless and giving him that kind of esteem which goes by the name of respect, this change can occur enabling the individual to confess, repent, and repudiate his sin. One dramatic portrayal of this in fiction is the conversion of Jean Valjean after he stole the silver candlesticks from the priest, as told by Victor Hugo in *Les Misérables*.

Since "forgiveness of sin" is the name I give to what causes this change which renders sin no longer a barrier to salvation even though the sin continues, and since this cause is creative interchange, therefore creative interchange is what forgives sin. This cause rendering sin no longer an insuperable barrier does not reside in the participant individuals who engage in creative interchange. Rather it resides in the creativity of this interchange because this is what creates in each that which enables the sinner to confess and repent and repudiate his sin.

So we reach the conclusion: The forgiveness of sin, namely, the cause producing in the individual the ability to confess and repent, is the creativity occurring in this kind of interchange between individuals. The forgiveness is not the work of the individuals concerned; it is the work of this kind of interchange. If this kind of creative interchange is equivalent to the work of God in human life, then the forgiveness of sin is the work of God and not of man. It produces the change whereby sin, while still continuing, no longer blocks the commitment of faith which is required for salvation.

After this analysis and interpretation of the evil from which man needs to be saved, let me restate the problem which concerns religion in five propositions to bring out the major points of the discussion.

The religious problem is to discover and give oneself in ultimate commitment to what will overcome the conflict of warning
parts within the self.

It is to give oneself in ultimate commitment to what will save
original experience from suffocation beneath the blanket of conventional experience so that one can develop the constructive
potentialities of his own unique individuality.

It is to give oneself to what will stop the indefinite accumulation of guilt issuing from the initial guilt of refusing to assume
responsibility for the conduct of one's life.

It is to give oneself in ultimate commitment to what will overcome loneliness by creating appreciative understanding of the
original experience of one another.

It is to find what will forgive sin so that sin will not be a barrier
excluding one from the saving and transforming power which
delivers from evil.

At the risk of repetition I must again state that this problem
thus formulated under five heads is never solved completely and
perfectly. It calls for continuing inquiry both at the level of abstract intellectual search going by the name of theology and
philosophy, and also at the level of practical, concrete daily living, where one critically examines his conduct and his state of
mind to discover how better to solve this religious problem.

This problem may be more clearly discerned if we examine
three different kinds of religion. They can be called the religion
of mental illness, the religion of conformity, and the religion of
creativity. All of these can be found in the various branches of
Christianity and in all the other religions of the world, hence
they cut across the major divisions by which religions and sects
are classified.

In the religion of mental illness we find beliefs which are
compulsive in the sense that they resist all modification by evidence or reason. The individual may profess a divine mission
utterly beyond the capacity of any human being. He may even
identify himself with Jesus Christ or God or some other religious
figure. Nevertheless, this is genuine religion because the individual is striving to resolve the conflict of warring parts within him-

self, trying to save his original experience from the deadening imposition of social demands, trying to stop the accumulation of guilt, trying to find some escape from intolerable loneliness and to attain forgiveness of sin. These attempts may be failures but, as said repeatedly, many attempts to solve the religious problem are failures more or less.

While this kind of religion is called the religion of mental illness it is not confined to the mental hospitals. It may be widely prevalent in the churches and also outside the churches. Perhaps we all have a streak of it because the three kinds of religion we are considering can reside together in the same individual in varying proportions. Mental illness like all kinds of illness can have all degrees of seriousness and in minor degrees is widely prevalent.

The second kind of religion in this classification is the religion of conformity. In this kind the individual does not cling compulsively to his religious beliefs and practices. This distinguishes his faith from that of the mentally ill. But he who adopts the religion of conformity does not examine his faith critically. No valid evidence may support his beliefs and justify his religious practices. He accepts them from his associates, from the authorities recognized by his fellowship of faith, and from the prevailing tradition. The chief feature of this kind of religion is the lack of any critical examination of the faith and unconcern for any inquiry or validating evidence beyond the accepted authorities and the consensus of opinion of the fellowship.

Until recent times in Western culture this religion of conformity has been by far the most common. While not so widely prevalent today it is still the dominant kind of religion. Throughout history it has been the chief agency in causing individuals to conform to the demands of the social order and the ruling authorities. This power to induce conformity derives not merely from fear of divine punishment, although that doubtless has always been present. But its penetrating and comprehensive power to bring the individual into conformity arises from the basic human problem which this kind of religion attempts to solve; and in some form or other, however inadequately, does solve. The

individual conforms to the faith because it helps him to suppress
or overcome his inner conflicts; it saves him from the pettiness
of conventional existence by giving him a sense of participation
in the destiny, the memory, the hope, and the worship of his
associates; it enables him to confess and repent and repudiate his
own unfaithfulness.

In addition to the two kinds of religion thus far examined is
the third kind, the religion of creativity. In it the individual commits himself to what creates his own original experience in depth
and fulness and vividness of quality; while it releases the individual from conformity it creates recognition of original experience
between individuals and thus reduces loneliness; it enables the
individual to master his inner conflicts to the measure that his
commitment is complete; it stops the indefinite accumulation of
guilt and brings about the change in the individual which is
caused by forgiveness of sin with the consequence that he is able
to recognize, confess, and repudiate his sin of unfaithfulness.

Throughout this writing I shall endeavor to interpret this religion of creativity because I think it goes farther than do the
other kinds in solving the religious problem.

Any discussion of the religious problem calls for an interpretation of "faith." As the term is here used it is identical with ultimate commitment. Faith is the act by which the individual commits himself in the wholeness of his being so far as he can to what
he believes will transform man as he cannot transform himself
to save him from evil and endow him with the greatest good,
provided that he meet the required conditions. The chief of
these required conditions is the act of faith itself. Obviously one
is incapable of the act of faith until influences have worked upon
him which render him able to give himself in whole hearted devotion to what he believes to be the saving power. In this sense
faith depends upon "grace."

What has just been said about faith can be put in more conventional language by saying that faith means to accept the
Saviour as Lord and Master. These words immediately suggest
a very popular and conventional form of Christianity. But the
same words apply to all forms of religion when "Saviour" refers

to *whatever* the individual may believe has the power to save from evil and when "accepting as Lord and Master" means to give priority over all else in one's daily life to the demands of this saving agency.

Faith always extends far beyond present knowledge, not necessarily in the sense that one claims to know what he does not know, but in the sense of commitment to what is much more than one's present understanding of it and in some respects likely to be very different from one's beliefs about it. It is easy to demonstrate that every concrete reality is more than, and in some respects different from, any statement which the human mind can make about it. All statements are abstractions.

In the religion of creativity, faith is based upon knowledge gained by intellectual inquiry and tested by predicted consequences under specified conditions. But at the same time faith reaches beyond the bounds of knowledge because one acknowledges that there is very much which he does not know about the reality to which he commits himself. Also one admits that his knowledge in respect to this religious problem is fallible like all knowledge. He aims at what can save from evil and endow with greatest good but his aim may miss the mark. Nevertheless, while his knowledge may fail, his intention is to commit himself with the wholeness of his being to what does in truth save from evil.

By reason of the mysteries which encompass our existence, one's religious commitment should take on a dual character, on the one hand guided by the farthest reach of his inquiry, on the other practiced as a faith in the sense of recognizing his liability to error and the tragic consequences of error in such a commitment as this. A man's religious devotion becomes a form of pernicious idolatry leading to dogmatic fanaticism and blind cruelty if he does not practice his ultimate commitment in this dual manner, on the one hand seeking the best knowledge he can get, on the other recognizing his fallibility and accepting the consequences of it. This dual character of religious commitment is required because otherwise one is committed to the limitations of his own mind. Nothing is worthy of man's ultimate commitment which is confined to the limits of his present comprehension, not to mention the malice and perversity always present to some degree in all human interpretations of the good and evil of human life.

Since the problem of man's ultimate commitment is so difficult and exposed to such tragic error, many refuse to make any profound commitment of faith. But when one does this he is nevertheless caught willy-nilly in some process of transformation and thereby backs blindly into his own fate without using his mind to find his way. Also when one does not give himself in full devotion to anything whatsoever, he inhibits, frustrates, or anaesthetizes himself because the whole self can be expressed and exercised only to the measure that one commits his whole self in faith. The ultimate commitment of faith in the religion of creativity is the only way to escape spiritual death when "spiritual death" means failure to live with the vivid qualities of original experience, with the full exercise of personal resources and with realization of one's constructive potentialities and with a deep sense of the worthfulness of life.

Creative interchange is that kind of interchange which creates in those who engage in it an appreciative understanding of the original experience of one another. One gets the view point of the other under such conditions that this original view derived from the other integrates with one's own personal resources. This integration modifies the view derived from the other in such a way that it becomes a part of one's own original experience. The understanding of the evils and errors in oneself and in others, brought about by creative interchange, will be prized as highly as the understanding of the virtues and the truths, because the understanding of errors and evils in human life is as great a good as to understand the virtues and the truths. Indeed to *understand* evil and error is itself virtue and truth.

Creative interchange has two aspects which are the two sides of the same thing. One aspect is the understanding in some measure of the original experience of the other person. The other aspect is the integration of what one gets from others in such a way as to create progressively the original experience which is oneself. This creative interchange creates the unique individuality of each person while at the same time enabling each to understand the individuality of others. Again I must repeat that all this is partial, incomplete, infected with error and distortion. Nevertheless it can be more or less complete, comprehensive, and correct.

The adjective "appreciative" attached to the understanding gained by creative interchange signifies that one prizes the original experience of the other as being very precious. The original experience of the other is highly prized because, for one thing, nothing contributes so much to the enrichment of any man's life as what he gets from the original experience of other people. It should be remembered that original experience is distinguished from the clichés, the stale conventions, and the automatic reactions which everyone reproduces in himself in order to adjust to the established order. Furthermore, the original experience of the other person is prized so highly because it is precisely this prizing of the original experience, namely the individuality of the other person, which is created by this kind of interchange. Creative interchange is not limited to the acquisition of information alone. One also gets from others appreciations, sentiments, hopes, fears, memories, regrets, aspirations, joys, sorrows, hates, loves, pieties, and other features of that vast complexity which makes up the total experience of every human being.

Creative communication in its most complete form is never fully attained although human nature craves it no matter how much conscious purpose may oppose it. In its most complete form it can be described thus: You express your whole self and your entire mind freely and fully and deeply and truly to other persons who understand you most completely and appreciatively with joy in what you are as so expressed; and you yourself respond to others who express themselves freely and fully and deeply and truly while you understand them most completely and appreciatively with joy in the spirits they are.

Over against creative interchange and opposing it are several other kinds of interchange. First is deceptive communication. This is the kind by which one conceals from his own consciousness and the consciousness of others what he does not want to recognize because it might break down his self-esteem or because it is dangerous or horrible or otherwise disturbing. To be able to preserve his sense of security, to be able to hold up his head among his fellows, to avoid neurosis and despair or other form of breakdown, everyone practices devices of concealment and deception in interchange with others. Obviously this is the opposite of creative interchange. Nevertheless it is one very large part of the social process.

Next is manipulative communication. In extreme form it is brainwashing. In milder form it is called propaganda or indoctrination in the derogatory sense of these terms. It is interchange by which one person tries to inhibit or suppress the thoughts and feelings of the other in so far as they run counter to what one wants to communicate. Instead of your communication integrating with the mind of the other and thereby increasing the resources of his mind, you use methods to inhibit the mind of the other so that you can control him. Hypnotism is an extreme form. Manipulative communication is thus seen to be opposed to creative interchange. Yet manipulative interchange is another large section of the social process.

Thirdly there is reiterative communication. In communication of this kind one does not communicate anything new nor receive anything new. He only gives and takes the signals by which the complexities of life are regulated. A very large part of the social process is of this sort. Commands, greetings, regulations, innumerable forms of interchange add almost nothing to the store of the mind but serve to regulate conduct and simplify what would otherwise be hopeless complexity. Traffic signals are a simple example.

Fourth is muddleheaded communication. In this kind of interchange one picks up all sorts of odds and ends, but the miscellany is not integrated. It is not creative. It tends to diminish the range and depth of what one can know, feel, and control because of preoccupation with trivialities. Here again we have a large segment of the social process.

Finally there is that kind of interchange which characterizes what David Riesman calls the "other-directed person."² In this kind of communication the individual puts on a false front which he changes whenever he meets different people and different situations in order to be pleasing or "get by."

I am not trying to analyze the social process into all the many different kinds of interchange which enter into it. I am sure that many other kinds could be added to this list. I am only trying to show how creative interchange is distinguished from the social process taken in its entirety. All these different kinds of interchange are woven together like so many strands of a rope. It is this rope, not the one strand of it called creative interchange, which can be called the social process.

When creative communication is understood I think it becomes obvious that it cannot be manipulated. "Creative" as here used means the emergence in the mind of what was not there before. But to manipulate one must have an aim or goal from the start which he tries to achieve by the manipulation. The outcome of creativity cannot be in the mind from the start. Therefore when-ever one practices manipulative interchange to produce an out-come which he has in mind from the start, the process is not crea-tive. To be sure, creative interchange and manipulative inter-change may be going on at the same time in the one single total process of communication between one and another person. The manipulative interchange may produce the end result sought by the manipulator but at the same time he may derive from the other insights and appreciations which never entered his mind before. In that case both the manipulative and the creative are combined in the social process then and there occurring.

Creative interchange provides the standard for judging what is good and what is evil in human life. The good is what sustains, promotes or favors the creation of appreciative understanding between individuals and peoples. The evil is what hinders or prevents this kind of interchange.

This standard is based on an interpretation of what creates in man all which is distinctively human. What is distinctively human includes the creation and use of a language with consequent ac-quisition of a tradition and culture accumulated through a sequence of generations. Language itself is created by the sort of interchange in which we detect what is in the mind of the other. Otherwise sounds could never become words in common usage. This kind of interchange makes it possible for individuals, peoples, generations, and cultures to learn from one another with that freedom and fulness which give to man all his distinctive attainments. Without this mutual learning and accumulation of knowledge, appreciations, skills, habits, customs, sentiments, aspirations, loyalties, loves, and pieties, the unprotected organism of man could not survive. Without this mutual learning there could be no tradition, no culture, no civilization, no science, no art, no ideals, no life at all at the level distinctively human.

Only by creative interchange is it possible for the individual to become self-critical and self-esteeming because in this way he learns what others think of him and thus becomes conscious of himself. Love in the sense of an appreciative understanding and cherishing of other persons, also love in the sense of a recognition of the unknown and unsearched depth of subjectivity residing in every human being, and love in the sense of deference and deep concern for this hidden subjectivity in every human person, all this is generated and progressively created to the measure that one is fully committed to creative interchange and allows it to dominate over other kinds in his life.

This is the answer which I suggest to the searching question of religious faith. The kind of interchange which generates appreciative understanding, with all the unsearched mystery in it, calls for the ultimate commitment of man because it saves him from the processes which impoverish and destroy the distinctive characteristics of his humanity. When he commits himself to it and meets other required conditions, it transforms him in the direction of the fullest development of his humanity and what lies beyond the merely human if there be such.

It will be said that man's destiny involves far more than creative interchange. That is true, but a certain misunderstanding must be avoided.

Certainly the depth and fulness of the Being in which we find our ultimate stay and trust may be far beyond anything covered in any account which can be given of creative interchange. But all we know of such a Being and all we can ever discover about such a Being must come by way of the creativity which widens and deepens our understanding and appreciation of what others have experienced and discovered and which then in turn enables us to understand our own experience. Such being the case, creative interchange must in any case command our ultimate commitment, whatever else may also be involved, and whatever may be the character of any Being to which it leads us.

Most of the people who hold to the idea of God claim that they know God by way of revelation and reject any idea of God not so derived because God in his saving and transforming power cannot be known in any way except by revelation. Therefore, say these people, any idea of God not received by way of revelation is a man-made God, not only false and idolatrous but also ridiculous because it is a human construction set up in the guise of deity. Since the common religious idea of God is thus tied up with belief in revelation, the idea of God and the idea of revelation cannot well be separated. This makes it necessary to examine the idea of revelation.

The idea of revelation has undergone great changes, especially in recent years. What the great majority of Christians in the past have called revelation is now rejected by contemporary theologians and a different interpretation proclaimed.

The "contemporary theologians" who are distinctively the outstanding leaders of the church in our time declare that revelation is not to be identified with any set of doctrines or beliefs or propositions of any kind. Revelation, say they, is not propositional. Revelation is the self-disclosure of the living reality of God, but no set of propositions can be identified with the living reality of God. God is much more than a true statement. This is almost unanimously the teaching of theologians in the higher seats of learning.

If revelation is not any set of propositions, then what can it be? Obviously it must be a creative transformation of human life occurring under such conditions that men become aware of the transforming power. For example, if it should be granted that

Deity is incarnate in Jesus Christ, this could not be a revelation to men unless it was at the same time a creative transformation of human life branching out from Jesus to his associates and from them to others in widening circles and onward to later generations. If this is revelation, then revelation cannot be a set of true propositions, otherwise called doctrines, about a divine life incarnate on earth. The revelation of God must be and can only be the very process of human life undergoing transformation in such a way that it saves man from evil and endows him with the greatest good. Unless one experiences this process of transformation in himself "the power of God unto salvation" has not been revealed to him. The historic Jesus can be the revelation of God only in the sense that his process of saving transformation spreads from Jesus down through the ages from man to man and group to group by way of the church and the Holy Spirit. But this kind of transformation is precisely what we mean by creative interchange. To what degree it originated in Jesus or is limited to that origin must be determined by historical research, as is any other assertion about events in history.

Creative interchange as here interpreted has many of the characteristics attributed to God in the Christian and other traditions. On the other hand many characteristics attributed to Deity it does not have. It is not supernatural *unless* by this term one means that it is the manifestation in human life of a Being whose total character is beyond the reach of human understanding and which confronts us with a mystery so deep that the human mind can never penetrate it very far. If one understands "supernatural" in this sense, then creative interchange between persons and peoples may be called supernatural.

This creativity is not a person for the very good reason that it works at the deepest roots of human personality to create, sustain, save, and transform as no mere person could ever do. For the same reason it cannot be limited in the way the human mind is limited. If one wishes to say that it is a "person" and a "mind" but with characteristics different from those of a human mind, then I suppose there is no harm in using such words provided it is understood that we do not mean "mind" and "person" in the sense in which these words apply to human beings. Certainly most people will symbolize this saving power in personal terms and do so quite properly because no better symbol is available to them.

I shall frequently be using the terms "it" and "thing" in referring to this creativity. It has become popular to insist that God is not a thing. It is true that the word "thing" is sometimes used to refer to what is less than human. But the word is also used to refer to anything which happens to be under discussion. The word is used in this sense in the sentence preceding and this is a common and perfectly proper usage. We all speak of "anything" and "everything" and in this usage nothing whatsoever can be excluded from what "thing" can designate, whether it be God or man, the Power of Being or the supernatural or anything else. So also with the pronoun "it." "It" is also used as the only pronoun we have which can refer to anything whatsoever, without limitation to physical or spiritual, personal or superpersonal. We encounter the limitations of language in dealing with these profound problems and so are forced to use very inadequate language.

The characteristics which creative communication has in common with those generally attributed to God can now be briefly listed. No attempt to demonstrate them will be undertaken at this point but some of them will be obvious and others will be discussed in following chapters. The first four of these have already been stated repeatedly. Creative communication *creates* the human mind and personality. The first beginnings of the human mind upon this planet must have emerged by way of this kind of interchange creating a language and with a language a tradition cumulatively developed through a series of generations. With this would come all the other characteristics of the human mind. In this sense "Adam" was created by creative communication. Also, as said before, without this kind of interchange with others no infant can develop the kind of mind called human.

This kind of interchange *sustains* life at the human level and without its continuous operation human beings could not continue to exist. It *saves* man from the worst which can happen to him on condition of faith when faith means commitment to it and not merely accepting the truth of a proposition. It transforms, that is to say, *saves unto* the best that man can ever attain, again on condition of faith and other required conditions which are the fruits of faith.

It is what is sinned against when sin is understood to be [1] original sin, in a sense shortly to be explained, [2] spiritual death, [3] pride and rebellion against what creates, sustains, saves, and transforms, [4] unfaithfulness to our commitment. In theological language sin is anything in the human personality which resists the saving and transforming power of God and for which human beings are responsible. If creative interchange be what creates, sustains, saves, and transforms, then sin appears as this resistance to creativity. This resistance is called original sin when it is acquired from the parents and other associates at the very beginning of the development of the human mind.[3] The psychology of personality, especially neo-Freudian psychology, provides ample evidence of original sin in this sense. Sin in the other three senses will be discussed in the following pages.

Commitment to creative interchange requires confession and repentance of sin. Creative interchange provides forgiveness of sin in the way which has been explained. Without confession and repentance of sin and its forgiveness the individual cannot be saved from spiritual death nor unto that creative transformation which is abundant life. He cannot because without these he cannot commit himself to what saves and transforms.

Religious commitment to this creativity requires worship in the form of rituals, symbols, and public assembly because worship brings the individual and the group more completely under the control of their ultimate commitment. It is the way people deepen their commitment and recover its strength when it weakens.

Creative communication answers prayer when prayer is understood to be worship plus petition; when petition is understood to be the outreaching of the total person after some good appropriate to him; when his worship conjoined with this outreaching has brought the individual more completely under the transforming power of creative interchange with others and with the environment generally.

Creative transformation performs miracles when miracle is understood to be a happening for human good which could not occur according to the order of things previously established but which now does occur because this order has been transformed. The order of the world relative to the human mind is transformed by creative interchange. By transforming the human mind relative to the environment and therefore the environment relative to the human mind, along with like transformation of interpersonal relations between individuals and peoples, events can occur which were impossible prior to such transformation.

Creative communication carries the promise of "the kingdom of God" by reason of its potential widening and deepening of appreciative understanding and sharing of resources between persons and peoples; its potential increase of qualitative richness; its potential increase beyond any known limit of mutual control and love as over against authoritarian control. It carries punishment for sin. This punishment occurs in the life of the individual, in society, and in history. It gives meaning to history as will be explained in the last two chapters.

In one special sense creative communication creates the universe. It does so in the sense that it makes possible whatever experience men are able to have of the universe. It creates the human mind and in that way creates the world relative to the human mind. To be sure, the world men experience would be very different if creative communication were not obstructed and its products corrupted by the sin of opposing forms of communication such as the deceptive, manipulative, and muddleheaded along with the malice, prejudice, pride, apathy, and other sins which corrupt the world. Nevertheless there would be no world at all relative to the human mind were it not for creative communication which makes it possible for the mind to experience a world.

Creative communication does what man cannot do, not in the sense of having a power quantitatively greater, but in the sense of having a power qualitatively different from the power of man. For example, man cannot think until interchange has created in him the ability to think; he cannot serve a high ideal until such an ideal has been created in his mind by this interchange with others; he cannot love what he hates until he has been transformed by this creativity in such a way that he loves where once vindictive hate ruled his mind. So with other developments and gifts. This does not mean that man has no power and no responsibility. On the contrary, man has increasing power and ever-increasing responsibility to provide the conditions required for the qualitatively different power of this creativity in his life.

Creative communication is the reality experienced in the great moments of the great mystics. This will be discussed in Chapter 4.

Creative communication generates moral obligation, is the source of the moral law, and gives to the moral law its authority and its sanctions. The moral law which issues from it might be stated thus: Act in every situation in such a way as to provide conditions most favorable for creative communication and appreciative understanding among all parties concerned.

Some may think that deepest and fullest appreciative understanding of other ways of life and other faiths different from their own cuts the nerve of missionary zeal. Quite the opposite is the case. The world is dominated by faiths, institutions, and ways of life which obstruct or prevent this kind of interchange which creates appreciative understanding among people. Therefore commitment to this kind of interchange generates zeal to convert others to this commitment and to change the ways and institutions which obstruct this kind of interchange, not to the end of uniformity but to the end of removing the barriers to fuller appreciation of diversities. Unless this is done, uniformity is the only other alternative in the world as it is now developing. This point will be elaborated in the next chapter.

Creative communication created the Christian church in the early days of Christianity and gives to the church its mission of evangelism, preaching, worship, counseling, and other forms of service. This will be more fully discussed in Chapter 8.

To him who commits himself to it most completely, creative communication provides peace, courage, consolation, and renewal of mind. To be sure, one is exposed to anxiety when he assumes responsibility for himself and others and faces up to the realities of human existence. There is a kind of peace sought by casting off responsibility and practicing the devices of evasion, distraction, and concealment. Over against this kind of peace based on deception is the kind which one must have in order to be able to assume full responsibility and face reality and endure whatever anguish is thereby incurred. This sustaining kind of peace is found when one gives himself quite completely to what satisfies the deepest and most comprehensive need of human nature. One finds this satisfaction of his nature in what creates, sustains, saves, and develops in man what is distinctively human. With this satisfaction attained through commitment to creativity, one can be deeply engaged in the troubles and responsibilities of life and yet have a sustaining peace. Without this, one cannot endure the heavier responsibilities nor face reality. He must either develop a callous indifference or refuse to assume the burdens rightly falling to him.

This peace can at times become ecstatic when anguish drives one to cease the struggle to protect his own false judgments about himself against humiliating evidence, either by trying to deny it, trying to conceal it, or trying to evade it by a pretended humility. These rare moments may never come to a person who is not driven by unendurable anguish to cast off all pretenses and simply give himself completely to be sustained or destroyed by the creativity which makes him human. But when this occurs there wells up into consciousness the ecstatic peace which this commitment can provide.

One last characteristic should be mentioned which creative communication has in common with those traditionally attributed to God. It takes the initiative in bringing on religious conversion. When Saul the Pharisee is changed to Paul the Christian, or Augustine the debater to Augustine the saint, the record of what actually happened indicates that creative interchange produced the transformation.

After listing all these characteristics in which creative communication is like God as traditionally conceived, may I say again and emphasize by repetition: This creativity which works between people in the form of interchange, and also within each individual, may be only a shallow, superficial manifestation of an infinite Being of mystery. It may be that this Being in its whole-ness is what creates, sustains, saves, and transforms human life toward the greater good. But obviously we can make no state-ment about that mystery except to acknowledge it, precisely be-cause it is a mystery. On the other hand, the creativity here under consideration can be known and studied and therefore can guide our commitment. Also it is knowable in the sense that we can find out many of the conditions which must be present for it to operate with power in human life. Thus it can be a guide in our conduct of human life in all areas: political, industrial, sexual, educational, scientific, artistic, in customs, courtesy, and care of the body.

Furthermore it should be noted that as the several forms of efficiency increase, human life becomes increasingly resistant to this saving and transforming power unless there is a proportion-ate increase in the intelligent practice of religious commitment to it. The several forms of efficiency which generate these resistances when religious commitment is not effectively and intelligently practiced are the following:

1] efficiency in controlling and directing society in any way the ruling group may desire;

2] efficiency in subordinating sexuality to pleasure without fur-ther involvement in the major responsibilities of life;

3] efficiency in the acquisition of wealth and in the increase of comfort, luxury, and leisure without any further overruling purpose;

4] efficiency in the exercise of violence and other forms of force by the military and the police without other purpose than either to defend the established order or to serve the will of the rulers;

5] efficiency in providing entertainment which diverts and dis-tracts but does not deepen insight into the realities with which man must struggle;

6] efficiency in the use of language and other symbols of com-munication to shape the mind and exercise control over others but not to deepen appreciative understanding of one another's motives and needs;

7] efficiency in organizing intellectual inquiry to serve the ends just listed but not primarily to understand what is good and what is evil, what is right and what is wrong, and what is the direction human life should take to reach the greatest good it can attain.

These are the dangers which threaten us today and these are the dangers from which we can be saved by commitment to the creativity which calls for religious faith. These dangers we shall now examine.

Chapter 2

FROM DRIFT TO DIRECTION

Drift and direction are here understood in a very special sense. Human life shows direction when controlled by some over-all agreement concerning what good is of such great value that striving after it with effort and suffering and fortitude is generally esteemed worth-while and is commended. Human life is adrift when not controlled by any such agreement. The agreement and consequent direction may be negative in the sense that people conform to a common way of life to avoid the danger and suffering of conflict, either among themselves or with an external enemy. On the other hand, the agreement and consequent direction may be positive in the sense of co-operative seeking for a good which all regard as having greatest value but which requires conflict and reconstruction to attain.

Agreement and co-operation under some ruling directive does not necessarily impose uniformity. The agreement and the directive might be to help each individual, or at least liberate each individual, to develop to the utmost degree his own capacity for appreciation and constructive action. Since appreciation and constructive action as here used are inseparable, I shall henceforth speak only of appreciation with the understanding that constructive action is included.

It is here argued that the good in human life which has greatest value is the development to the highest degree possible in each individual of his capacity to appreciate most profoundly and comprehensively everything which his mind is able to appreci-ate.

The good just stated requires radical and progressive transfor-mation of each individual continuously throughout his life or so long as he is able to undergo such transformation. Therefore the greatest good is to undergo that kind of transformation which enables the human mind to appreciate most profoundly and com-prehensively everything appreciable. The same thing can be said more simply: The good in human life which has greatest value is love. But "love" like other common words is highly ambiguous. When used in this context it must be understood to mean the ut-most reach of appreciative understanding. It is not intimacy when intimacy is a nuisance and interference in the affairs of the other person. It is not doing good before you know what the other per-son actually needs and what is appropriate for you to offer. Fur-thermore the word "love" must be extended to include apprecia-tion of inanimate things as well as the animate and the personal. The greatest obstacle standing in the way of attaining this maximum development of the individual's capacity for apprecia-tion is something which happens to every individual more or less. It happens to him because of the kind of relation he has with other persons from infancy on. Interchange with other persons is necessary to develop within the individual this capacity; but this relation is always imperfect in the sense that to some degree it always does the opposite. In many cases, perhaps to some degree in all cases, the individual must react to others in a way to prevent the development of his capacity to appreciate. Also after this capacity has been awakened and developed to some degree, the appreciations of the individual are deadened or anaesthetized by the demands made upon him by society and intimate associates. The individual is always forced more or less to suppress and over-lay his appreciations by an assumed conformity to the accepted pattern of thought and feeling.

All this is not to be understood to mean that interpersonal re-lations are hostile to the development of the individual's capacity to appreciate. The previous chapter made plain that exactly the opposite is the case. The full capacity of the individual to appreciate can be developed only by way of a kind of interchange with others. The trouble is that there are many kinds of interchange besides the kind which is creative. These other kinds always occur more or less and produce the evils noted in the first chapter.

This problem of releasing and developing the individual's full capacity to appreciate takes on a different form in different ages. The particular kind of difficulty to be overcome in our time has been intensively studied by such men as Erich Fromm, José Ortega y Gasset, Paul Sartre, Simone de Beauvoir, and other existentialists as well as many psychologists and other social scientists. While these all disagree on many points, they seem generally to agree on the one point we wish here to emphasize, namely, the form of the obstruction which society today imposes upon the development of the individual's capacity to appreciate.

The following statement does not include the many qualifications and exceptions required for accuracy but it does point up this problem as it appears in our society today.

> . . . the peoples of Western Europe and America . . . have become . . . much more uniform, stereotyped, group-minded, and susceptible of mass manipulation and regimentation. They are less differentiated, and have less personal energy, initiative, and ambition. They are less individualistic, enterprising, adventurous, self-reliant, with less sense of personal responsibility, more passive, more concerned with security, more indifferent to freedom, more cooperative, compliant and dependent. They are more open-minded, less disposed to be dogmatic about ideas or principles, with greater capacity for compromise. Relativism is their prevailing philosophical attitude or way of thinking about intellectual and moral, political and economic problems. In almost every aspect of their life and work and ideas one may see emerging among these people a more and more collective form of thought, emotion and action, which expresses itself not only in such things as the importance attached to public opinion polls, but in international and industrial relations, and in scientific, professional, and cultural activities.

All these things, abstractly described, reflect, for one thing, a kind of decline in individual creative vitality that would be expected to express itself not only biologically, in an indifference to the future of the race and a receding birth rate, but also more immediately in a revaluation of individual economic incentives, which is already evident. Clearly the monetary, financial, or acquisitive incentives to work, thrift, enterprise, saving, investment, and ownership of property—even possession of personal property—which were the main motive power of the economic expansion, of the machine age, are evaporating and are being replaced by a kind of collective search for automatic security, which is increasingly thought of in terms of free or effortless consumer satisfactions and passive spectator pastimes and amusements. The rapid and steady drift toward socialization of finance, production, and consumption appearing in England, Europe, and America, as well as the movement toward international economic and political collectivism, are merely superficial manifestations of these changes in the character and motives of the human material in the community.[1]

This quotation seems to say that the individualism prevailing in the nineteenth century was superior to the conformism of our time. This, I think, is a mistake. Individualism (of a kind) and conformism both obstruct when they do not corrupt or break, the development of the individual's capacity to appreciate. But since they are different they pose a different kind of problem. So far as concerns this problem the great change coming over the life of man, most rapidly in the United States but also in Europe and extending to all peoples, might be characterized in the following way.

As man acquires mastery over subhuman nature, interpersonal and other social relations absorb more of his attention and energy. This follows for many reasons. For one, the mastery of the sub-human world can be exercised only by many millions of people working together, with increasing specialization and division of labor, with more intricate and far-reaching interdependence between each and all, with the consequence that more time and effort must be given to the problems of organization, adjusting interpersonal and other social relations, keeping up morale and goodwill. In sum, the problem of life becomes less and less one of dealing with material things and more and more dealing with associated individuals. Also individuals have more wealth and leisure and if these are not to be disintegrating they must be used to seek and find what is interesting to the individual. This freedom from labor with material things and this need to spend wealth and leisure on what is interesting, produces organized, professional occupations devoted to all manner of entertainment and service. But entertainment and service are concerned with pleasing people. Also individuals who are not professional entertainers must spend a great deal of leisure time with one another and the problem of not boring or irritating one another becomes increasingly the problem of life. Besides all this the wealth and leisure combined with space-conquering instruments of travel and communication, require all the different kinds and classes of people to live in close proximity and interdependence.

These are some of the developments which are causing the problem of interchange between persons and peoples to absorb ever more of the time and energy and thought of everyone. Interchange has always been important but never before could it loom so big and dominate so completely the life of man, because never before did men exercise so much control over subhuman nature.

When people must live together in great numbers with ever-changing relations and ever-changing associates, it is to their mutual advantage to avoid irritation and boredom and snatch whatever convenience and pleasure is possible from the shifting contacts. The easiest way to do this, if not the only way in many cases, is to manipulate oneself and others into a smooth running system of adaptive responses. One tries to be the kind of person who is "warm," "personal," and "sincere." He does not allow himself to feel anything deeply, nor express strong feeling, nor become so involved in any personal relation that he cannot easily break it or change it.

A fine study of this development in our society has been made

by David Riesman and his associates.² We do not need to accept their view of the phases of population growth correlated
with these changes in American character nor need we think that
the problem is largely one of the proper use of leisure as over
against work. However much we may criticize the theories of
this book we can at least recognize the value of their descriptions. They note that the mind of every man is shaped partly
by the tradition he inherits, partly by the ideals acquired in
childhood from parents and other associates, partly by the social
demands made upon him by the changing contacts of daily life.
When these three are all shaped by tradition, the individual is
"tradition-directed." But when the demands of tradition in one
instance and the demands of newly developed ideals in another
seem to be doing in our society, then it would seem possible
to say that one or another of these three influences might dominate more or less over the others in shaping the character of
an individual. In this sense it can be said that some are predomi-
nantly tradition-directed, some inner-directed by newly developed
ideals or goals of some sort, while some will be other-directed
by the changing demands of daily life. With this understanding
of the matter I see nothing to dispute with Riesman's teaching
on this point and the distinctions should be useful in social
analysis.

When the dominant forms of industry become too large to be
subject to the control of one man but must be directed by a large
staff of managers, engineers, and other specialists; when competition in price gives way to competition in salesmanship, ad-
vertising, and general attractiveness or charm; when machines
do most of the hard work and success depends upon one's ability
to get along with people, win their favor and manipulate them;
when service, entertainment, and glamor become the profession
of increasing numbers because wealth and leisure provide a market for their goods; when these and other like conditions develop,
the other-directed person makes his appearance. His ruling concern is to detect the likes and dislikes of his associates and adapt
himself to them.

Throughout most of human history, excepting privileged individuals at times and places of advanced civilization, tradition has been the dominant factor shaping the minds of men. Generally speaking this held true until the end of the Middle Ages. But then came the Renaissance and the Reformation, Puritanism, the increasing use of money, the rise of the business man, and the industrial revolution. With these the inner-directed man began to come to the front with his individualism and his private ideals or other purposes. With the turn of the century the third kind of character began to develop more numerously. This third kind is called the other-directed. To repeat, every man is influenced by all three: tradition, personal goals, and the striving to win the approval of associates. But developing social and historical conditions can make one of the three increasingly dominant. In that sense and in that sense only we seem to be moving into the age of the other-directed man.

If this interpretation of the problem of our time was defended only by Riesman and his associates, it might not be so significant. But many others in different language and from different viewpoints have noted the same development.

One of the most vivid descriptions of this change in American life is given by Robert Jungk,[3] a journalist who has spent most of his life fighting the developments of totalitarianism in Europe, first in Germany under Hitler and later from other centers. His background and training have made him highly competent to see what is happening in the United States. His purpose is not to tell us that our problem is becoming increasingly that of the "other-directed" man and the "glad hand society." But what he says unintentionally points to the same fact and hence his testimony is all the more convincing.

> For the Americans today are concerned with bigger things than land ownership. They are fundamentally more ambitious than even their sharpest adversaries believe. Their efforts do not aspire to the mastery of continents, still less to that of the entire globe, but to higher things far then these. America is striving to win power over the sum total of things, complete and absolute mastery of nature in all its aspects.

This bid for power is not directed against any nation, class or race. It assails no particular way of government but the ways of creation, which have scarcely fluctuated within the memory of man. Clouds and wind, plant and beast, the bound-less heavens themselves are to be subjugated. The stake is higher than dictators' seats and presidential chairs. The stake is the throne of God. To occupy God's place, to repeat his deeds, to re-create and organize a man-made cosmos accord-ing to man-made laws of reason, foresight and efficiency; that is America's ultimate objective. Toward this her chief efforts are directed.[4]

This quotation may be extravagant and it is not saying what Riesman and his associates are saying. Mr. Jungk is making a different point. But the kind of organization, interchange, and adaptation required to achieve and exercise the power mentioned by Jungk requires the same kind of conformism which Riesman describes under the head of the other-directed man.

These three overlapping and mingling in each individual—the tradition-directed, the inner-directed, and the other-directed—should be distinguished from the creatively-directed which we have been describing under the head of creative interchange. Traditionalism, individualism, and conformism are all deviations, limitations, and obstructions imposed upon the creatively di-rected. This is easily demonstrated. The infant must learn to use the signs and symbols of his culture and this requires the sort of appreciative understanding of his associates which can only be produced by creative interchange. The other-directed person does indeed learn to sense the moods, the tastes, the likes and dislikes of his associates and adopt them as his own. But this is all at a superficial level. These likes and dislikes are put on and taken off much as one puts on and takes off different styles of clothing in adaptation to the demands of the changing situa-tion or changing fashion. Beneath this changing pattern of con-formity is that capacity for appreciation peculiar to the indi-vidual which might be developed to some maximum degree by creative interchange with others but which is deadened and anaesthetized or suppressed or never allowed to develop under the regime of conformism.

The regime of individualism is no better because the rigid organization of personality under the domination of a relatively changeless goal or ideal will not permit the individual's capacity for appreciation to develop any more than conformity to the wishes of others. So also a rigid and dominating tradition will be obstructive in the same way. On the other hand, every human being to be human at all does develop his capacity for appreciative understanding within limits. Neither a confining tradition nor a confining ideal nor the diffusive adaptation to all manner of people (the other-directed), can prevent the development of individual capacity for appreciation and constructive action. But they can obstruct it and they can corrupt it. That is the reason for saying that these three are deviant forms of creative interchange. They confine and limit and may corrupt, but they cannot altogether prevent, the directive control exercised by creativity.

So far we have been looking at superimposed conformity standing over against creative interchange as a problem internal to our own society. But it is also the most important problem arising in the world community which is just now for the first time in the history of the world coming into existence. We must examine it in this context also.

Perhaps nothing now happening is more fateful for the future life of man than the swift and irresistible tightening of the bonds of interdependence among all the peoples, all the cultures, all the faiths and nations and classes and races on the earth. All these divisions of humanity with their hates and fears toward one another, with their resentments and conflicting interests, with their envies and suspicions, are being compelled to live together in a tight little community where the action of any one is bound to make great difference to all the others.

In this tight global community not only are the misery and welfare of each major division of humanity determined by what the other divisions do; every individual human being is likewise dependent upon millions of others, not only for material goods, but also for his sense of security or insecurity, for his happiness or distress, his achievement or frustration. Furthermore, this kind of interdependence is bound to increase very rapidly beyond its present state if civilization continues. It cannot be stopped nor the speed of its increase diminished because it is driven by science, technology, and mass production. Civilization as we know it cannot continue without these. These three are leaping forward at terrific pace and every forward leap carries with it a proportionate increase in the closeness and complexity of inter-dependence. Also the political rivalry between Russia and the United States, each trying to win the world to its way of life, is swiftly binding all parts of the world more closely to one side or the other; and, paradoxical as it may seem, the very rivalry between these two giants results in closer bonds between them.

Increasing interdependence forces increasing control and di-rection over the activities of men. When individuals and peoples are separated from one another, and when each lives by getting what it needs from the raw state of nature, each can live in its own way without regard for the other. Under such conditions there is minimum exercise of control and direction by one peo-ple over the way others shall conduct their lives. But the closer the bonds of interdependence, the more will the life of each be regulated relative to the others. Hence the necessity for exercis-ing direction and control over the conduct of human life.

Only now in the twentieth century, and increasingly from now on if civilization endures, the whole of humanity is brought to-gether in such close interdependence that direction and control must be exercised over all peoples and all individuals as members of a single society. In this sense humanity will now pass from the ages of drift to the ages of direction or destroy civilization. No longer can any people or any individual go its own way regardless of others. Henceforth the whole of humanity must find a way of life which all can live together. This does not necessarily mean uniformity, as said before; but it does mean a direction of striving so ordered that one group or individual will not wholly frustrate the others. In the end it will mean an ultimate commitment which all will share, hence a common faith and the acceptance by all of certain general principles so regulating conduct that one individual or group shall not reduce the others to misery or death.

The wider and tighter the interdependence and the greater the diversity of those included in these bonds, the less tolerance can there be for any deviation from what the common life requires. Only when individuals and peoples are widely separated and relatively independent of one another, can we tolerate other ways of life which are opposed to our own. When interdependence increases, the oppositions which could formerly be tolerated become so frustrative and destructive that tolerance is impossible. Interdependence increases the conflict of interests which could previously be accepted but which now becomes unendurable. With increasing interdependence my own personality is deranged by conformity to customs which previously did not reach me. When my home, my children, and my own person are corrupted and degraded by alien ways of life, tolerance can no longer continue.

Tolerance, therefore, cannot solve the problem posed by the diversities of human life when interdependence swiftly increases, folding us tightly into close association with all the peoples of the earth. The proclamation of tolerance as a way of dealing with this problem is not only an illusion; it is an illusion which will bring us all to ruin if widely accepted. To be sure, many diversities can be tolerated and in many cases must be; but there is a better and more creative way to deal with diversity. Only when this better way fails may tolerance be accepted as the second best; and even when thus endured as second best, the margin of endurance swiftly narrows as interdependence increases.

So we conclude: There is no escape from the imperative demand of our time. We must establish a chosen direction and way of life for all. Humanity as a whole must accept a way of life which permits us all to live together in close association. This will require a measure of control, of planning and directing never before exercised over the global expanse of human life. As said before, it requires a major shift in the conduct of human affairs, from the ages of drift to the ages of direction.

Uniformity within limits is a necessary and indispensable condition of all associated living. For example, the correct pronunciation of words, so that one person can understand another, is a kind of uniformity necessary for the exercise of creative interchange. So also are the rules of logic; so also are certain forms of courtesy and many rules of conduct and routine habits all of which serve to release the mind from petty matters which can be taken for granted to the end of interpreting the insights and innovations which open the way to the further enrichment of experience and fuller control over circumstance. In certain matters uniformity is always necessary. Life cannot be lived without it and especially life in a complex society. But there are two totally different ways of dealing with uniformity. In the one case, it is the end sought. In the other case, uniformity is the means and required condition for creative interchange between individuals, cultures, and ways of life which are unique and diverse.

To appreciate the full significance of the decision which hangs over us, let us look down each of two roads which are open before us. First examine the consequences ensuing if we do not deliberately choose to make creative interchange our ruling concern, and if we do not give ourselves over to it personally and socially with that measure of completeness whereby it becomes a form of religious commitment.

When uniformity is forced upon all, not as a means and within the limits required to provide conditions most favorable for creative interchange, but in disregard for the latter and as the one and only way to iron out conflicting diversities, people divide into two kinds. One kind, generally a small minority, fights and rebels against the imposed uniformity. These fight for the freedom to find and do and be what they must in order not to become inhibited, suppressed, suffer inner conflict, and put on a false front which kills their own individuality. The others, generally a large majority, submit to the imposed pattern of mechanization. Look first at what happens to those who rebel and then to those who submit.

When uniformity is forced, they who rebel will be compelled to submit, not because the rulers in the beginning are necessarily cruel, but because dangerous and destructive conflicts cannot be permitted. When appreciative understanding of individuality is not the ruling concern, there is no way to deal with individuality except to iron it out. Hence deviation from the imposed pattern becomes destructive and must be eliminated. The rebels must be beaten down. The difficulty of doing this and the instruments required to do it gradually bring about a change in the total social system when imposed uniformity is the method used to solve the problem of opposing differences. The grinding down of the imposed uniformity generates more resistance; rising resistance brings forth methods increasingly coercive. The men who apply these methods become increasingly brutal because persons who are not brutal are incompetent to apply them. Sensitive and compassionate people are sickened by the torture and the concentration camps and so rendered unfit to exercise control over the social system. So they step out and more brutal men take their places. In every society are some who enjoy the sense of power experienced when tightening the screws on tormented victims and in determining the fate of persons subjected to their power. Gradually people of this sort take over places of high command in a society which regulates conduct by imposed uniformity.

In such a society many methods are used besides physical torture. Social disapproval, deprivation of employment, refusal to promote, barring the way to honor and opportunity, mob violence and slander, control of the agencies of information and propaganda, and all the devices which modern science and technology have put into our hands can be applied. In this way the rebels can be kept under control when and if they are permitted to survive at all.

So much for the rebels. Now look at the great majority who do not outwardly rebel against the imposed uniformity. A fate awaits them even worse than the fate of the rebel. Studies of personality have taught us that outward conformity which suppresses the inalienable demands of individuality engenders rebellion which may be unconscious. Inwardly and unconsciously the native individuality of each fights against the uniformity. Below the level of consciousness such persons suffer inner conflicts and these generate anxieties. In some these anxieties are expressed in hates and fears, suspicion and resentment, and may break out in mob violence and in individual acts of cruelty against any one who is unable to fight back. Helpless people who can be safely attacked serve as scapegoats against which to vent the ill will secretly boiling within these suppressed individuals. These conformists slavishly obey the authorities above them, but cruelly and despotically treat the people occupying subordinate positions.

A society ordered and controlled after this manner will not permit the development of that kind of intelligence and that kind of sensitive concern for others which leaders in a democratic society must have. Hence such leaders will not be available. Individuals who might develop in this way will not be allowed to rise above the lowest levels of social rank. Thus a vicious circle is generated. The rulers make the society worse and the society makes the rulers worse. This may continue for generation after generation. We know that this can happen because we know that some societies have been unbelievably cruel, not because of a special biological nature, but because successive generations have moulded the minds of men in this direction.

A world-wide society which lives under an enforced uniformity will not have any people able to liberate it from the outside. The whole world will be dominated and controlled in this way and after a few generations men will have forgotten what it is like to live in a society where freedom and creativity have free play. Some inside the society will rebel but they can always be beaten down. The great majority will conform although many may have suppressed resentments, hates, and fears. But they will ordinarily play safe by venting their hidden hate and fear in acts of cruelty upon helpless individuals who cannot hit back. Since small children are the most helpless, they will be the chief victims in such a society.

This is what we see down one of the two roads which fork in front of us and between which we must choose. One of these two roads or the other we must surely travel. We cannot escape the way of superimposed uniformity if we do not choose and give ourselves in religious commitment to the way of creative interchange. This is so because uniformity is the consequence of inertia and refusal to choose. However, even choice is not enough to escape the way of uniformity when interdependence and power increase with the speed we now observe. It must be a choice of religious commitment. Religious commitment is required because of internal psychological resistances to creative interchange which have been built up within us; also because of the resistances to it which have been built up in our social institutions.

On the other hand, the interdependence and power now increasing will enable creative interchange to lift human life to richness of experience and amplitude of personality not before possible, if and when creative interchange is recognized and accepted as commanding the ultimate commitment of man. Why this is so and what this involves was partially stated in the first chapter and will be more fully developed in later ones.

There is a creativity at work in human life which is always ready to break through the resistances set up within the individual person and in social customs and institutions. When these resistances are removed the creativity begins to transfigure the life of man and the world in which he lives. This transfiguration is in the form of appreciative understanding between people, in some cases approaching the depth and fulness of love. It is also in the form of magnified power of mutual control through concern for one another's needs and interests, thus reducing when not removing the coercions of authoritarian control from above. It is also in the form of enriching life with felt qualities found in all things, activities, persons, and situations, this enrichment approaching at times the aesthetic forms of beauty.

To say that this creativity is always ready to break through and transfigure does not mean that one act of transfiguration will bring the world to complete perfection. Rather what is meant is that the life of man can reach a higher plateau of being when the obstructive and destructive resistances to creativity are reduced or corrected. We know this break-through can occur because it has occurred to a high degree in the case of a few rare individuals on certain occasions. But it cannot rise triumphant until the break-through occurs in the lives of many associated individuals and continues more or less indefinitely.

In this sense the eschatologies, Christian and otherwise, concerning a golden age in the future, have validity. Human life as now lived is instable and transitional to a level of being not yet reached. But there is no guarantee that this break-through will occur. It depends on the major decisions made by men and the kind of religious commitment they finally choose. But once the break-through is well-started it rolls on to larger dimensions, even as the opposite alternative of superimposed uniformity gathers momentum and finally becomes irresistible.

The condition making possible this break-through to a higher level of being was brought on by the origin of civilization and the life of the city. Civilization and the city also made possible the degradation of man to levels of misery and corruption and destruction not previously possible. The present moment in history has magnified the dimensions of these alternatives and is forcing a decision which may be final. We may be moving toward a time when the period of transition and instability will end and we shall have passed over either to a final commitment to creative interchange or to the point of no return under the grinding wheels of a superimposed uniformity.

The past seems to indicate that out of defeat and despair creativity brings forth the higher levels of life provided that in such a time men are driven to commit themselves without resistance to the creative interchange with one another. In that sense, our age is not only one of great peril but also one of great promise. The magnified powers and interdependence of our time can be used to provide conditions for the most fruitful and enriching interchange between diverse and unique individuals and cultures, provided that the faith which prevails among men and the practices of religious commitment all direct the self-giving and the devotion of our lives to creative interchange. But nothing short of a religious faith to this end, with searching self-criticism and confession and repentance of the sin of not meeting the conditions required for this interchange, will save us. So long as we insist that all the major obstructions to this interchange are on the other side of the iron curtain, we are doomed.

No matter how false the view of the other may be in my esteem, and no matter how evil his ways, nothing is so enriching, nothing so empowering, nothing so generative of wisdom, as this appreciative understanding of another person or people. Nothing is so corrective of error and evil, nothing so expands the vision, nothing so effectively overcomes hate, fear, resentment, and envy, nothing so liberates the unique individuality and its potentialities for greatness as this kind of interchange regardless of the virtue of the other party.

Creative interchange is going on all the time where human beings are associated, otherwise they cannot act humanly toward one another, and cannot recognize that the other individual has a subjectivity. Not to recognize the other as having thoughts and feelings of his own is to fail to recognize him to be human, because self-consciousness and a rich subjectivity are what distinguish the human from the nonhuman. While this kind of interchange is going on all the time, it cannot prevail over counter forms of interaction until it commands our ultimate commitment and thereby is lifted to dominance over all else. This is the great transition which must be accomplished before the human level of being is fully attained. This is the next plateau which historical development must reach if the human way of life is to continue.

Perhaps every human being engages to some degree in all six kinds of interchange with others, the creative, the deceptive, the reiterative, the brain-washing, the clutter-minded, and the other-directed. But one of the six may dominate over the others. The destiny of man in the sense of attaining that plateau of being where the human can prevail over the non-human depends on creative communication dominating over the other kinds.

The ability to learn what others have learned, to appreciate what others appreciate, to feel what others feel, and to add all this to what the individual has acquired from other sources, and finally to form out of it all a coherent unity which is one's own individuality is what distinguishes the human mind from every-thing else. This kind of interchange and progressive integration makes it possible to expand beyond any known limit what man may know, feel, and control. It makes it possible to increase beyond any known limit the variety of forms and situations yielding aesthetic quality or feeling appreciation. It makes it possible to increase beyond any known limit the appreciative understanding between individuals, groups, and cultures. Crea-tive interchange makes it possible to increase beyond any known limit mutual control as over against authoritarian control, since mutual control is exercised by way of appreciative understanding and responsiveness to one another's needs and interests. This kind of mutual control achieved by way of creative interchange is the only way to escape the ever-tightening, degrading and corrupting coercions of authoritarian control. Also it delivers us from the "glad hand" society in which "other-directed" people put on false fronts to be pleasing and where all depths of individuality and depth of understanding die out.

Resistances to creative interchange are built up within the in-dividual psyche as self-protective devices against the hurts and sufferings endured when one expresses himself freely, fully, and truly, and exposes all his sensitivities to receive appreciatively from others what they express. But the protective devices de-signed to guard against this suffering generate anxiety caused by the failure to develop one's own capacity to appreciate. Since the individual's own unique capacity to appreciate conflicts with these protective devices, they generate inner conflicts, suppres-sions and inhibitions, neurosis and psychosis, and other ills of personality. Therapeutic treatment of these psychic ills consists in removing to some degree these internal barriers set up as pro-tective devices against the hurts of creative interchange, thus opening the way for this interchange to produce more apprecia-tive understanding in interpersonal relations.

These barriers to creative interchange are not only internal to the individual. They are also social. Barriers are built into all our social institutions. Of course the opposite is also true. Social institutions provide the conditions which make it possible to carry on sustaining interchange. To provide such conditions is the human function of home, school, church, and government. But since human beings have psychological resistances to creative interchange, with all the fear, suspicion, hate, envy, and other antagonisms and hostilities thereby engendered, social institutions must protect individuals and groups against one another. But social protection, like the psychological, hinders creativity and often prevents it quite completely. Also social institutions are used in various ways by individuals and groups to dominate, suppress, exploit, and destroy others.

While all these obstructions do exist and have always existed in human life, both psychologically and socially, the great cultural achievements in history have occurred when these obstructions were relaxed sufficiently to allow individuals and groups to learn from one another more widely and freely and to allow individual minds to integrate creatively what was learned, when learning is understood to include not only information but also the acquisition of feelings, appreciations, skills, and techniques.

The relevance of all this to the present moment of history has already been indicated. The magnified power exercised by man today and the ever-tightening bonds of interdependence have brought the human race to the point where this kind of interchange will be suppressed unless we deliberately choose to commit ourselves finally and completely to it in the sense of striving above all else to provide the conditions most favorable for it to occur in every situation where it is possible.

If this kind of choice and commitment is not made, the alternative will inevitably follow. If creative communication is not made dominant, only one other way remains for the peoples of the world to live together without mutual destruction. That other way is the regime of a superimposed and coerced uniformity.

The creative communication, which up to this time has been allowed very largely to take care of itself, must now be deliberately chosen as the ruling concern. The basic institutions of home, school and government, industry and commerce will have to be deliberately shaped to serve it. Religion must lead men to commit themselves to it without reservation. One religion may give the name of "Christ" to this kind of interchange which produces the appreciative understanding of love between individuals and peoples. Another religion may call it the will of God as revealed in the Torah or the Koran. Other religions may find that this kind of interchange between men is the burden of the teaching of the saints and sages of Buddhism and Hinduism and Confucianism, or whatever may be the chief authority in the religion under consideration.

However much the various religions may otherwise differ in doctrine and belief, in ceremony and ritual, in organization and government, this creative relation between human beings should be made central in them all if we are to find the way of salvation from degradation and dehumanization.

We have called this movement in history a shift from the ages of drift to the ages of direction. The same interpretation of our times is expressed when we say that it is a transition from relative irresponsibility to greatly increased responsibility. This increased responsibility concerns the commitment of human life to what in truth has the character and power to transform man as he cannot transform himself. This increased responsibility means that we must have more accurate and reliable knowledge concerning what calls for this commitment. It also demands more knowledge of the conditions which must be met for this transformation to occur. But first of all must come the personal giving of the whole self to this creativity which transforms the mind. This is necessary to overcome the internal psychological resistances to creative transformation which are present in every person. Also this must come first because otherwise one will not devote himself to providing whatever other conditions lie within the competence of the individual.

Since the choice before which we stand involves an ultimate commitment, we shall seek in the next chapter a better understanding of such a commitment and what the potentialities of human life may be which depend upon it.

Chapter 3

LIVING RICHLY WITH

DARK REALITIES

—————————

W$_{\text{HEN}}$ $_{\text{HOPES}}$ and plans come to nothing or seem trivial within the limitations of our finitude we have the experience variously described by the existentialists. It is sometimes called the experience of "nothingness." It is what we experience when the scope and content of possible achievement appear as nothing compared to what we demand and seek. All this can come to a focus in the knowledge that I must die, since the end of individual existence is the ultimate limitation and denial.

Some of the existentialists call for resignation and acceptance of an ultimate "No" imposed upon human existence by this encounter with nothingness, anxiety, guilt, fate, and meaninglessness. Others call for the exercise of freedom in making decisions into which one casts his whole self, thereby creating himself ever anew. For still others this encounter with dark realities generates the leap of faith whereby one identifies himself with an alleged Being unconfined and unlimited by the processes of existence.

Different from all of these is the way here set forth for dealing with finitude, anxiety, despair, and death. This further way is to treat the experience as the means of deliverance from those preoccupations which hinder the emergence of insights leading to ways of life more rich and comprehensive than those previously attained. Creative transformation in depth requires, however, the unity and wholeness of the self which is unattainable unless one casts off the deceptive and evasive devices built up to conceal the major evils. A glance at these evils will help to explain what is meant.

Dread is felt when the most beloved is threatened. Anxiety assails when we are aware of a blessedness endangered or missed. The deeps of evil never reach consciousness except in opposition to the heights of good. Sin is rebellion against transfiguring righteousness. Fear and anxiety are involved in all which is most lovable. Consequently to be aware of evil is not only instrumental to the end of protection; the full reality of good is not unveiled to the human mind until the full reality of evil is exposed to the appreciative consciousness. This is so because of the close conjunction between good and evil which our statements have been indicating. This conjunction does not in any way make the evil less evil nor the good less good. On the contrary, the utmost opposition of the one to the other cannot be discerned until we see them in close relation to one another.

All this shows that there is no way to live richly except in the presence of the dark realities. When we try to secure peace, comfort, and happiness by concealing what we fear and resist and by suppressing below the level of consciousness our reaction to these evils, we impoverish our lives. The fulness of reality with all the richness of felt quality which it yields can enter consciousness only when we face it openly with our full capacity for apprehending it.

Sharp distinction must be made between the actuality of evil and the awareness of it. It is good to be aware of evil provided it does not cause one to resort to the evasive devices which dull the mind, sap the energy, misdirect effort, darken vision, and bring on apathy. Nothing is more important in the treatment of evil than this distinction between the actuality of evil and the being aware of it.

Dark realities emerge as the mind matures. They are evil in themselves but their evil is multiplied when one refuses to recognize them for what they truly are. After many social contacts I discover that others condemn, dislike, and otherwise judge me in ways radically different from what I myself consider to be the truth about myself. I find that I speak and act in ways to wound others and give them experiences very different from what I intended. What I seek and prize and promote above all else with the utmost devotion, for which I would live and die, may not be, indeed most probably is not, as impeccably perfect and glorious as it appears to be in my starry-eyed gaze. A sequence of punctured illusions leads me at last to recognize the fallibility of my evaluations. Experience demonstrates that I am surrounded on all sides with dangers, not merely physical dangers, but the danger that a friend may turn against me, that I may be rejected by my people, that all I have worked to achieve may come to nothing. I may discover that I have already been rejected where I thought my place secure.

This list of evils might be extended indefinitely, but the ones mentioned will serve to illustrate the area of positive value which is always threatened and often devastated by accident, guilt, and the other destroyers.

There is a kind of good, however, which these evils never reach. I have called it creative good to distinguish it from created good.[1] Created good includes beauty, love, friendship, power of achievement, and all the values commonly sought and prized by human beings. Creative good is the creativity which creates the human mind and all its values. It is the internal integration within the individual of what he has derived from others when this internal integration progressively creates the original experience of that individual.

When created good is destroyed or sinks to triviality and one is left with a meaningless blank, three alternatives are open. One is despair. Another is some device by which one conceals the evil and deceives himself into thinking that it has not happened or that it is neutralized by a Being who transcends time. The third alternative is to give oneself more completely than ever to creative good. When created good is wiped off the surface in great part, creativity can do its most magnificient work, because one can commit himself to it more completely under such conditions. The great Hebrew prophets lived in this way

and under such conditions. Perhaps never in human history has
there been a more fruitful transformation of the human mind
than occurred with the prophets and their followers. So likewise
Jesus struggled with the Devil for forty days and nights in the
wilderness before he came forth with his gospel. Those were
the days when he confronted the limitations of his finitude and
pondered whether he should try to transcend them, as many men
attempt to do with diastrous consequences, or commit himself
most completely to that creative interchange with fellow men
which works within the bounds of human finitude.

The human mind seems to be so fashioned that one cannot cast
himself into the keeping of latent creativity and find his blessedness there so long as honor, success, love, beauty, and the more
material goods seem readily available. When these fade out,
however, some men, perhaps not many, can realize that creativity is the Lord and Master of life and the only Saviour from
what would otherwise be the conquering power of darkness.
This does not mean that created goods are evil or should not be
sought and enjoyed; it does mean that another kind of good
can alone satisfy the whole being of man and must be given
priority if created goods are not to pall and turn to "nothing,"
as the existentialists so eloquently affirm.

Ordinarily creative transformation does not occur in a time of
deep trouble unless one has practiced ultimate commitment to
creativity prior to the hour of darkness. But if one has this faith
in creativity, events which otherwise might drive to despair or
to illusion or to apathy or to fury, become occasions of rejuvena-
tion. This does not mean that new creations burst forth in time
of trouble. One may have to struggle forty days and nights before the vision comes. The time of waiting may be longer. New
creations of importance are slow in gestation and may require
years, even centuries, to ripen. But the time of waiting is not
lost time. It is the time for practicing those rituals of commitment by which one is brought more completely into the state of
readiness for whatever the latent creativity may eventually
bring forth. It is a time when one can strive to purge himself of
resistances to creative transformation. Periods spent in such prac-

tices of faith and devotion can yield a profound satisfaction even though the mind as yet can see no glimmer of the new creation. When such times are used to bring the mind to full realization of the infinite value of creativity as over against the finite values of created good, one can endure such seasons without turning to self-deception or other devices of desperation.

Western man may be entering a time when the bright possibilities which have sustained him will no longer do so. If this is to be our experience during the next century or so when the power of other peoples rise to dominance and our power relative to theirs declines, this period of decline can be fruitful and rewarding if it teaches us to reverse the order of priority by which we have lived heretofore and devote ourselves to seeking out the conditions most favorable for creative transformation of the human mind. If we do not do this, evils in our midst will mount as we try to divert our minds from our fate either by dissipation and frivolity or by desperate ventures. People who have reached some high level of good fortune and have cherished a vision of increasing it indefinitely experience the extremes of frustration and meaninglessness when this vision fades and this good fortune slips away. There is evidence to indicate that this may be the experience of Western man during the years ahead.

The statement just made does not lead to pessimism nor to the apathetic nor defeatist attitude if one can turn the experience of such a time to fruitful practice by cultivating commitment to what transforms the human mind creatively so that other goals can enter human consciousness which are now beyond our imagination but which will be more worthy of human effort than any heretofore prevailing.

The values of Western culture are precious and we shall not relinquish them if they can be retained. But human life at its depth, a depth shared by all humanity and not alone by Western man, has another kind of good more precious and of greater promise. It can be uncovered and released for its divine work in time of cultural decline as may not be possible in times of security and prosperity because, in times of prosperity, created good dominates the mind. The proper order of priority as between created good and creativity cannot be sustained when the mind, without further transformation, seems to be able to seek and get and imagine an ample sufficiency. Creativity cannot dominate human concern until it is seen that the mind of man is unfit for life except as it submits itself to creative transformation.

Our purpose in taking note of the dangers and evils which threaten us is not to produce gloom, but to examine a difficulty which needs to be overcome before anyone can give himself completely to any ultimate commitment, least of all to that kind of interchange which progressively creates and enriches the mind of man and the world which he can experience. We are about to examine what may be the chief source of man's self-destructive propensities, the chief destroyer of his integrity, the chief cause of his spiritual impoverishment, his weakness, his sense of futility, his irrational compulsions and follies.

This source of perversion which keeps man from realizing the great good for which his nature fits him, can be put into a single word: Evasion. It is man's refusal to face up to the dark realities. When he does not allow these matters to enter conscious awareness with all the depth and fulness of their being, he cannot let anything come into consciousness in its true character and in the fulness of its being. He cannot, because these dark realities are woven into everything; therefore, in order to cast the veil of concealment over what causes anxiety, he must conceal the true character of everything which is inextricably merged with the fearful presence.

A glance at the dark realities above listed will show that they enter into the essential character of everything which we seek and enjoy, indeed into everything whatsoever which we can experience. Consequently, when we evade the complete awareness of them, we exclude the full consciousness of everything. Most of all we reduce to a feeble flicker of appreciation what would give us greatest joy if we did not dim our vision to conceal the lurking evil. What is most loved and honored, prized and sought is precisely what involves most fully the dark presence. When we love most profoundly, death, disgrace, rejection, defects in the beloved, the inability to share what is truly our own, the wounding and the misunderstanding, and all the others, close in upon us. Beauty, love, honor, praise, comfort, pleasure, anything and everything most prized by men, are clutched and encompassed by these dangers. The more highly anything is prized, the more darkly do these realities hover over it.

The point of all this can be simply stated. One can never enter into the great good which his nature permits and demands until he is able to allow the dark realities to come to his consciousness in all their magnitude and do it without the kind of fear, horror, disgust, or revulsion which is evasive. Please note the last word "evasive." One cannot help but experience fear and other forms of anxiety when he stands in the unveiled presence of the greatest dangers and other evils. But there are two kinds of fear or any other form of anxiety. There is the evasive kind and the kind not evasive. The evasive kind is sometimes called the fear of fear. It is also the refusal to accept responsibility or to admit a fault in oneself which is truly there. These evasive anxieties are more shattering than fear fully accepted and acknowledged. The kind of fear which is not evasive, which does not cause one to conceal the reality which causes the fear, nor drive to the many kinds of compulsive behavior which weaken, impoverish, corrupt, distort, and falsify, is illustrated by the following. A young sergeant with other soldiers was waiting to charge into deadly fire, and his knees were shaking. An old and seasoned soldier noticed this and called out, "Hey, bud, your knees are shaking." The young man replied, "Sure they are. But they would shake worse still if they knew where I was going to take them."

The awareness of evil is not evil; on the contrary it is one of the supreme goods because only when one is fully cognizant of it can he act intelligently toward it. More important still, only when one allows evil to enter awareness in the fulness of its reality can one experience most fully the most precious realities in love and beauty, in creativity of all kinds. No one can think, feel, and act with his whole self if a part of himself must be deadened or suppressed to exclude from consciousness what the whole self experiences. No one can live fully and abundantly unless he can take into his consciousness all the evils and dangers which are truly and presently involved. This statement does not attribute any virtue whatsoever to the imaginative construction of evils which are not truly present or involved in the precious realities with which one is dealing. Indeed there is much evidence to indicate that the false construction of imaginary evil is one of the devices unconsciously used to conceal the real dangers and evils. It is one of the many evasive devices practiced by the human mind to exclude from consciousness the true character of all realities, even the most precious and glorious, because the full appreciative understanding of them would have to take into account the evils which threaten and infect them.

In order to make the study of this problem specific and concrete let us take death to be representative of all the other dark realities. It is not the only one, to be sure, but it is perhaps the most obvious and universal in its threat to every beloved and beautiful or otherwise highly prized object including the existence of one's own self. Death can serve as a symbol of all the dark realities because it stands behind them all as the last fatality, either the climactic evil from which we try to escape or else the lesser evil into which we escape when life becomes unendurable. Also it is the one last fatality from which no one can escape. Thus it symbolizes all the limitations which frustrate human endeavor. It represents all those happenings which man cannot control but which fall destructively upon his plans and hopes and all his strivings, upon his loved ones and upon things and places dear to him. Hence death is pre-eminently the symbol of finitude. Obsession with this so-called nothingness or finitude is just as evasive as the attempt to exclude it from consciousness. In both cases one is excluding the full appreciative understanding of what truly is. The most precious realities in their finitude truly have being; and to call them non-being because they must come to an end is as perverse as to ignore this threat and this ending. The irresponsible obsession with death and nothingness, which we see in some existentialists, is a subtle and dishonest trick by which the mind evades the appreciative apprehension of precious reality and responsible action in dealing with it. But just now we are considering the opposite kind of evasion which is more common, namely the exclusion of these dark realities from appreciation and thereby dimming our vision of matters of greatest value because of the intimate union of the evil and the good.

Death is woven inextricably into all that makes life rich and full, noble and heroic, tragic and triumphant, soaring and declining. Death is inextricably woven into all these because they all must come to an end. One cannot receive the beloved or other prized object into appreciative consciousness if he cannot recognize death in the depth of its meaning, because the true character of every precious thing is defined in part by its relation to death. To appreciate anything one must discern it in its true character. But the true character of everything appreciable is finitude. Therefore we fail to appreciate the great good of the most precious realities when we shrink from recognizing their relation to death.

This evasiveness renders all life superficial, relatively barren, casting over all things a pretence and a veil which dims the luster. When we refuse to face death along with all the limitations and frustrations which it represents, we refuse to face the full reality and significance of ourselves, of every other person, and of all things whatsoever which we can prize in the embodiments of space and time. This is true not only because all things perish but because we ourselves must die and thus bring to an end our experience of whatever we love. Finitude when rightly understood and recognized does not cast a shadow over the world but quite the contrary. It adds a brightness and a vividness to every precious thing.

We need to understand and appreciate finitude if we are to love what is most lovable in its true character and with all the fulness and depth of devotion of which we are capable. The same applies to all the dark realities which go along with finitude. We cannot throw ourselves unreservedly and with joy into the most difficult undertakings if we shrink from failure. We cannot move with the full tide of love if we are unable to accept the possibility of being left alone. We must take death in full stride if we are to live life to the full. This is a recurrent theme in the writings of Ernest Hemingway, perhaps never stated better than in his short story, "The Short and Happy Life of Francis Macomber."

This evasiveness in some form or other is the cause of all the psychic ills and most of the corruption. Perhaps nothing drains away so much of the energy which we might have for action, thinking, and feeling. It saps the enthusiasm for life and gives to all things a drab and pallid hue.

The evasive attitude toward death is revealed by the way we refer to it. We speak of "passing on." We say, "We must all go some time." There are many similar expressions by which we practice concealment of the dark reality.

The expression "We must all go some time" is especially significant because it reveals one of the most common ways in which we try to conceal from ourselves the realities of human existence which cause anxiety. This most common method is that of anonymity. It is the merging of my self with the mass of humanity or with some group so that I no longer feel the impact of the dread reality upon my own individual self. By mixing in the herd and losing the sense of self-identity, becoming what has been called a mass man, I can acquire the feeling that the danger, the evil, the burden and load of responsibility do not fall upon me individually. I am only one among many and so I can generate the illusion that what falls upon me will be only a very little blow. It happens to everybody, I say comfortably and so to get the feeling that it does not exactly happen to me because I am not everybody. This flight into anonymity is an evasion and an illusion. It is a failure to face up to reality and consciously assume the burden which truly weighs on me. It is a refusal to accept into full conscious awareness the reality which is truly there and which cannot be escaped but only concealed by the devices of evasion.

Besides anonymity, there is a second device by which men keep out of mind the full and deep experience of the greatest good which human life can have because this greatest good involves the dark presence of hovering evil. This second device might be called evasive preoccupation. It is perhaps even more corrupting than anonymity because it infects it with penetrating rottenness all the most holy, noble, and creative undertakings. Nowhere is it more pronounced than in religion, in sex love and friendship, in moral striving and idealism, in the pursuit of beauty. It appears also in work to support the family and to make money, in industrial enterprise, in patriotism and group loyalty, as well as in numberless trivial activities. As good a place as any to examine it is in love between the sexes.

One may cultivate love between himself and his mate as an evasive preoccupation. A most lurid portrayal of love pursued in this way is the story by Dorothy Parker called "Big Blonde." Love pursued in this way will insist on keeping out of consideration the difficulties, troubles, pains and sorrows encountered by either party. One must be gay, happy, entertaining, attractive in person. Everything must be as pleasant and pretty as it can possibly be made. There is certainly a place in love for beauty and charm, gaiety and pleasure, and all the arts. Deliberately to be disagreeable, whining and complaining, morose and sullen is out of the question. But the love which constantly shies away from the real dangers and troubles, responsibilities and burdens of life is an evasive device. Sex love is peculiarly fitted to serve in this way because it can be made so delightful and obsessive, so varied and inclusive of many interests, and yet be practiced to keep the dark realities out of mind. So long as it is practiced in this way, there can be no genuine appreciative understanding of the other person but only a fictitious representation falsified in such a way as to keep all disagreeable matters and responsibilities beyond the reach of apprehension. If love is understood to be the fullest appreciative understanding of the other person, then this evasive practice which goes by the name is not love at all. Yet it is probable that this corruption enters to some degree in almost all instances of love between the sexes, in which case the persons concerned are cut off from one of the deepest, richest, and most complete satisfactions which life can yield, namely, love in all the depth and fulness of its reality.

Sex love when it is genuine and not an evasive device is perhaps more effective than anything else in overcoming one of the greatest difficulties standing in the way of creating progressively the mind and its world with richness and fulness of satisfactions, scope of knowledge, and power of control.

This difficulty which must be overcome if any individual is to undergo the creative transformation of the mind leading to maximum richness and freedom of living can be most briefly described as the *id*. Sigmund Freud gave it that name and while his idea about it has been considerably revised the word still serves to indicate this greatest difficulty. The id is that large part of the self which refuses to learn along with the learning self when "learning" means not merely acquisition of knowledge and skill but the integrated development of all the capacities distinctively human. Consequently one's total capacity to think, act, and appreciate is never enlisted so long as there is an id not integrated into the progressive, creative transformation of the total self. The creative transformation which might increase joy, power, and insight indefinitely is held down to meager limits because this large part of the psychosomatic individual refuses to undergo these developments. Thus life falls short of what it might be.

Freud claimed that this part of the total self which refuses to go along with the learning mind is fixed and unchangeable. The neo-Freudians are generally agreed that Freud was mistaken on this point. While the total capacity for meaningful experience latent in the individual is never brought into action, there is no known limit in the degree to which the individual in the wholeness of his being might be awakened to sustain and enrich the conscious mind.

Now sex love to the measure that it casts off evasive devices and accepts the other person fully and truly as he is, seems better able than almost any other experience to overcome the resistance of the id and draw more of the total individuality into that creative transformation of the mind which occurs when the lovers learn from one another. In sex love the total capacity for biological response can more readily than in most other forms of interchange between persons be merged with the total capacity for psychological response. This statement applies not merely to the sex act itself but to the interchange going on between the lovers about all the matters which may concern them as individuals, their sorrows, troubles, and difficulties as well as the opposite of these.

Since more of the individual's total capacity for experience is awakened, individuals in love often find that everything they perceive and do is glorified with richness and vividness of felt quality. This integration of communicable meanings with the organism's total capacity for experience is the spiritual achievement of sex love. This is the contribution of sex love to the creative transformation of the human mind.

While sex love can make this contribution to the realization of the constructive potentialities of human life, very often it does the opposite. Perhaps most commonly it is practiced as a way of escape from the problems and responsibilities of life. Men turn to love to keep the dark realities out of mind.

What has been said of love applies also to beauty. It can be sought, cultivated, and experienced as a device for concealing the depth and the horror, the misery and the glory, the richness and the pain of life. It seems quite probable that many people who cultivate the fine arts either as aesthetes or artists and who surround themselves with beautiful things, do it to distract the mind from dangers, anxieties, and responsibilities which cannot be escaped but can be concealed. How much art is produced to this end, how much of it is contemplated and prized to this end, and how much beauty in all manner of situations outside of art is sought and prized in this way, it would be difficult to say. But there seems to be much evidence that this evasive enjoyment of beauty is widely prevalent.

Yet beauty like love is one of the chief ways in which communicable meanings can be integrated with the organism's total capacity for experience and thus serve creative communication to the end of transforming the mind of man and his world in the direction of the greatest good for which human existence is fitted. Perhaps the standard for distinguishing great art from all lesser forms, once the technique of art is mastered, is precisely this. Great art is not évasive, lesser art is. Obviously evasiveness is a matter of degree. Hence there can be all degrees of excellence in art by this standard. Great art is the practice of a technique by which the evasiveness of the mind is overcome so that one can discern the true character of what he is experiencing. By enabling us to face the dark realities, great art enables us to appreciate what is precious and noble as we cannot do when we refuse to recognize how all things dear are enmeshed in pretense, pride, fear, corruption, and the constant threat of destructive power. Art uses fiction; but if the art is truly of high excellence, the fiction is the device used to tease and coddle and circumvent the evasive devices so that one can experience the full richness of quality which is there amid the fearful forms.

Comedy as well as tragedy exposes the face of reality which we ordinarily conceal. In ordinary life we exclude from conscious awareness in great part the follies, blunders, futilities, and limitations which are merged with the noble, the strong, and the triumphant. Comedy exposes these blunders and pretenses which ordinarily escape consciousness. *Don Quixote* is a good example and so also is *Bouvard and Pécuchet* by Gustave Flaubert. The following verse by Gilbert Chesterton is a simple illustration.

> The men who fought for England,
> Following a fallen star—
> Alas, alas, for England,
> Their graves are strewn afar.
>
> The men who rule in England,
> In stately conclave met—
> Alas, alas, for England,
> They have no graves as yet.

High comedy enables us to look straight into the face of foibles, weaknesses, pretenses, and the falsity of standards which we do not ordinarily recognize in ourselves and in our fellows. But all this is great art, not the evasive kind which may be more common and popular.

Fine art is not the only agent which draws the veil from the face of reality, but it is one. On the other hand, as said before, much art does exactly the opposite. It conceals the truth about

life in order to be pleasing and beguiling and help us do what
we are striving to do—live evasively. No distinction in the field
of art, I judge, is more important than the line which separates
evasive art from exposing art. The same applies to evasive love
and exposing love, evasive morality and exposing morality,
evasive religion and exposing religion. Perhaps the most common in all these cases is the evasive kind. Especially is this true
of morality and religion.

Perhaps morality is always evasive when practiced as an end
in itself and not as the necessary discipline required to serve a
higher devotion. The personal satisfaction found in one's own
moral rectitude, in being a Christian governed by an ideal given
of God and not of man, is probably in many cases a satisfaction
derived from successfully evading the truth about oneself. So
also with science or patriotism or idealism. These can be enjoyed and practiced by separating them in consciousness from
the total context of existence in which they play their rightful
part. When not thus separated, when practiced in the context
of reality where they properly operate, they expose the dark
realities while enriching and empowering the life of man. When
separated from this context they become evasive practices.

All human life can be lived evasively and to some degree perhaps it always is. But it might be lived not with face averted but
face full front, freely and richly lived with full release of all the
capacities for experience and all the powers of control and all
the exercise of intelligence. It *might* be lived in this way but it
cannot be until men learn how to accept the dark realities as
inseparable characters wrought into the structure of what is
precious, lovable, beautiful, and holy.

They who live evasively are starving the hunger for life within
themselves. They are inhibited and suppressed; they are anxious
and troubled with a hidden anxiety which disturbs their dreams
and impairs every joy; which impoverishes every experience of
love and every experience of beauty; which corrupts every noble
thing they undertake and reduces to triviality what might otherwise be grand. Three-fourths of their total capacity for thinking,
acting, and feeling, perhaps nine-tenths, is starved and dead-

ened. Their joy is pallid, their sorrow is half a mockery; their hour of triumph is shrill without any of the resonance of deep hallelujahs. They cannot love with the depth and power which transfigures the world. They cannot act with passions free and flowing in tides of power.

On the surface such men may be merry but deep within is the void and the darkness, the emptiness and the hunger. So pleasures must be many; love and beauty must be very artful, work to support the family or make money must be very strenuous; the fight against traitors and the defense of the homeland must be wildeyed; the struggle to dominate the world must become a consuming passion.

They who will not receive in open experience the full depth and power of the dark realities cannot throw their total selves into anything because a large part of themselves must be deadened in order to keep these matters out of consciousness. To release the full power and passion of the total self one must face up to all the realities which are truly present in the form of truths and meanings and concrete existences.

The practice of evading and concealing is not peculiar to individuals alone. It is the practice of whole cultures. Perhaps all cultures are of this kind more or less. Such a culture shapes the mind, focuses the attention, directs action and impulse so as to evade awareness of the full depth of experience. Language is constructed and endowed with meanings in such a way as to keep these deeper concerns out of mind. Words, sentences, and elaborate statements do not designate realities in the form in which we can truly experience them. Customs and moral standards, manners and respectability, all are slanted in the same direction. Consequently our habits and impulses, focus of attention and structure of consciousness, are shaped and ordered to conceal what is there in the full richness of its qualities. Social judgments of approval and disapproval are determined to the same end. Thus the total culture and the minds created and shaped by the culture are designed to conceal and evade. The great artists struggle to tear the veil away. Their struggle to uncover the depth and richness of quality in matters of human concern is evidence that this depth and richness are concealed by the culture of daily life.

This facing up to all which is dreadfully real must not be confused with the kind of courage displayed by one who lightly risks his life and dies with slight concern about his end. A soldier may be trained so that he will die without much thought of it. Many others who are not soldiers may die in this way. But this is exactly the opposite of what is here under consideration. Facing death without a qualm and dying without anxiety is the consequence of anesthetizing the human capacity for experiencing the depth and fulness of the meaning of death. It is the consequence of practicing anonymity or some other device by which appreciative consciousness loses its capacity for feeling any qualities beyond trivialities. This is the peculiar way in which man dehumanizes himself and trains himself to deny his own destiny.

Man is made for creative transformation as a bird is made for flight. To be sure he is in a cage much of the time. The bars of the cage are the resistances to creative transformation which are present in himself and in the world round about. Also, like most birds when long confined, he settles down in time and loses both the desire and the ability to undergo creative transformation. But in childhood creativity dominates. The mind expands its range of knowledge and power of control, its appreciative understanding of other minds and its participation in the cultural heritage. At no other time is there so much expansion and enrichment of the mind and of the world which the mind can appreciate. But resistances are encountered which bring on anxiety, frustration, failure, and misunderstanding. To avoid suffering, the mind becomes evasive and creativity dies down. The bird ceases to beat against the bars of the cage.

The demands of the existing world imprison, suppress, and distort that outreaching expansiveness of the mind which would occur if the whole psychosomatic individual could undergo creative transformation by the use of langauge and other symbols to interpret and give human significance to what the whole self is experiencing. But the conventional language and the established order of life do not permit this. Consequently there is conflict between what the social situation demands of one and what is needed to preserve and develop the constructive potentialities of the individual. Out of this conflict the dark realities emerge. On the other hand, one cannot escape the conflict by abandoning society because interchange with others is necessary for any creative transformation of the mind at the high human level.

All this shows that man is made not for human life as it is but for the creativity which transforms life. Therefore he must seek his freedom, his peace and his power, and all the great human values by commitment to a creativity which overcomes the world as now existing by giving to it a dimension and form of possibility beyond the compass of human ideals.

No Utopia can ever satisfy the individual in the wholeness of his being. The best possible state of existence ever to be attained will be a world which yields most readily and continuously to the transforming power of this creativity. But even such a world will not satisfy the whole self. It will be the best possible not in the sense that it satisfies in itself but only because it is more subject than any other to that creative transformation which alone does satisfy the nature of man. Hence the greatest good for the human being is not any state of existence whatsoever. Neither is it any possibility in the form of an end result. Neither is it any realm beyond the existing world. Rather this greatest good is the creativity which everlastingly transforms every state of existence toward more richness of felt quality, more comprehensive knowledge and power of control, more appreciative understanding between individuals, and more mutual control. But this it can do only when required conditions are present. The required conditions are never all present in perfect completeness. Even when they are most fully present such a state of affairs is extremely instable and cannot long continue. The most important of these required conditions in human life is the exclusion of all evasiveness. This in turn depends upon the most complete self-giving of associated individuals to that kind of interchange between each and other which expands and enriches what each can know, feel, and control.

Nevertheless, while all this is true, there is a supreme good to be had with its joy and peace and power. This supreme good is precisely the most complete commitment to the creativity just described.

There is a Kingdom of God to be had with all the blessedness ever proclaimed by prophets and saints. But the way to it and the form of it and the kind of good which it is must be accepted and appreciated. It is not any future state of existence either in this world or in any other. It is not beyond history nor beyond time. We are on the road to defeat and frustration when we look beyond this world for our greatest good. It is to be found in what is going on more or less all the time in human life. But the joy of it and the peace and power of it cannot be known until commitment to it is most complete and perfect, when evasiveness is cast out, when the dark realities are recognized for what they truly are, and the appreciative mind in consequence is fully open to all the qualities which life can yield.

Still another feature of human life shows that man is made for this creativity and not for the existing state of the world at any given time. It is the predicament of human choice. When an individual decides between alternatives, he finds in many cases that he must choose one good to the exclusion of others. The good excluded may be so precious that it is anguish to reject it. Also, no matter what he chooses, the chosen good is never perfect. Evil is always mixed into it, partly because of the good which had to be rejected.

This predicament of human choice is partly due to our ignorance. Even more it is due to our inability to act with the whole self. It is due to the false fronts and shams by which life is conducted not only in oneself but also by others throughout society. It is due to the incompleteness of our commitment to the power which transforms creatively. While all this is true, this predicament has a further significance. It points to the destiny for man which we have been describing. It shows that man can find his most complete satisfaction only when he lives for creative transformation and not for any achieved state of affairs now present or ever to be attained. The analysis of time in the next chapter will further support this claim.

The predicament of choice arises from inability to find any-thing in the world which completely satisfies the whole nature of man. It shows that every existing set of conditions confines human potentiality to narrow and distorting bounds no matter what course of action may be chosen. This reveals an expansive-ness of human potentiality which beats against the bounds of the existing world. It demonstrates that man is made not for the world as it is but for the creativity which transforms the world. Every decision except the decision to commit himself to this creativity, every course of action which is chosen and every good which is achieved, lacks the amplitude and expansiveness required to open the way for the full realization of the po-tentialities resident in the wholeness of each human self. Ex-cepting commitment to creativity, every choice demands that the self be forced into a channel too narrow, confining, and distorting for the wholeness of man's being. Thus we know that man's freedom is found only when he gives himself to this creativity with full acceptance of any suffering involved in undergoing its transformations.

Choices deficient in freedom after the manner indicated must be made constantly throughout life. Indeed so constantly must they occur that the self in the full range of its demands and potentialities is beaten down into the unconscious and can-not be brought to consciousness except in the form of an anxiety and restlessness which no achievement can assuage. Even this discontent can be driven into the unconscious so completely that the conscious mind becomes a puppet moved here and there by the mechanisms of change without any conscious sense of re-bellion against this fate. But hidden beneath this placid surface of the mind is the turmoil of the total self, stirred up and driven by a creativity which finds no release. It is a creativity reaching forever beyond the bounds of every actual existing state of the world.

All this shows that human destiny extends beyond the horizon of what we are able to imagine with the minds we now have. It shows that we are pilgrims not to another world beyond the skies nor to any supernatural realm but to the continuous re-making of this world. It shows that a creativity resides in man and works through him with a reach which the human mind cannot comprehend and which the human mind at its peril tries to control or direct or confine to the limits of any human purpose or ideal other than the purpose to serve this creativity and undergo the transformations which it may accomplish.

The good for which we live, which might enter conscious awareness with proper commitment and deliverance from evasive devices, is too vast to be realized in any social organization or movement; too vast for any ideal or course of action when these are confined to the limits of human imagination and purpose. But peace in the only form available to man, a peace which dwells in the midst of struggle and suffering, combined with power and freedom, love and beauty, all these are found by the most complete self-giving to the creativity which continues everlastingly in time. All the dark realities can be accepted when we know that they are intrinsic to the creative expansion and enrichment of the appreciative consciousness.

This creativity operates in human life but it is necessary to recognize that it is more than human. This can be easily demonstrated as follows.

No man can cause to come into his mind an idea which he has never glimpsed; nor extend goodwill where he feels ill will and his sense of justice forbids such extension. Neither can any one achieve a higher ideal when it contradicts the one he thinks highest. Yet new ideas, extended brotherhood, and higher ideals do enter human life from time to time. So also do experiences of love and beauty which the individual could not have imagined nor intended before they occurred. Creativity is the name we give to this process of emerging ideas, wider brotherhood, higher ideals, richer forms of beauty, and love more profound. Therefore this creativity is more than human in the sense of doing what man cannot do when human doing is defined as producing what man intends and imagines before it occurs.

This creativity is more than human in the sense that it has lifted man to the place of dominance which he now holds on this planet. It has brought forth the best which man has ever attained; and it opens up to man his highest possibilities.

After advancing civilization has brought every other process under human control, supposing that possible, this process of man's own transformation will still remain beyond his control in the sense that he cannot direct it to produce an idea which has never entered his mind, nor a higher ideal which contradicts the one he now holds highest, nor an extension of brotherhood condemned by his moral standards achieved to date, nor a vision of beauty he has never imagined, nor a depth of love alien to all his present ideals.

Here, then, we have the one master reality which will always be beyond man's control and yet which determines a destiny more glorious than anything else in the universe. If this is true, man's greatness is attained not by devoting himself to the exercise of control over what commands his ultimate commitment but to the very opposite. His greatness is attained by giving himself over to be controlled, shaped, and progressively created by it. Also, if this is true, all attempt to find what should command the ultimate commitment by peering into the depths and heights of Being outside of human life, or into eternity or the supernatural, is to seek where it can never be found. What transforms human life toward the best possible must operate in human life and in time, where man is, not in an eternity where man is not.

This claim involves us in the whole problem of time. The problem is pressing and acute because religion in our tradition has generally pointed to eternity beyond time as the realm of man's highest attainment and as commanding his last commitment. So in the next chapter we shall try to deal with this problem of time.

Chapter 4

TIME AND MAN'S ULTIMATE

COMMITMENT

———————

THE EXPERIENCE of time is the experience of a present changing into a past while being continuously created by innovations so that a new present is always with us. Furthermore, this present always carries with it the anticipation that innovations now emerging will display the character which the past has taught us to expect. This anticipation we call the future. Confusion arises, however, when we speak as though what we anticipate already has some kind of existence called future existence, or future events. To speak of future existence or future events is to use an idiom which is harmless enough if we understand that it should not be taken any more literally than the idiom which says the sun is in my eyes. The sun is not in my eyes. It is millions of miles away. So also the future is not another world where events are occurring now and which will be repeated again in my experience when the future becomes the present. The future does not become the present if that expression is interpreted to mean that the future already exists and merely changes its status so as to re-enact itself in the present after having somehow occurred before it occurred. To speak in such language is to speak in terms as self-contradictory as square circles.

What we have said so far, however, only introduces the problem of time. We need to break down this problem into its com-

ponent parts and treat them in order. First, we shall consider
change because time certainly involves change. Then we shall go
on to examine the mystic experience because it allegedly transcends time. Also it claims to direct man's ultimate commitment
beyond time. Therefore we must examine it with care. Next we
shall explain what we understand to be the meaning of the present, then the meaning of the past and future, and finally the
creativity necessarily involved in time. After that we can make
our statement about man's ultimate commitment.

If we examine carefully our experience of change we find in
this experience two things which should be distinguished. We
not only find something changing but also a law or order to which
the process of change conforms. This law of change can also be
called the structure or form of change. This structure or form
does not itself change, but it is present in any process of change.
This we shall try to demonstrate, namely, that the experience of
change is impossible without a structure, law, or form which
does not change.

Any existing thing can change only if it continues to exist as
the same thing throughout the period of change. The moment
it ceases to be the same thing, it is no longer changing because it
no longer exists. A table, for example, is always changing with
change of colors as the lighting varies, with changes due to
scratches and nicks and tear until at last it disintegrates
into pieces or ashes and so ceases to be a table. When the changes
cease to maintain the form, structure, or law of change which
is characteristic of the table, change continues but it then takes
on another form. This other form of change is characteristic of
broken pieces of wood or smoke and ashes but not of the table.
Always when we experience change we experience some law or
structure distinguishing that particular kind of change from
other kinds of change.

This law or structure or form is the changeless element in all
change. To be sure, one structure may give place to another, so
that we have a sequence of structures. The changing table gives
way to changing pieces of wood and the changing pieces give
way to chemicals. But each structure, so long as it characterizes

the change, is itself changeless. It is changeless in the sense that it preserves the identity of the something-or-other which is changing. The law of gravitation, for example, is one law of change which is always present in changes of material bodies. The law of gravitation does not change but is the changeless law to which all changes of material bodies conform. If the form of change called gravitation should cease, there would not any more be any material bodies because that form of change constitutes the identity of material bodies.

What is true of the table undergoing change, and what is true of all material bodies under the law of gravitation, is true of everything else. Wherever you find change, you find some structure characterizing the change and this structure is not itself changing.

Let us shift from material things to a human person. I myself since birth have been changing. But I am the same person now as I was at birth and will continue to be the same person until I cease to be myself. This self-identity which persists through all change is a certain order, structure, or law of change which distinguishes me as over against all else. That is to say, I have certain distinctive ways of feeling, thinking, acting; and these ways are the forms of change, or the law of change, which mark me off from everything else.

No hidden underlying substance can preserve my identity because no underlying hidden substance is ever perceived, but these persistent, self-identifying characteristics are perceived.

It is true that during certain periods of time I may display one form of change, and then for another period of time display a very different form of change. At one time, for example, I am eating breakfast and at another time I am reading a philosophical paper. But if I retain my identity from birth to death, there is a basic, constitutive law of change underlying all these breakfast forms and paper-reading forms. This basic, constitutive law of change is what constitutes my personal identity. I am the same person because certain ways of thinking, feeling, and acting are characteristic of me. This constitutive structure of my individuality preserves my identity through all transformations. When any change occurs which deviates seriously from this law of change constituting my personal identity, there appears in place of myself a decomposing carcass.

What is said of the form of change characterizing the table, and the form of change characterizing gravitation, and the form of change characterizing my own person, applies also to the universe as a whole. The universe is a universe only because throughout all its changes there is a constitutive structure whereby we can call it a universe. It is true that the universe displays first one form of change and then another; but these are transitory parts and epochs within the universe as a whole. The universe as a whole can continue to exist and thus continue to undergo change only because, beneath all these forms of change which are present for a time and then are not present, there is one basic form which is always present and must be present because without it the universe would not be a universe. This form of change always present in all changes which can ever happen in the universe is the constitutive character of the universe apart from which there can be no universe. If this constitutive structure of the universe should fade out of experience, there would be no universe. Neither would there be any mind. Neither would there be anything at all, because we can speak of anything at all only in terms of some structure. When all structure ceases, mind itself ceases and there is nothing.

This constitutive structure of the universe can likewise be called the constitutive structure of the knowing mind, because the mind can have experiences only within the confines of that structure which constitutes the human mind. Any form of change which deviated from the necessary structure of human experience could never be experienced. It could not even be called a form of change, because "form of change" means a form of change which might conceivably be experienced. Thus it can be said that the constitutive structure of the universe is identical with the constitutive structure of the mind.

The statement just made does not entail that the universe is a kind of mind. It only asserts that the mind can know at any one time only what the resources of the mind at that time enable it to know. Therefore the universe which any individual can experience can only be the structures and qualities which his mind at that time enables him to experience. Aristotle finds one kind of cosmic order, Newton another, and Einstein still another. If this continues, the universe as known to the cognitive powers of the mind after ten thousand years have passed will be very different from what it is now.

One may object by saying that over and above all these changing forms of the universe as experienced by individuals is the real universe. But we can have no knowledge and no experience of any reality except what we have knowledge and experience of with the forms of thought and feeling which at the time characterize our minds.

One can state the matter otherwise. There is a great night of darkness which is the mystery of reality; but in that night is a spotlight which is the human consciousness with whatsoever forms of thought and feeling are available to it at the time. As generations pass this illuminated area seems to expand, generally speaking. But it not only expands. It takes on a very different structure as we pass from primitive man to the early civilized man to the man of later civilization, say of Greece, to the modern European and on to civilized experience in A.D. 20,000. Throughout all these changes and all other change which may ever occur, the human mind will never know anything about this mystery of reality except what the human mind is able to know at any one time. This ability to know is the constitutive structure of the mind as the term is here used. This constitutive structure of the mind corresponds to the constitutive structure of reality in the sense that the mind can have no experience of reality except what the constitutive structure of the mind permits it to have. This is the "egocentric predicament," if you will, but it is coercive and inescapable.

So far we have spoken only of the changeless order necessarily involved in all change. But if the order does not change, then what does change? What is the content of change? What changes in such a way as to conform to the changeless order?

What changes continuously in our experience is quality, not

only sense qualities but a myriad of ever-changing felt qualities. In conscious awareness, if we examine carefully, we find a continuous flow of sensed qualities and felt qualities. This flow is always richer in content than those relatively few qualities which conform to the changeless structure which happens to hold attention. For example, when I look at a table or tree I am at the same time always experiencing far more qualities than those which fit into the form of the table or the tree. Even love and friendship have structures which distinguish them from hate and malice, although it is quite evident that laws of change distinguishing love and friendship are much more vaguely and indefinitely determined than are the laws of change characterizing qualities which we call a table or a tree. Also these structures of felt quality which distinguish love and friendship are much more inclusive of felt qualities than are those structures which define tables and trees. The more inclusive of felt quality any structure may be, the more vague and indefinite it becomes. That is the reason that the exact sciences reduce to a minimum the qualities entering into the structures which they seek to know because the richer the content of quality, the more difficult to determine accurately the precise structure of change.

The flow of felt quality always seems to be richer in content than any structure can contain. Always there is a surplusage, an overflow, which is as yet unstructured. It is true that it is difficult to bring to consciousness any quality which does not fit into some structure, but on the fringes of awareness these unstructured qualities seem always to be present. Furthermore, art and the mystic experience bring to conscious awareness a rich content of quality and thus testify to a flow of quality vast and massive and perhaps inexhaustible, waiting to be brought to conscious awareness by the creation of structures of art, structures of love and friendship, and all the structures which ever may be created in human experience to the end of including more of this depth and fulness of quality.

It should not be forgotten, however, that these structures created to bring to conscious awareness ever more of the inexhaustible depth of quality are opposed by the creation of the opposite kind of structures, namely, those of exact science and of technology. These two opposing kinds of structures might conceivably be reconciled and developed in a way to magnify one another. But very often, it seems, they compete with one another so that an age or culture or area of life devoted to the creation of scientific and technological structures crowds out and impoverishes the qualitatively rich structures of love, friendship, worship, devotion, loyalty, art, and all qualitatively rich forms of awareness.

If I may put what we have said in a figure of speech it might be expressed thus (but please remember this is only a figure of speech): There is a formless, vast, unfathomed ocean of quality waiting to be structured in such form that it can be brought to awareness. A creativity works in human life creating structures or forms of thought and action which bring to appreciative awareness this depth and richness of quality. The creation of these structures creates the human mind on the one hand and the world which the human mind knows and feels on the other. In small children and in primitive society these structures are almost all shaped to create mind and world over against one another in such a way as to render the mind most abundantly appreciative of qualities and the world most rich with felt quality. But as life becomes more complex it becomes necessary to create, along with structures rich with quality, other structures relatively barren of quality but useful for accurate knowledge and efficient action. Ideally, these two kinds should support and enhance one another, but often the opposite occurs. Human life even reaches the stage in many cases where men become so absorbed and obsessed with the problems of accurate knowledge and efficient action that they are diverted, not to say perverted, from life devoted to appreciative awareness, and become obsessed with barren structures of knowledge and power. In such cases the barren structures of accuracy and efficiency throw off the yoke of servitude to structures rich with quality. In time, however, the barren structures exhaust themselves because all the deep satisfactions of life are found in the progressive enrichment of experience by way of structures designed to bring to conscious awareness more qualities from the inexhaustible depth of quality.

Life dominated by concern for accuracy and efficiency, knowledge and power, when these exclude the creation of structures
rich with quality, can be called perverted or corrupted because
it generates subconscious rebellion appearing in the self-destructive tendencies now being described by the psychology of personality under such labels as the authoritarian personality, the
market personality, the one who seeks anonymity, and many other
forms of internal conflict. The point is that human life has its
own constitutive law or form of development. This constitutive
law requires that human life be creatively transformed by way
of structures rich with felt quality. When people at the level of
conscious purpose try to live in any other way, the subconscious
propulsions constitutive of the human way of life rebel. These
subconscious propulsions struggle, so to speak, to balance or
compensate for the deviations from the intrinsic demand of human nature. This internal conflict between the constitutive propulsions of human life and the conscious purpose can be called
corruption or perversion or sin.

This brings us to a consideration of art, aesthetic experience,
and the mystic experience because these are the forms in which
it is most easy to recognize richness of felt quality. It is a mistake,
however, to think that fine art is the form in which we achieve
most appreciative awareness of felt quality. On the contrary,
what fine art contributes is microscopic compared to what is derived from living with the baby you love, the woman you love,
the tragedy or triumph of the great man you admire, your home,
your native land, and innumerable other things. But in art this
richness of quality is most easily examined, so we turn to it.

Preliminary to this examination of art and mystic experience
a statement previously made should be emphasized, namely, the
richer in content of quality any structure may be, the more vague
and undefined the structure becomes. There are, however, two
very important exceptions to this. One exception is the work of
art. A work of fine art not only brings to conscious awareness a
rich content of quality but does it within a structure precisely
defined and formed. The other exception is an experience not of
art but of all manner of things. Individuals without skills and
techniques of the artist can still develop forms of perception and

forms of experience in which a rich content of quality is experienced within the confines of precisely defined structure. These richly qualitative forms of experience are the forms of aesthetic perception. They can be had in observing the lives of fellow men, in observing a human individual, in doing certain practical things, in observing the scenes of nature, and in many other situations.

While these exceptions must be recognized, it is still true that life as lived in any culture is streaked and interlaced with forms of experience very vaguely defined but very rich in content of experienced quality. These forms may be those of love and friendship; they may be forms of comradeship; they may be certain traditional festivals; they may be forms of worship; they may be forms of doing certain kinds of work; they may be forms of loyalty, of the love of native land, of hero-worship for certain outstanding leaders and saints, of folklore, myth, and legend and much else.

These ill-defined structures rich with quality, which are present in every culture more or less, are the raw material with which the artist and the aesthete work. The creative artist and the aesthete reconstruct some of these richly qualitative but ill-defined structures to the point where they become more precisely defined and structured. A culture which is poor in these ill-defined structures of traditional loyalty, love of the land, hero-worship, love and friendship, and the like, is a culture where fine art cannot flourish because it does not have the raw materials which the artist must have to do his work.

On the other hand, it is conceivable that a culture having the structures of thought and action throughout everyday life most richly endowed with appreciated qualities, and with conditions favorable for their further creation, would have no supreme achievements in fine art. This might follow if creative genius should find its greatest opportunity in creating ways of abundant living outside those narrow and technical fields in which great art is brought forth. This absence of the supreme achievements of fine art in such a culture would not necessarily follow, but it is quite possible. In any case, it is important to emphasize again that the richness of human experience is found in every day life. Fine art makes its own contribution, but this contribution is small compared to other sources.

This brings us directly to the problem of mystic experience because the great mystic, as we shall interpret him, is an originator of forms of thought and action in everyday life which are most rich with felt quality. Not all mystics and not every mystic is of this order but some are.

The great mystic is one in whom creativity is so reconstructive of the organization of the mind that the experience is relatively inchoate until the new structure in process of formation is more fully developed. In some mystics the new structure may never be developed beyond this first beginning and so never reaches a form that can be carried into everyday life. In such case the experience remains a flood of felt quality without practical significance, all structure submerged with unformed feeling. On the other hand, some mystics have come forth with a gospel and a new way of life more rich with "love" than the prevailing culture has previously permitted.

This new way of life brought forth by creativity in transforming the mind of the mystic is more richly appreciative of the qualities in persons, situations, events, kinds of work, classes of people, in poverty, humility, sorrow, loss, and tragedy, in power, luxury, heroic achievement, splendid mastery, in scenes of nature, periods of history, and human destiny. Such mystics have opened the minds of men to what is blessed in the poor in spirit, in the meek, in those that mourn, and even in being reviled and persecuted for righteousness' sake. They have spoken of a new heaven and a new earth and have even claimed that they had a glimpse of it.

When life becomes profoundly appreciative of the qualities in all manner of things, it is sometimes called the life of love. But "love" in this context is a very inaccurate expression. Rather, what is meant is a way of life in which structures have been created, otherwise called meanings, which enable one consciously to experience and profoundly appreciate the qualities to be found in persons, in ways of life, and in all the world of things.

In this sense and with this qualification we say that the great mystic may be one in whom creativity occurs in such a way as to initiate the beginning of those structures which characterize the life of universal love.

In the mystic creativity generates only the beginnings of this most appreciative way of life. The new way of life does not get beyond these beginnings because the prevailing habits both of the mystic himself and of his associates resist radical and immediate transformation. The mind cannot suddenly take on new forms of appreciative consciousness radically different from those of the prevailing culture because every human mind is shaped by creative communication with associates. While the individual can make his own unique contribution, it is always a contribution, not the sudden creation of a totally new kind of mentality. New forms of thought, action, and appreciative awareness are created by co-operative and communicative interchange between individuals. Forms thus created and prevalent we call a culture or way of life. Hence, when creativity in the mystic experience breaks through the bounds of these cultural forms, the new forms cannot depart very far from those of the culture. The institutions, the way of thought, and the perception already established in the society, resist sudden change. Even the mind of the mystic is held in bondage to his culture although he advances somewhat beyond it. The qualitative richness of his experience overflows the bounds imposed by the customary way of life but when his experience passes very far beyond these bounds it becomes formless, ineffable, and inarticulate. His understanding of it and his expression of it fail. But it gives him a sense of glory, love, and beauty beyond his power to grasp.

This mystic awareness of beatitude is no illusion because glory, love, and beauty beyond the reach of the mind as now formed are in truth the forms of appreciative awareness yet to be created which can contain a richness of felt quality beyond the capacity of any forms presently accessible to the human mind. Such forms of appreciative awareness would, of course, be correlative with a world having such qualities in such forms.

It is impossible within the lifetime of a single individual to transform the culture of a people into the forms of universal love. Also without co-operation and communication with other likeminded persons it is impossible to transform the mind of the mystic himself into forms of appreciative awareness greatly different from the culture in which he lives. But the great mystic is one in whom creativity produces the beginning of this maximum appreciation of qualities. To carry this beginning to completion would require a new language, new institutions, new habits and customs, and a new culture fit to contain this increase in beauty and love.

What is brought forth in the experience of the great mystic is the beginning of a new creation, not only a new creation in the form of a mind more capable of loving appreciation toward all persons and things, but also a new creation in the form of a world relative to such a mind. But this is only a tendency. To repeat, the mind of the mystic cannot undergo the degree of transformation required to complete the new creation apart from a corresponding transformation of other minds in creative communication with his own and, along with this, a corresponding transformation of social institutions and physical conditions. But the mind of the mystic undergoes a transformation in this direction sufficient to give him a sense of the glory which might be.

In this sense the great mystics can be viewed as the first promise and intimation of what may in time be attained, somewhat as the first bird in late winter or the first bud in wintry weather is the promise of spring and summer. Spring and summer are not inevitable, however. An ice age may ensue. Yet if the great mystics are "the first born of many brethren," the new heavens and the new earth might in time appear. In any case, this interpretation recognizes the cosmic and divine significance of certain forms of the mystic experience.

Since the experience of the creative mystic goes beyond the bounds of all established structures and forms of thought and world, he is likely to think that he is experiencing eternity. This is a very natural illusion. With one understanding of the word it is no illusion at all. If eternity is the potentiality of all the beauty, love, and glory yet to be attained in time, it is no illusion. In any case, the mystic must either be silent about his experience or else use symbols which do not properly describe what he is experiencing. This is necessary because all intelligible symbols have been created to refer to the established forms of experience. Hence there can be no language to tell about an experience which goes beyond these forms with a richness of felt quality vaguely outlined by forms yet to be developed in a glory not yet attained. So, if the mystic is to talk about his experience at all he must use words which do not properly designate what he experiences but do suggest great fulness of felt quality and some high peak of life's attainment. "Eternity" in its religious usage seems to carry the suggestion of what might be experienced, very wonderful and very mysterious and very blissful. Consequently, it often appeals to the mystic as suitable to use when he tries to tell what he experienced.

As the cognitive powers of the mind develop in the form of developing science and philosophy and other forms of apprehension, the order which the human mind discovers in reality becomes more extensive, more accurately fitted to the data and the data themselves more precisely defined. In the other direction of love and aesthetic quality, structures may arise yielding an ever greater abundance of experienced quality.

This brings us again to the question previously asked. Is there some ultimate structure of all reality which the human mind can never know because it is independent of the human mind in the sense that it can never be known? Such a claim is a self-contradictory statement for reasons already stated. Structure is a word used by the human mind and can have no meaning except what the human mind gives to it. Otherwise it is a meaningless sound. But the only meaning which the human mind can give to the word is the meaning which "structure" has for the human mind. An unknowable "structure" in the sense of not being related to the cognitive powers of the human mind is therefore meaningless. The inescapable limitations imposed upon the meaning of the word makes it self-contradictory to affirm a structure other than a structure which the human mind at sometime or other can conceive and discover. Certainly there are structures yet to be discovered. But they are structures only in the sense that the human mind can in time think them and can find data conforming to them. But this can happen only after creative interaction with the physical world and between human minds has produced the state of mind and the physical and social conditions making it possible for the mind to discover such an order in some realm of being.

From all this we conclude that the ultimate constitutive structure of reality is creativity itself because the order of creativity is the only order necessarily present in all knowledge and in all forms of experience and changelessly present through all changes which human experience can undergo. It is the only order which is logically prior to every other order. No other can be ultimate because every other may be supplanted by creative transformation of the mind with corresponding transformation of the world as experienced by the mind.

The structure, form, or order of creativity is very imperfectly known to date but it is defined by the conditions which must be present for new insights and expanding structures to emerge, whether these be structures of felt quality, vivid, varied, and abundant, or whether they be structures with minimum quality such as those sought by science. We know there must be some order in the sequence of emerging structures because it is impossible to leap from the order of the world as known by primitive man to the order as known by a highly educated man in the twentieth century, not because the native ability of the primitive man is inferior to that of modern man but because a certain orderly sequence of conditions must develop before the view of the world as held by Thales can be transformed into the view held by Aristotle and this again into the view held by modern thinkers. The law of change which describes this creative transformation of the human mind and of the world as experienced by the mind is the structure of creativity. I hold this, on the basis of the reasons I have given, to be the ultimate constituent structure of reality.

So we conclude: The reality underlying all others in the sense of a changeless structure of felt quality and knowable order is creativity because it is necessarily prior to every other form of experience. It is also the reality which alone can bring to supreme fulfilment all the creative potentialities of human life when man gives himself over to it in religious commitment of faith. Thus it is ultimate in two senses: It is metaphysically ultimate because it is logically prior to all other knowledge and experience; it is religiously ultimate and valuationally (axiologically) ultimate because it brings forth the greatest human good which man can ever experience on condition that man accepts it as his saviour and creator and allows himself to be creatively transformed by it. It is the only "eternal" order in the sense that it must always be changelessly present through all change and all time which man can ever experience.

This interpretation of the constitutive structure of all reality as being determined by the ability of the mind to gain knowledge and have experience is not a form of subjectivism. It does not represent our experienced world to be a mere creature of the mind over against an objective reality which is other than this mental creation of ours. Such would be the case if it was here affirmed that reality had a structure independent of the mind because then this structure independent of the mind would be the objective reality. But what we are affirming is the exact opposite of this. There is no structure other than what the mind can discover; therefore this structure which the mind can discover is objective reality.

Also this interpretation of mind and reality should not lead one to deny that a world existed long before any human mind inhabited it. We have every reason to believe that the universe existed for millions of years before any human mind had being. But we know this only because the structure of our minds today and our ability to gain knowledge in our time discovers the past to be of this character. The past has this character relative to our minds today and relative to the data now accessible to us. It may be that thousands of years hence the best science of that time will give a very different account of the cosmic past, even as our statement about it differs radically from that of a thousand years ago. Those concepts and those propositions which meet the most rigorous tests of science and logic ever to be attained present the structure of reality relative to the human mind.

Another misunderstanding should be avoided. This view does not say that the human mind creates its world. On the contrary, it is here claimed that creativity creates both the human mind on the one hand and the world relative to that mind on the other. After this parenthetical statement about the structure of reality in relation to the structure of the mind, let us turn again to the problem of time. We are now able to examine more analytically than we have thus far done the nature of time in terms of past, present, and future.

The present cannot be considered apart from the past and the anticipated future, any more than a smile or a frown can be considered apart from the face that smiles or frowns. The present might be considered the smile or the frown on the face of that period of time which includes both past and one's anticipation of the future. No man's present ever includes the future but only his anticipation of it.

This period of time called the present is always a flow of structured quality as we have already seen from our previous analysis of change. This flow of structured quality may be more or less extensive and more or less rich with quality, depending on the structure which happens to be at the focus of attention and the ruling concern. In some cases the structure may extend the period called the present to include years and centuries; in other cases it may be limited to fractions of a second. In some cases the present may be so rich with felt quality and so ecstatic that one loses the sense of the passage of time and may describe the experience as entry from time into eternity, although this can never be more than a figure of speech no matter how literal the individual may think his language to be. Again the present may be so barren of quality that it is almost unendurable. But all these variations in the period called the present, whether it be maximum extension or minimum contraction, and whether it be greater richness of felt quality or greatest poverty, all depend upon the structure which holds the attention and determines the magnitude and content of what is called the present.

All the past of which I am aware is always included in the present in the sense that I am aware of it in the present. But whether I call the past of which I am aware a part of the present or a part of the past again depends on the structure which holds my attention. If my attention is given to a foot race now being run, while the past of which I am aware consists of other foot races previously run, these other foot races are called the past, while the present is the period of time required to run the present race. On the other hand, if the structure which holds my attention is the entire history of modern foot racing in contrast to that of ancient Greece, then all of modern foot racing may be called the present while that of ancient Greece is the past.

The past is always changing in two very important ways. Any event of the past is always becoming more remote and thereby changing its character in my view. Secondly, the total structure of events which joins any past event with the present is always being reconstructed by the creativity operative in all human experience. This order of events continuously reconstructed by this creativity gives a different meaning and character to the past event. The event which once seemed tragic may now seem funny, or vice versa; and in various other ways all events change their character with the passage of time.

When we turn to consider the future, we have something very different from past and present. There are no future events although we may use that colloquialism in speaking of the future. The anticipated future can only be conceivable structures which may or may not characterize events when the present and past are different from what they now are.

To say that a certain time is characterized by the same structure as the present and yet is different from the present, is not to make a self-contradictory statement, because a structure is always an abstraction; the events which it may characterize are always vastly richer in content than that one structure. Also concrete events always participate in other structures besides the one which happens to be at the focus of attention. Furthermore, the concrete experienced event is always a flow of qualities; and qualities are not structures at all even though they are distinguished and are related to one another by structures. As said before, they are the changing content of the changeless structures.

Let us summarize what we have said about past, present, and future. The present is always a period of time in which we experience a flow of quality. It always includes a past indistinguishably merged with the present or, if you prefer to put it that way, a present indistinguishably merged with a past. Past, present, and the anticipated future are all determined by the structures which command attention. The past and present are concrete events having structures. The anticipated future is of anticipated structures which may or may not characterize events when the present becomes different from what it is now.

One last thing should be said about the creativity which is always present in time, and is creative of time, even as it is creative of our minds and of the world which our minds are able to experience. This creativity is always present in the sense that new structures are always being added to those which have characterized events in the past. This addition of added structure may be reduced to the minimum, but it seems that it is never altogether absent. Indeed we would have no sense of time if there were no creation of structures in our experience. The addition of new structures may vary from the minimum discernible, to some unknown maximum. Thus creativity can be more or less creative.

This creativity is not cumulative if the structures which have characterized events in the past become inaccessible to human knowledge and human awareness, and if this loss is as great as, or greater than, the addition of new structures brought forth during a given period of time. In such case creativity is not cumulative although it continues to be creative. On the other hand, creativity may be cumulative in the sense of adding more and more structure to the flow of experienced quality.

Still another distinction should be made in respect to creativity. Cumulative creativity may enrich experience or impoverish it. If the new structures added to the old are rich with quality, and if they vivify and clarify the total content of quality in the growing system of structures, then cumulative creativity enriches experience and progressively reconstructs the mind of man and the world he can experience in the direction of universal love as enunciated in the great summarizing commandment about love of God and neighbor. On the other hand, if the new structures added to the old, rendering life increasingly complex, are more barren of quality than the old structures were, and if they obscure and confuse the total content of quality in the growing system of structures, then cumulative creativity impoverishes life.

The relatively barren but instrumental structures of science and technology are needed in a complex society to provide enough to eat, to protect health, to make communication wide and free, to increase the range and variety of association by means of travel, to provide leisure from grinding and exhausting toil, to maintain relations of peace and goodwill, and to devise and uphold many other conditions required for the cumulative creation of structures rich with quality.

While the cumulative creation of accurate and efficient structures is thus necessary in a complex society, and may be developed and used to sustain and promote the enrichment of life, they may also be used and developed in a way to impoverish life. Whether they are used and developed in the one way or the other depends on the ruling policies and aims which control the conduct of human life. Above all, this most important issue is determined one way or another by the ultimate commitment. Only if man's ultimate commitment is given to the cumulative creativity which enriches life in ways leading to maximum increase of appreciative awareness can human life in a complex society be saved from conflicts internal to the individual personality and internal to society. These self-destructive conflicts arise within the individual person and within society when cumulative creativity impoverishes life. The reason they arise is because the basic, constitutive, universal, and imperative need of human nature, unconscious as this need may often be, is for enrichment by way of creativity.

What human life is all about is to achieve forms of thought and action which are as rich as possible with felt quality. Examples of such structures rich with felt quality are love, beauty, productive work which is deeply satisfying, and all forms of appreciative awareness. If the goal of life is determined by what is most satisfying to the whole being of man then the goal of life is to achieve the richest possible content of felt quality in the structures of thought and action by which we conduct our daily lives.

These structures of thought and action cannot be created merely by human striving. They can only be brought forth in human life by a creativity which creates the human mind and the form of the world which the human mind can experience. This creativity should command the ultimate commitment of man because it creates the human mind with its distinctive nature, it saves man from his destructive tendencies, and it satisfies the constitutive need of his nature when required conditions are present. Chief of these required conditions is that man commit himself most completely in religious faith to this creativity, to be transformed continuously by it and to serve it at any sacrifice by providing the other conditions which must be present for it to operate with greatest saving and transforming power.

This creativity cannot occur apart from time, hence is necessarily temporal. Therefore man's ultimate commitment should be given to what is temporal and not to eternity or the eternal. On the other hand, if "eternal" refers to a reality which preserves its identity through all the changes of time but has no being apart from time, namely, the creativity here under consideration, then it can be said that "the eternal" commands the ultimate commitment of man. But when such expressions as "time and eternity" are used, the necessary distinctions should be kept clear. Creativity is eternal not in the sense of being out of time or beyond time but in the sense of being continuously creative of the emerging present.

Chapter 5

THE GUIDE TO GREATER GOOD

R ECENT thinking about good and evil and right and wrong has been much disturbed about the meaning of the word "good." I shall, therefore, proceed at once to state what I mean by greatest good. It is the most complete satisfaction of the individual that is possible when the individual is viewed in the wholeness of his being. Any good less than the greatest is some approximation to this most complete satisfaction of the individual. The greater good is an approximation beyond some prior state of existence. In some cases great suffering can be a greater good than pleasure or other form of enjoyment, provided that the suffering is one element in a situation which upholds the integrity of the individual and satisfies that integrity more than any alternative available at the time.

In defining the greatest good the words "in the wholeness of his being" expose a serious problem with which human beings must struggle in seeking the greater good. It is the conflict within the human personality between opposing propensities and demands. It is the conflict which clinical psychology and psychiatry are describing. The interests which possess the conscious mind at any given time may find satisfaction in a way which defeats other interests of the same individual. When these latter dominate the conscious self the previous "satisfaction" may be evaluated as the extreme opposite of satisfying. Also the unconscious drives and demands which are being frustrated by conscious striving may never reach consciousness in such form as to be understood by the individual himself but may manifest themselves in fits of melancholy, in various forms of anxiety, and in self-defeating behavior.

All this has been said before but is here repeated to bring out the full significance of the words "satisfy the individual in the wholeness of his being so far as that is possible."

Much controversy has raged over the fact that any discussion of good and evil and right and wrong must begin with a definition of good and any such definition can be resolved to the statement: Good is good. Of course that is true but it applies to inquiry into any subject whatsoever and not only to the study of values. One must always begin with these words and these words must be defined. Furthermore these words must state what it is that one intends to examine. The subject matter may be specified by words which are arbitrarily defined because no words in current usage with conventional meanings are fit to designate with accuracy the field of inquiry. In other cases such arbitrary definitions are not required; but when words are used with their conventional meanings one needs to select some one of the conventional meanings and define it more precisely than is done in common conversation. To this end I have stated the sense in which I shall use the word "good" although further discussion of the subject is required to make the meaning more definite.

When anyone states what is good, the conventional practice in recent times has been to make the rejoinder: But suppose someone says that for him that is not good! So acutely have people become aware of the diversity of evaluations in different cultures and by different individuals and so violent has become the opposition against imposing uniformity that this reaction against any attempt to state the nature of good is almost automatic. This reaction presents a difficulty in any attempt to inquire if there may not be some kind of good which is common to all men and greater in value than all the diverse goods which also must be recognized. Any good common to all and greater in value than all the diverse goods must, of course, provide for diversity because diversity is required to satisfy the unique individual in the wholeness of his being. But such diversity cannot be had unless there is a good common to all which provides for it. Therefore it is an error to think that a good common to all must necessarily impose a uniformity denying those diverse values necessary to satisfy the unique demands of the individual. Exactly the opposite is the truth of the matter. The individual cannot have those values peculiar to himself unless there is a supervalue which sustains this kind of freedom.

Sometimes the objection raised against any statement about the greatest good common to all can be resolved by defining words. The objector may attach a different meaning to the word "good" than the meaning it must have when it designates the supervalue here under consideration. When that is the case there should be no dispute, once the parties concerned understand one another. Common words like "good" and "pig" and "man" have many meanings attached to them in current usage. No one of these meanings is more right than another. "Pig" means not only a certain animal; it also means a greedy person. Then there is pig iron and the piggy bank. Even more diversified are the meanings attached to the word "good." For any man to insist that no other meaning can be given to the word "good" except the one he attaches to it is foolish obstinacy.

The objection to what is here called good may, however, be of a different sort. The objector might mean that if he were put in a situation where he was most completely satisfied in the wholeness of his being, he would, if he had opportunity, reject that situation and choose another which would be less satisfying, even though he knew at the time that it would be less satisfying. If that is the contention, the objector is appealing to empirical evidence gathered by experiment. It might be impossible for the objector to undertake such an experiment self-consciously because he might feel that his own self-esteem depended on proving himself right. In that case his own state of mind would make it impossible to experience the more complete satisfaction.

There are other complexities of the total self which make it difficult to conduct this kind of experiment. Chief of these is the conflict between the different parts of the total individual, making it impossible for one to experience any satisfaction which approximates satisfaction in the wholeness of his being. Not being able to experience it, he can form no judgment about it.

Despite these difficulties many experiments and observations have been made upon human groups dealing with this problem of satisfaction. The observation is always made upon a group, at least a group of two, because the observer is himself a human being and his relation to the individual under observation makes a group of two. What he observes is always the individual in relation to him and himself in relation to the individual. Harry Stack Sullivan develops the implications of this idea very fully and shows that this involvement of the observer can be an aid and not a hindrance to the correct observation and understanding of the human being.[1]

These studies and experiments seem to indicate that the human being finds the most complete satisfaction of his individuality in its wholeness so far as that is possible in certain interpersonal relations when other conditions are favorable.[2] This kind of interpersonal relation we have tried to characterize, calling it creative interchange.

The term "greatest happiness" is not used to designate the greatest good because the philosophers from Aristotle down to recent times have not recognized the radical nature of inner conflict exposed by psychiatry and other social and psychological studies. They did, of course, recognize conflict within the human being; but the depth and complexity of it and the distinctive features of it developed by intensive and controlled studies were not known to them. Consequently their discussions of happiness have given a meaning to that term which makes it inapplicable to what is here called satisfaction of the individual in the wholeness of his being. Especially is this true of John Stuart Mill who, more than any other, has given currency to the idea of happiness as the ultimate goal of all human striving.

When happiness means most complete satisfaction of the interests which dominate consciousness, it cannot be the greatest good as here conceived because of the conflict between these interests and others which do not control consciousness but which are constitutive of the individual. Thus happiness in the sense of satisfying the interests which dominate consciousness cannot be a guide to the greater good unless qualified in a way which Mill inadvertently recognized without developing its implications. Because of this inner conflict, the pursuit of happiness without qualification can lead to the extreme opposite of greatest good.

A further distinction should be noted which characterizes the good as here interpreted. The good is not subjective when subjective means an experience which excludes environmental conditions and other persons. When inner conflict is modified in such a way as to yield an experience which satisfies the total self, so far as that is possible, this experience always includes environmental conditions and other persons. The other persons may not at the moment be physically present. Experience of other persons, when we experience their humanness, is always more than experience of their physical bodies. This further experience comes by way of signs and symbols which convey meanings shared in common by the individuals concerned. When one experiences these shared meanings he is experiencing the other persons even when they are not physically present. Sometimes the depth and fulness of these shared meanings cannot be experienced except in solitude and in such cases the experiencing of others is more profound in solitude than when they are physically present. Of course this fullest experience of other persons is not always in solitude, but it can be.

The experience of the good is an experience which includes both the total individual having the experience and the total effective environment, including other persons. Thus the good is not inside the individual. Neither is it outside. It includes both the organic individual and everything outside the individual which must be in existence for him to have the satisfying experience.

Such a statement does not mean that the good thus experienced is the total universe. An experiment can reveal what in the universe enters into the experience of the good and what does not. If anything in the universe can be changed without diminishing the good which is being experienced, it is not included in that good. Obviously enormous changes can occur and innumerable things can be changed without modifying the experience of the individual even when he is experiencing the most complete satisfaction of his individuality in its wholeness. On the other hand, many things cannot be changed without reducing this satisfaction. What cannot be changed without changing the experience is a part of that experience even though one can have no consciousness of it and will never know what it is. It is nevertheless a part of the total situation which yields the experience and in that sense is experienced. Therefore what is experienced as the greatest good is unknown to the individual in great part even when he can know certain features pertaining to it by which it is distinguished from other forms of being.

Experience in this sense can extend beyond the bounds of conscious awareness and beyond the bounds of knowledge. This should not be confusing or sound paradoxical. Every concrete thing we ever experience includes far more than ever reaches consciousness or is discovered by intellectual inquiry.

Relative to the greatest good which any human being can ever experience, the totality of all being should be distinguished in three ways. First is the totality of all which must have being for the experience to occur in the character of greatest good. Second is all which is irrelevant to the experience and all those orders of being which oppose the greatest good to all degrees of evil. Finally is the basic structure necessary to any being whatsoever. This basic structure is sometimes called "being as such."[3] It underlies all the changing forms of existence. It sustains the greatest evil as well as the greatest good. Therefore it cannot be included in what distinguishes the greatest good from the greatest evil.

If one claims that non-being is the greatest evil, the rejoinder is that one could not have the experience of anticipating non-being without sufficient being to enable him to have such an experience. Therefore the basic structure of all being is a part of what we experience when we experience the greatest evil, namely, the anticipation of non-being. If one goes farther and talks about good and evil apart from all human experience, and in that sense says that being is better than non-being, his words become meaningless, because we cannot discuss anything whatsoever except in relation to human experience.

As a necessary condition for the greatest good, being as such participates in the greatest good. As a necessary condition for the greatest evil, being as such participates in the greatest evil. Being as such is neutral with respect to the greatest good and the greatest evil. It can be neither guide nor support in seeking the greatest good or any good. He who perpetrates the greatest evil and becomes the greatest evil can depend upon it as reliably as he who serves the greatest good and undergoes transformation into the greatest good. To say that being as such is good when it means the basic structure upon which everything must depend in order to exist at all, is to make a false statement. Being as such can do nothing for man except to serve as the ground which is utterly indifferent and neutral to whatever happens. It is even more irrelevant to the good life than Aristotle's Unmoved Mover. The Unmoved Mover could at least serve as the ideal after which men might aspire. Being as such has no such relation to human life. If there is any validity in the concept at all, being as such is eternal. The word "eternal" has come to connote some being that is superior in goodness to human existence. If that is the necessary connotation of the word, it should not be applied to being as such. But being as such endures without change when all else changes.

When one says that being is better than non-being, no matter how men may evaluate their experiences of being, he is generally introducing surreptitiously and perhaps unintentionally his own experience of being and his evaluation of that experience. If so, he is contradicting himself when he says that being is better than non-being no matter how men may evaluate their experience of being. Indeed I do not see how anyone can discuss the subject except in terms of human experience of being. Only in those terms can we speak of being as good or bad. When being is evaluated in this way, it is found to be bad in those forms which oppose the satisfaction of the human individual when he is sufficiently unified to experience satisfaction in whole-ness. It is found to be good in those forms of being which do the opposite. But to say that being as such is good is contradictory to all human experience.

Another claim must be rejected which is often made when the subject of human values is introduced. It is often said that one cannot discuss the good and evil of life with any consistency unless he assumes without evidence that life is good. I see no justification whatsoever for such a claim. Rather such a claim introduces not consistency but self-contradiction into the entire discussion. Life is not good merely because it is life. Exactly the opposite is true. The greatest evil can be experienced only in life. Without life there would be no evil except in relation to life, and also no good. Precisely because life is not good but can be made either good or evil, there is sense in discussing the problem of good and evil. But to assume at the start that life is good regardless of how it develops and what happens, renders the discussion absurd.

Since life can have all extremes of good and evil and is the source of all evil just as much as it is the source of all good, reverence for life cannot be a guide to greater good. Reverence for the process which makes life good can be our guide; but just as surely reverence for life in the form of the process which creates maximum evil will make us the promoters of greatest evil. The greatest good is not a changeless state of being. The most complete satisfaction can only be found in a process of change but this change must have the character which satisfies. If the process ceases to be the kind of change which satisfies and becomes the kind of change which frustrates and reduces satisfaction to a minimum, it is no longer good. The kind of change which is excluded from the good is this kind.

The process of change which satisfies has been repeatedly described. It is that creative transformation of the individual which enables him to enter into fuller and more enriching inter-change with other individuals, which enables him to find more to appreciate in a greater diversity of situations. What is ap-preciated may be beauty or integrity; it may be intellectual brilliance or nobility of character; it may be simple humility or devotion; it may be physical, biological, psychological, social or historical; it may be any of the innumerable values which human beings can appreciate when the mind is properly cultivated, when the personality is rightly organized, when sensitivities are multiform and acute.

This process which expands and enriches the appreciable world cannot stop if the individual is to experience the greatest good. No matter what range and depth of positive value the individual may have reached, he cannot find satisfaction of his individuality in its wholeness unless the expansion and enrichment continue. If it stops at any level, no matter how rich his life may be at that level, misery, frustration, and desperation can occur if the creative transformation does not continue. Indeed life at the lower levels of stupor, dullness, and limited range cannot suffer so acutely as they who are frustrated at levels where sensitivity and appreciative awareness and eager anticipation have reached their maximum. Therefore the greatest good is a process of change. But not every change is good. Some kinds of change can be the greatest evil.

The controversy over whether change is better than changeless being is entirely futile. If changeless being refers to a definite kind of change and excludes other kinds of change, then the greatest good is a kind of changeless being. But if changeless being refers to a condition wherein change has been reduced to a minimum, it can engender misery and desperation. When creative transformation has lifted the individual or the group or the civilization to the higher levels of sensitivity and appreciation and then stops, the great evils known to history break forth. The execution of these evils is itself a process of change, but the desperation expressed by this behavior may have been induced at a prior period when creative transformation ceased for a number of individuals and the vacuity of life then ensuing had to be filled by fighting, rebelling, and orgies of various kinds.

Another distinction must be made if misunderstanding is to be avoided concerning the guide to greater good. The distinction is between the process of creative transformation and what this process creates. The greatest good is the process itself although it cannot be separated from what it creates. Evidence that the process of creative transformation is itself the greatest good has been set forth repeatedly. When this process ceases, the ensuing passivity is intolerable, no matter how great may be the enrichment of life attained at that level of development. This enrichment can be called created good. But if this enrichment cannot be used, or is not used, to promote further creative transformation, it is used to waste, to destroy, and to dissipate. This shows that created good, no matter how great it may become, cannot satisfy the individual in the wholeness of his being, but rather induces inner conflicts. The individual must commit himself to creative good, here called creative transformation, to find satisfaction. This seems to be an iron law, wrought into the nature of man. He is made for creativity and not for created good.

This does not mean, of course, that created good should not be enjoyed and used to the full measure of all the positive value it can yield. Not to enjoy and use all the good thus far created and do it to the utmost limit of one's capacity, is itself a delinquency. But a much greater delinquency occurs when one enjoys and uses created good in such a way as to obstruct creative good. This greater delinquency brings on all the major evils of human life and history.

This distinction between creative good and created good shows that there are two ways of speaking about the guide to greater good. One can mean the guide to that way of life in which the individual with more of his total being undergoes creative transformation. One can also mean the guide which leads to a greater magnitude of created good. Creative transformation is itself the guide to greater magnitude of created good. Striving to accumulate more created good in any other way than by creative transformation of self and society leads to frustration. Greater good attained thus by way of creativity demands religious commitment. This commitment requires action to modify all the conditions of human existence in such a way that this creative transformation can operate most effectively throughout society and human history.

The religious problem of commitment to creativity can be better understood if we examine what Harry Stack Sullivan calls "security operations."[4] These are devices by which the individual protects his self-esteem. The individual ordinarily is not conscious of his own security operations; but he uses them to protect that sense of his own self-worth without which he cannot live with any hope nor any confidence. These security operations, however, do not give the individual a correct knowledge of himself nor of his own worth. They are essentially deceptive. This becomes plain when we note how they develop.

Security operations are developed to protect one's self-esteem over against the ideas of oneself which other people have or which one thinks they have. One is never correctly understood in the wholeness of his being by other people; and in most cases one is approved or disapproved in terms which grossly misrepresent one's true self.

This approval and disapproval based on misrepresentation and misunderstanding of oneself begins in early childhood and continues throughout life. Against these false approvals and disapprovals the individual must protect his self-esteem. Yet the individual's own idea of himself is very largely shaped by what others think of him, not that he necessarily agrees with what others think, but what he thinks of himself is built up in defense against their judgments. Consequently security operations are ways of thinking, feeling, and acting performed to build and perpetuate a false picture of oneself, a false picture of other people and of the social situation.

These security operations which misrepresent oneself and others and the conditions of human existence cannot guide one into situations which satisfy the individual in his true character and wholeness. They do the contrary. They mislead. Yet these security operations determine in great part what the individual thinks is his own worth and the worth of other people and what he thinks are the good things to seek and cherish in life. Yet, so far as security operations dominate the individual, he seeks the opposite of what can satisfy himself in the wholeness of his being.

The individual is unable to correct the security operations which mislead him because they are largely automatic and un-conscious. This difficulty is further magnified by the individual's attaching his own self-esteem and his whole system of values to these devices. They determine what he is able to recognize as good, to seek, and to cherish. Consequently, if they should be suddenly removed, he would be able to recognize nothing as good either in himself or in others or in the world. The result would be a plunge to the depths of despair. So the removal of security operations is a slow and painful process. Yet the in-dividual can never find what satisfies him in the wholeness of his being until he is released from the domination of security operations. Until he is released, he cannot commit himself to what does satisfy that wholeness.

All this is a matter of degree to be sure. The individual can be released more or less from the control of security operations and perhaps no one is completely free of them. As it should be understood that the use of protective devices against the misunderstanding and misrepresentation of oneself by others does not mislead and is not an evil when deliberately employed to that end. This everyone must do in some measure and in some situations.

The chief evil of security operations is that they disrupt the unity of the self. Evidence seems to indicate that the newly born are unified as individuals and continue to have this unity until it is disrupted by security operations. Again this is a matter of degree. Some children are reared under conditions which disrupt the unity of the self much more than occurs with other children. The same applies to individuals at all stages in their develop-ment.

A unified self does not mean a self free of all conflicts. It does mean a self free of conflicts which cannot be treated in such a way as to promote creative transformation. The unified self is not a static or completed condition but the very opposite. It cannot be achieved or approximated except by commitment to creativity. Only by learning from others in depth and others learning from oneself in depth, thus releasing the wholeness of individuality in each, can man be unified and this unity be satisfied. But this involves continuous creative transformation with inner conflicts continuously undergoing modification.

This seems to indicate that man in his present condition is transitional to something beyond what he is now. He must either destroy himself or rise toward a level of being not yet within reach of his imagination. This was the teaching of Nietzsche and of many others. But the imaginative picture of the superman set forth by Nietzsche cannot be correct precisely because no man in his present state can imagine what that higher level of being may be. The chief thing to be transformed in man is his imagination, not his biological organism. Since the higher being will be chiefly distinguished by a transformed imagination, the imaginings of man today, including the imaginings of Nietzsche, cannot picture that transformed imagination.

When the creativity which accomplishes this transformation is seen to be the supreme good, everything should be condemned as evil in oneself and others and in social institutions which hinders it. Thus one will disapprove lying and stealing when they hinder creative interchange more than some practical alternative, but will not condemn them otherwise. One will condemn as morally wrong sexual promiscuity for the same reason and on the same condition. He will approve the lifelong bond of marriage between one man and one woman if this more than any practical alternative creates the most profound and comprehensive appreciative understanding of the unique individuality of one another.

Moral judgments with this standard are based on knowledge. The knowledge determining such judgments will be knowledge of the conditions which are most favorable for the kind of interchange under consideration. Conduct is morally right which provides conditions most favorable for the creative transformation of man both as an individual, as a society, and also as development throughout human history. When the requisite knowledge is unattainable, the intention so to act is morally right even when the act misses its goal. All the sciences can be enlisted to the end of obtaining the requisite knowledge to guide action which is morally right when right and good are determined by their relation to creative transformation and its required conditions.

An article in *The Bulletin of the Atomic Scientists* by E. A. Burtt shows how science might serve the cause of man in this way.

But may science refuse to give us the kind of knowledge that is desperately needed in our search for the way of life which leads to man's highest fulfillment, on the ground that her present concepts and methods are unable to yield it? Or is it her business to modify her methods when necessary, in order that she will be able to attain the understanding that might spell the difference between life and death, stable well-being and its opposite. . . .

To summarize. My contention is that it is one of the great tasks of scientists and philosophers of science—indeed, the most insistent task at the present moment in history—to distinguish between different sorts of order that can be discovered in the world, and to envision the type of order that is appropriate on the one hand to the scientist's material and on the other to the valid human ends which that material should rightly serve. Any other order, whether we wish it so or not, will inevitably serve some less valid or even undesirable human end. What this means is that science will need to adopt an over-all postulate of predictive order that is appropriate to any subject matter whatever; then, within this general framework it would distinguish the various types of orderly relationships that can be discovered, according as one's end in dealing with the objects and processes thus related varies. The aim will be to detect and clarify, in the case of each kind of subject matter, the pattern of order that will provide an effective means for achieving the ends distinctively appropriate to that field. It is in the area of psychological and social science that this is a crucial challenge.

To accept the challenge will mean a rather drastic revolution; it may require us to throw aside many of the habits and presuppositions that have governed our thinking in the past. But only thus will a stable coherence be established between our clearest ethical ideals and the methods by which we study the significant truths about man. The problem is not merely to establish a sound moral control over the application of scientific discoveries reached by our present techniques. The whole structure of the science of man, theoretical as well as practical, must be reconstructed so that it will harmonize with our moral and spiritual vision, and will become an effective instrument for its progressive realization.[5]

The satisfaction found in creative interchange stands in contrast to satisfaction which leads to quiescence and unconsciousness. Hunger and thirst are example of the latter. One ceases to be conscious of the satisfaction shortly after these appetites are appeased. Striving to escape from uncomfortable cold or heat, to escape from physical danger, and to recover physiological equilibrium are further examples. These satisfactions relieve a tension; when the tension is relieved consciousness of satisfaction sinks away.

Satisfaction found in creative transformation does not issue in quiescence and unconsciousness. It is satisfaction found in widening horizons; in changing qualities both felt and sensed which vivify one another; in insights which emerge with more inclusive integrations of experience. Friendly and stimulating conversation, discussion which unfolds wider ranges of meaning with distinctions more clearly defined; scientific research; artistic production; love in the form of continued companionship which deepens continuously the appreciative understanding of the unique individuality of one another; work which develops increasing mastery leading to more complex problems solved with magnified power of control, all these are examples of the kind of satisfaction experienced when one commits himself to creativity. It is not limited to the works of talented men. It can be found in any walk of life if conditions are favorable.

An objection to this understanding of the guide to greater

good comes from those who point to the ideal as providing this kind of guidance.

This objection stems from a confusion. An ideal is an abstraction but satisfaction can be found only in a concrete situation. A contemplated ideal may be very satisfying but this contemplation cannot occur apart from an existing situation which enables the individual to engage in that kind of contemplation. Therefore it is the existing situation which is satisfying. Not the ideal by itself, but the contemplation of the ideal is satisfying and this involves a very complex process of interchange between the individual and environmental conditions. When thus enjoyed, the ideal is not the distinguishing feature of some future state of existence but is one component of the present situation, an ornament of present actuality.

When ideals are valued not as objects to be contemplated but as possibilities to be actualized, they may seem to be better than the present state of affairs. But the possibility in the abstract, apart from actualization in the form of a concrete situation, is not good except as a utility. Abstract ideals and other abstract constructs are useful because they instruct us concerning certain elements by which to identify one situation as better than other. But always it is the concrete situation thus identified, never the abstractions apart from the situation, which can be called good. Therefore the guide to greater good is the actual process of transformation by which the present situation is transformed into a better one. It is not the ideal by which this better situation may be identified when attained.

There is another reason for saying that the ideal in abstraction and apart from an actual existing situation is neither a greater good nor a guide to greater good. Creative interchange transforms the individual and his situation so that his ideals become better than they were before. Ideals in this sense are better when they inform us more accurately concerning those features by which to identify concrete situations which will be better than the present when they are actualized. Since creative interchange improves the ideal as well as the concrete situation, it is the guide to greater good and not the ideal.

This problem of guidance to the greater good has become

urgent because of the way modern technology has modified the appreciative consciousness of man. Men are more confused and uncertain concerning what is better and worse and right and wrong than they were when a single, coherent, and unquestioned tradition shaped the mind and determined evaluative judgments. Increasing numbers feel that they have no guide to the greater good. Still others propose many diverse and contradictory guides. Men in other times may have been just as mistaken concerning better and worse as they are now, but they did not know it. Consequently they did not seek a guide to greater good because they thought they had it. Today they are seeking or at least do not claim to know. Still others deny that there can be any guidance except arbitrary judgment.

Recognition of the conflict between the different divisions of the total self has rendered the problem more baffling. Conscious rational inquiry itself becomes a barrier to finding the greater good when reason is not informed of the unconscious demands of the total self and the conditions required to attain that degree of integration which must be attained for any approximation to total satisfaction. When not instructed concerning these matters, the conscious mind using all the resources of reason will judge that to be good which cannot satisfy the total individual and which often conflicts radically with any such satisfaction. For this reason rational inquiry with its rational ideals must seek the greater good indirectly if it is to be successful. It must seek it by striving to provide conditions most favorable for creative interchange and then allowing this creativity to bring forth the greater good rather than going after it directly.

This procedure cannot be followed very far if the problem is limited to individual conduct or to groups of individuals. It must extend into the organization and conduct of basic institutions such as industry, government, education, institutional religion, and organized institutional science. This institutional problem and the opportunity it affords to magnify the power of creative interchange throughout our society will be examined in Part Two.

The argument of this chapter ends with a summary of the

major values derived from creative interchange and which can be had in no other way. The sixteen listed might be extended, but these should reveal the fundamental importance of this process going on in human life.

1] Human beings find satisfaction in being appreciated and understood by those whom they esteem to be significant persons.

2] Creative interchange tends to alleviate the conflict between superimposed conformity to impersonal standards and the demands of the concrete individual, thus reducing conflict between conscious and unconscious levels of the total individual.

3] Creative interchange enables each individual to make a larger contribution to the pooled resources of the community.

4] Creative interchange makes possible more intelligent and devoted co-operation in the complex enterprises of industry, government, and other large organizations which prevail in our society.

5] Creative interchange reduces the amount of coercion required in maintaining social order.

6] Creative interchange releases self-expression of the individual and thus provides for personal integrity.

7] Creative interchange conserves and accumulates more of the cultural resources transmitted through a sequence of generations, thus increasing the significance of history.

8] Creative interchange opens the most promising way to resolve the conflicts between the diverse cultures which are now forced by our technological society to live in close interdependence and intimate association.

9] Creative interchange creates the human kind of mentality throughout infancy and childhood, without it there can be no human mind.

10] Creative interchange creates the universe when universe means everything we can know, feel, or imagine.

11] Creative interchange provides the sense of personal security in interpersonal relations without which individuals resort to self-defeating and socially destructive behavior. Such behavior in some of its forms is called criminal, neurotic, or psychotic.

12] Creative interchange opens the way to appreciation of the tragedy and pathos, degradation and grandeur of man thus enabling one to experience life in all its dimensions of depth and fulness and vivifying contrasts of quality. Life thus lived may be called a rich life or an abundant life.

13] Creative interchange when given priority over all else is a guide to conduct enabling one to deal constructively with a greater diversity of situations, gather meaning and value from greater extremes of variation, and find a way through more radical changes of fortune than any other guide can do.

14] Creative interchange creates the only kind of love which can be extended to all men over the barrier of diversity and hostility, can be fully intelligent in dealing with them, and can provide maximum freedom for all participants.

15] Creative interchange creates maximum freedom for each to exercise his powers.

16] By bringing forth new patterns for living when disaster and social change render old patterns worthless, creative interchange provides ultimate security and spiritual renewal on condition that one give himself over to it with complete devotion.

Chapter 6

SOURCES OF MORAL CONFUSION

T HE TERM "moral confusion" is here used to refer to uncertainty, ambiguity, and contradictions not only about standards for moral judgment but also about all other standards for evaluating good and evil and better and worse in the diverse areas of human concern. This confusion has many sources but I shall here examine only a few philosophical theories and theological doctrines which I believe contribute to the confusion. Thereafter I shall indicate some of the distinctions which must be made if the confusion is to be cleared.

One way of seeking a standard for evaluation is the dialectic of question and answer made famous by Socrates and Plato. In this way ideals are discovered in the various areas where good and evil and better and worse must be distinguished and these ideals are accepted as standards for evaluation. In criticizing this approach I do not fail to recognize the indispensability of this dialectic in all thinking nor do I deny the great contribution which this procedure has made to our judgments of value. But ideals in bare abstraction cannot guide to the greater good. Kant sought his ultimate moral standard by this dialectic of reason and reached the conclusion that rigorous, universal rational consistency was sufficient in itself to make valid moral judgments. The limitation of this method appears when we note that the human mind undergoes creative transformation from infancy to old age, from one period of history and culture to others, and from one group of associates to another. Prior to modern times this way of seeking the good life did not encounter the difficulties it does today because social change was not so rapid and diverse traditions were not so closely bound together. Today all the cultures of the world are intermingled and social change is very rapid. Also the power to actualize the ideal was very limited in earlier times. Consequently the abstract rational ideal could float in the realm of dreams where it could not do great harm. But when men have the technology, the devices of propaganda, the skills and mechanisms of organization now available for moulding human life into the likeness of an ideal, the evil consequences become apparent. The abstract rational ideal differs from man to man and culture to culture and age to age even when the same word is used to express it. Note the difference in meaning conveyed by the abstract ideal of democracy when the word is used by Communists as compared with its use in the Western democracies. With closer interdependence of peoples devotion to opposing ideals produces moral confusion and endangers coexistence. Also the abstract ideal can never deal adequately with the complexities of the concrete situation nor meet the demands of individuality in its growing wholeness.

In sum, the abstract rational ideal is unfit to deal with the ever-changing concrete fulness of life, with the intricacy and subtlety of interpersonal and intercultural relations, and with the unpredictable creative transformations of the human mind.

A second area of inquiry where reason has sought guidance to the greater good is represented by the utilitarians. Here it is no longer the realm of abstract ideals which is searched, but rather the throng concrete fulness of life. In some of the modernized forms of this approach the procedure seems to be this: One inquires into all which he now likes and dislikes and into all which he can imagine himself liking and disliking in the consequences flowing from the alternatives before him. This should include all which he is now able to approve and disapprove in the interests of other people throughout the expanse of humanity and history so far as his imagination can extend. Then he should choose the alternative which yields the greater balance of what he favors and approves as over against what he disfavors and disapproves.[1] In this way he seeks the most inclusive, liberal harmony of all interests. "Liberal" in this context means that each individual should be free to choose what his own unique individuality demands so long as it does not hinder like privileges of others.

An outstanding present-day representative of his way of seeking guidance to the greater good was the late Ralph Barton Perry.[2] His theory of value, called the relational theory, is, perhaps, more widely held in philosophical circles at the present time than any other although the existentialists are in strong rebellion against it and so are many others. A very clear and simple statement of this approach is found in a book by Ian McCreal, *The Art of Making Choices*.[3] In this treatment of better and worse and right and wrong important contributions have been made to the problem of evaluation but my present purpose is limited to indicating how moral confusion arises from it when certain distinctions are ignored.

Professor McCreal defines the meaning of "good" by examining the word in a great variety of contexts. Following is a selection of diverse uses which upon examination reveal an underlying meaning identical in all cases.

"He is a good man." "This is a good hammer for driving nails." "I feel good all over." "What a good pie!" "Life is good." "Two o'clock would be a good time."[4] The list might be extended indefinitely but analysis of many cases reveals one single meaning for the word underlying all the differences. This one single meaning might be stated thus: An entity is good if under specifiable circumstances a person would favor it, provided he possessed knowledge of it or about it in certain respects. The word "entity" is used to indicate that what one favors might be a feeling, an action, a belief, a motive, an ideal, a human person, a society, a system, a method, a process, an existing material thing, or anything whatsoever which can be imagined or thought about. With this understanding, an entity might have great value although not favored by any person if in such case no person had yet discovered that aspect of it and those circumstances which arouse the attitude of favoring it. Good money is still good even when thrown away under the mistaken idea that it is counterfeit. A faithful friend is still good even when one mistakenly believes that he has been betrayed. Delicious food is still good to eat even when rejected because one has not yet tasted it and thinks it is not good. This is McGreal's own interpretation.

This idea of good identifies value with that relation between a conscious mind and some entity in which the entity is favored or disfavored by the conscious being. In Perry's language, any object takes on value by reason of the interest in it on the part of some conscious being. The interest may not be actually conscious here and now, but if an object is qualified under specifiable circumstances to excite interest in it when some conscious being becomes aware of it, then it has value under those circumstances and in that relation whether or not any conscious being has yet actually favored it.

My argument against this way of using reason as the guide to greater good can be summarized under two points.

1] What one can enjoy or imagine himself enjoying and what he can imagine others enjoying, with the experience and knowledge acquired to date, and with the help of tradition and custom, is no indicator of what he will be able to enjoy with more experience and more knowledge and with that progressive reorganization of his personality which interchange with others will produce. Neither is it any reliable indication of what others enjoy either now or later. The very mind he calls his own will undergo changes in capacity and form of appreciation which he cannot possibly anticipate. The same applies to other pers: s with whom he must reckon, both those with whom he is now associated and those with whom he will associate in years to come. Therefore to choose in terms of anticipated enjoyment of future situations for himself and others is to choose in a way that is doomed to error and disappointment. This does not apply to short-range choices such as food for dinner, gifts to buy for Christmas, and similar matters. But it does apply when one seeks that way of life which will lead through the years and generations to a greater good; and it applies to decisions which determine national and social policy effecting the lives of men in all the cultures of the world. Above all it applies when choosing a life commitment to which one gives his total self in trust that it will make for the greatest possible good for himself and for all men in all times.

All revolutionary increase in the number, variety, and integration of entities favored must come by way of new experiences which, prior to their occurrence, the individual cannot imagine. Therefore if the individual orders his life with maximum efficiency to have and promote only those entities which he can now favor, and exclude all which he disfavors, he will cut himself off from those entities which he would favor in the future if he could have access to them. But he never can have access to them because he has ordered his life in service only of what at a given time he can favor. Thus he shuts himself in a prison, so to speak, and shuts out the greater good which might have been attained in the future by the very zeal and ability with which he pursues the greater good within the limits of his ability to imagine it at the given time.

From observation of others and from the records of history, literature, and psychological studie , the happy life is most likely to result from new enjoyments arising unexpectedly, which could not be anticipated except in the sense of knowing that if one lives in such a way as to expand and deepen his capacity for appreciation such glad surprises will occur. But this cannot be accomplished by way of any calculus of specific favorings now accessible to knowledge and imagination.

2] In many, if not in most cases, pleasant feeling is caused by giving attention to some entity other than the pleasant feeling, say a friend or a baseball game or the future imagined in a dream. Therefore if one gives attention to his own pleasant feeling in order to evaluate it and not to the entity which causes the feeling, attention thus diverted from that entity which causes the enjoyment will result in its fading out. When attending a dramatic production or solving a problem or contemplating a sunset or conversing with a friend, full attention must be given to the production, problem, sunset, or friend if the value is to be experienced. Preoccupation with one's own favoring, therefore, shuts out the values. Such being the case, to find the greater good one needs to forget his own preferences and feelings of enjoyment and devote himself to what creates progressively in his own person and in his associates the capacity to appreciate a wider range and diversity of entities even though at the time he cannot imagine what these entities might be, and is totally unable to enjoy them until after the capacity to enjoy them has been created in him.

Still another way of judging better and worse is causing confusion. One accepts the standards of the culture within the society where that culture prevails. Here again we have guidance which applies to minor matters. One cannot safely ignore the common practices of the people with whom he may be associated. But in a world of tight-bound interdependence the standards of diverse cultures prescribe opposing ways of life. The Communist way of life conflicts with that of the Western democracies. The white and the Negro in South Africa find it difficult to live together and the diverse cultures of Asia conflict with one another and with the standards of people who live in other parts of the world. This conflict calls for adjudication by something other than the standards prescribed by the several conflicting ways of life.

The conflicts and confusions resulting from the standards thus far described, namely: the abstract ideal or universal principle, the harmonizing of diverse favorings, and the tradition and culture of a people, have led some to assert that the guide in making wise choices must be intuition. Certainly intuitions are indispensable but people have diverse and conflicting intuitions and the problem is to ascertain which intuitions point the way to the greater good and which do not. Furthermore, the intuitive

judgment of the total self in its wholeness, so far as this is approximated in human life, is very different from intuitions arising
in one level of the self—as opposed to other levels.

Nothing is good for the whole self if it is only good for a part
of the self when this part conflicts with other parts. Consequently
no evaluation of better and worse which the self can make is
valid unless it is the total unified self which does the evaluating.
But no human self ever is completely and perfectly unified.
Therefore no intuitive judgment can be said to be a judgment
made by the total self, although some individuals can approach
wholeness sufficiently to reveal the conflict between judgments
made in behalf of "security operations" and judgments made by
a self more or less unified and more or less free of security operations. This reveals the unreliability of intuition.

The confusion arising from these different standards for
judging better and worse and right and wrong has driven some
to declare that we must make our decisions without accepting
any standard. The existentialists are making this claim with Paul
Sartre reaching the greatest number of people with this declaration. Many who do not align themselves with the philosophical
existentialists nevertheless assert that decision is imperative but
cannot be made with the integrity and freedom required if they
accept any standard which reason or empirical evidence can
justify.

Every one of the five forms of judging right and wrong thus
far examined (namely, abstract ideal, harmony, mores of the
culture, intuition, existentialism) has made an important contribution, but they cannot deliver us from the confusion which
now prevails concerning right and wrong and better and worse.
Let us now glance at some of the theological doctrines which also
bear responsibility for the confusion of our time. Those to be
considered are: the appeal to God's will and biblical faith; the
appeal to the Christian tradition; the moral imperative to love;
the ontology of being; the leap of faith.

The first theological doctrine to be examined is the declaration
that God's will must be the guide. The difficulty here is to know
what God's will may be. Since no human mind can know God's

will in its scope and depth and fulness, the person who makes this claim is thrown back on some unquestioned authority. Generally this is the Bible as interpreted by the Catholic hierarchy or as interpreted by the sect to which the individual belongs or as interpreted by himself with some measure of independence. But all these several ways of interpreting the Bible contradict one another on many points. Some of the greatest scholars, such as Shirley Jackson Case and James Muilenburg, are diametrically opposed in their understanding of the message found in the Bible.

It should be added that some of the most scholarly theologians of our time, notably Professor Paul Tillich, deny that God has a will in any literal meaning of that word. He and others with him deny that God is a person, even though people generally symbolize the "power of being" by picturing the reality which engages their ultimate concern as though it were a divine person having thoughts, feelings, and a will. Belief in a divine person is theism, says Professor Tillich, and he rejects theism.[5] People symbolize in the form of a divine person the being upon which they are ultimately dependent for courage and hope, not because the symbol is descriptively true of this being but because of the psychological need to represent the "power of being" in this way. I refer to this teaching of Professor Tillich not because I think he is in error on this point but to show the contradictions and ambiguities arising in present day theology and in human thinking generally when God's will is said to be the guide to greater good.

A second source of moral confusion arising from religion is the appeal to Christianity as the standard for judging right and wrong and better and worse. Christianity is closely allied to biblical faith but it differs in two ways. First, it includes all the diverse and contradictory interpretations of the Bible when Bible is understood to include the Old and New Testaments. Second, and more important, Christianity stands in contrast if not in opposition to all the other religious traditions. When people appeal to Christianity as their standard they almost always mean a distinctive tradition, uniquely different from all others. The difficulty with this is that we are fast moving into a planetary society in which the majority of people will not accept this tradition peculiar to Western culture. Multitudes in Asia and Africa have a religious and cultural tradition of their own which they cherish as fondly as Christians cherish theirs and of which they are just as proud. Also, increasing numbers in Western culture do not look exclusively to the Christian tradition for guidance to the greater good. Furthermore, Christianity includes such a diversity of standards concealed under the use of common words such as "love" and "Christ" that reference to it as a standard for evaluation is unintelligible unless one knows the particular form of Christianity which the speaker represents.

For these reasons the declaration that Christianity or the Christian tradition can be the standard, generates confusion and is very misleading. This statement does not imply a repudiation of Christianity. No man can repudiate the religious tradition in which he has been reared if he engages in moral and religious inquiry. He may reject it verbally but the chief source upon which anyone of necessity must draw is the tradition which has created the symbolized meanings with which his mind operates in thinking about the guide to greater good. Karl Marx is an outstanding example of one who verbally repudiated his tradition but obviously embodies in his life's work one interpretation of the values and standards of his inherited faith.

A third form of religious teaching widely proclaimed in these days is the declaration that love is the supreme moral imperative. But it is impossible to love at command. Any attempt to obey a moral principle of that kind can only bring on hypocrisy and self-deception. This is quite obvious in the cases of many persons who accept "love" as the rule by which they live. However, there is something which one can do about love. It has been stated several times through this writing. One can seek to provide the conditions most favorable for that kind of interchange which creates appreciative understanding of the unique individuality of the persons involved. Under favorable conditions this may reach the level of love. But love must be created in us if we have it at all. To put this in theological language, love must be given to us by the grace of God.

A fourth source of moral confusion in theology is exemplified by the distinguished scholar and religious thinker, Professor Paul Tillich. He has done magnificent work in clearing away large blocks of misleading theology and his profound insights are abiding contributions of great significance. But I believe that his attempt to interpret the greatest values of life in such a way that they can be found in "being as such" or "being itself" or "the power of being" can only magnify the moral confusion of our time.

He has attempted to give an ontological interpretation to love, power, and justice.[6] Ontology as understood by Professor Tillich is inquiry which seeks by analysis of experience to discover what is necessary for the existence of anything whatsoever. What is thus necessary and common to all existence he calls "being as such" or "being in itself" or "the power of being." Being as such is made up of those structures which are necessary to all existence and to all possibilities of existence. These structures which enter into being as such must be sharply distinguished from those other structures which are peculiar to different kinds of existence. Structures which distinguish stars from apple trees, human beings from goats, and every kind of thing which can be distinguished from other kinds, are excluded from being as such or the power of being. In that sense being as such is not a thing. That is to say, it enters into everything and, therefore, does not distinguish any one kind of thing from other things.

> Ontology . . . separates those elements of the real which are generic and particular from those elements which are constitutive of everything that is and therefore universal. It leaves the former to the special sciences or to metaphysical constructions, it elaborates the latter through critical analysis.[7]

.   .   .   .

> . . . non-being is not foreign to being, but . . . is that quality by which everything that participates in being is negated. . . . Being which includes non-being is finite being. 'Finite' means carrying within one's being the destiny not to be. It designates a limited power of being, limited between a beginning and an end, between non-being before and non-being after.[8]

Professor Tillich says that the love, power, and justice experienced in human life are present in the power of being, but only in a metaphorical sense. "Metaphorical" must be emphasized because the only kind of love, power, and justice which can be found in being as such must be identical with the love, power, and justice to be found in moons and stars, in atomic explosions and dinosaurs and in everything else which ever existed or ever can exist in *so far as these all participate in the power of being.* This follows from Professor Tillich's definition of being as such, namely, the being which enters into everything which exists because otherwise it could not exist.

Now the love, power, and justice which are the great values to be sought by creative transformation of human existence cannot be the love, power, and justice fully present in that initial form of existence out of which the human level has arisen by a long sequence of creative transformations. Yet this initial form of existence, like everything else, must have had in it the power of being fully as much as the highest attainment of human life.

There is another interpretation of the power of being which would avoid this confusion, but it would contradict the above quotation in which Professor Tillich defines the power of being. According to this other interpretation, the power of being would be more fully present in, say, the saint than in the germ which kills the saint. But if that should be granted, the power of being would help to distinguish one kind of being from other kinds and that contradicts the definition of the power of being as stated in the passage above quoted. The power of being can in no way distinguish one kind of existence from other kinds.

It would be contradictory to Professor Tillich's idea of being as such to say that it contains in potentiality all the highest values ever to be attained in the development of particular kinds of existence whereby they are distinguished from other kinds as, for example, the human kind of existence. Furthermore, this would entail that all the potentialities of utmost evil also reside in being as such. Also "potentiality" in this sense is not intelligible.[9] Apparently Professor Tillich's purpose is to provide an ontological ground for love, power, and justice and thus give them eternal validity and ultimate authority. But in attempting to do this he creates moral confusion because the ontological ground sustains in existence the very worst as much as the best. The process of degradation to the last demonic level participates in the power of being as much as the creativity toward the highest.

Professor Tillich recognizes the confusion and the evil which result from the theological teaching that our guide to greater good is the divine will of a supernatural person.[10] His logic and his insight in correcting this theological error deserve our gratitude. But his own ontological treatment of love, power, and justice is no less a source of confusion in evaluating the alternatives which determine the course of human life.

One may derive courage from the belief that love, power, and justice are eternally present metaphorically in the being which forever conquers non-being. But the metaphor confuses the moral issues as I have tried to show. There is another way to peace, joy, and courage while accepting the inevitability of non-being in the forms of guilt, chance, and death. In this other way the moral issues are not so confused.

In this other way to courage one gives himself as completely as possible to the best that is or ever can be. This best is not a future state but the actual, present process of creativity. Guilt, chance, and death are accepted as helpers in making this commitment because these limitations imposed upon one's existence enable him to gather up his total existence in one package, so to speak, and deliver it entire to this greatest good. To be sure, no one can do this perfectly; but the recognition of guilt, chance, and death in their full and inescapable reality enables one to do it most effectively. This becomes obvious when one compares the limitations of his existence with the opposite. If he were infinite in power to overcome non-being and thus self-sufficient and perfect, he would have no inducement to give himself in such devotion nor would it be possible. The finite individual, on the other hand, can find courage to the measure of his devotion by giving himself just as he is with all the weaknesses and evils which characterize his total existence. Guilt, death, and chance do not sap courage when they are accepted as inescapable elements in life and are given along with all the rest of the total self in service and devotion to the limit of one's ability, however limited that ability may be.

One final source of confusion in current religious thinking should be examined.

Soren Kierkegaard and his present-day followers have made a great contribution to our understanding. They have revealed a depth in existence which is concealed from awareness by conventional ways of thinking. They rightly teach that the self in its wholeness, otherwise called the authentic self, makes demands vastly beyond those consciously acknowledged. Also demands are made on the total self far in excess of the responsibilities ordinarily assumed. Furthermore we achieve freedom only when the authentic self acts, making these demands and assuming these responsibilities. The existentialists have further shown that good and evil are not merely the relations between conscious mind and object which generate satisfaction or dissatisfaction. Neither can good be identified with conformity to an abstract principle. Rather good and evil are states of existence. Good is that state of existence where the authentic self acts, assuming its full responsibilities and making its demands in their full magnitude.

For this teaching we should be grateful to the existentialists. But they have been so concerned to demonstrate the depth and richness of concrete reality and to show how abstract theoretical thinking ignores this depth and richness, that they provide no general principles for guiding moral decision except the demand that decisions be made by the authentic self and not by any one part of the self to the exclusion of the rest. They are correct in saying that no abstract ideal and no abstract principle can be identified with the good which we seek nor the good which we should become. This good must be the total authentic self in some state of being. But to know how to act and what to seek we must have guiding principles. To be sure these guiding principles can only indicate the course of action. They cannot comprehend the wholeness of the self and the depth of being which is the good that we should become. This wholeness and this depth can never be comprehended by any theoretical formulations. But theoretical formulations we must have to guide action and decision. These the existentialists have not provided.[11] When they are religious they give us only some form of the leap of faith.

The story told by Kierkegaard of Abraham going forth to kill his son at God's command reveals in a very vivid way both the truth and the limitation in the teaching of the religious existentialists. In this story the whole self of Abraham acts without concealing any of the dreadful realities involved. But no guiding principles distinguishing right and wrong and better and worse are recognized. In some of his later writing Kierkegaard tries to recover from this moral anarchy but never succeeds nor do the other existentialists.

This completes the examination of the sources of moral confusion found in various forms of contemporary philosophy and religious thinking. The most popular of these views is the "liberal harmony" represented by Ralph Barton Perry and Ian McGreal. Liberal harmony is the standard which has been identified with our Western democracy and is most congenial to our way of thinking. On that account it is difficult to see the danger in it. To expose this danger further criticism is required.

When judgments of better and worse are made by many people these value judgments cannot be readily ordered into a liberal harmony if they are judgments made by the total self in all the uniqueness of its individuality. Consequently the standard of liberal harmony tends to develop judgments of the partial self. These value judgments of the partial self can become pernicious when they do not generate conflict between associated individuals. The associates thus in agreement may be a small group such as a family or neighborhood or they may include an entire nation or even the whole of humanity. Such an harmony is pernicious when all the associates support one another in judging to be good what is evil relative to the whole self of each. This collective judgment makes it exceedingly difficult for any individual or small minority to break through the crust of conformity thus imposed. Especially is this true if the mass agreement is about a matter mistakenly held to be of supreme importance for the nation or the total culture or, as it might be, for all humanity. In this way men are caught in a trap of collective judgment and driven to seek evil under the illusion that it is good. To some degree, perhaps, we are all caught in this kind of trap; but this corruption of the moral judgment caused by the mass judgment of partial selves is a matter of degree. Some societies are much better than others in this respect and under favorable conditions the evil can be corrected through indefinite degrees short of perfection.

One does not escape from this predicament of the divided self in agreement with other divided selves merely by rejecting the judgment of the majority and becoming a dissenter and individualist. Mere dissent does not restore the unity of the self nor enable the individual to recognize what is good for the total self. The individualist in rebellion against the judgment of the group or in arrogant assumption of superiority is likely to be just as much divided in himself and, in consequence, incapable of sound judgment. Neither in mass conformity nor in individualistic opposition to the mass does one find unity of the self and what satisfies this unity.

The self can be unified only by what satisfies the total self. What satisfies the total self is that creative transformation which enriches experience by expanding the range of what can be appreciated, understood, and controlled by learning from other people through appreciative understanding of them. This is the work of creative interchange.

Individuals who are unconscious of being divided selves and who do not know that the good they seek is evil relative to a unified self cannot, except to slight degree, engage in creative interchange because only one level of the self in conflict with other levels can communicate. How, then, is deliverance possible? When I speak of deliverance I do not mean a sudden leap to perfection but I mean a development in the direction of greater good.

Ordinarily deliverance is not possible unless something happens to the society which produces the following chain of consequences. The event disrupts the harmony of evaluations achieved by partial selves. This generally requires some degree of breakdown in the social order which sustains the harmony. This may be caused by conflict with an opposing way of life which causes individuals and social leaders to examine critically their accepted goals and goods and see the evil in them. Under these conditions some individuals may begin to engage in the kind of interchange with one another which makes them aware of the need of being made whole and the worthlessness of what they have heretofore prized as good. This group by creative interchange gradually develops in the direction of the greater good and spreads its influence, gathering others into this same way of life.

This deliverance from the divided self and from the pursuit of what satisfies one level of the self in opposition to other levels can be translated into theological language. It is salvation initiated by confession and repentance of sin brought on by suffering of the Cross and consummated by forgiveness of sin in interpersonal relations. The whole procedure is the work of divine grace because it cannot be initiated by volition of the individuals concerned but is given to them by creative interchange when required conditions are present. The deity operating in this way is the creativity repeatedly described.

The suffering of the Cross is any suffering which induces confession and repentance of sin. Sin at its deepest level is inability to commit oneself to the creativity which saves and transforms. Confession and repentance of sin is initiated by divine grace after some breakdown has brought individuals to themselves. The story of the prodigal son illustrates the way in which this occurs. Confession and repentance of sin lead to forgiveness.

Forgiveness in this context is not merely a judgment upon oneself by a supreme Being. Rather it is a change wrought in oneself. It is change *from* a state of being in which one cannot enter into appreciative understanding with others. It is change *to* a state in which one can have this appreciative understanding of the other despite wrong done and wrong suffered.

This change in oneself is wrought by divine grace. This means that in the state of bitterness and resentment or in the state of arrogance and assumed self-sufficiency one cannot by deliberate volition change himself in a way to open the channels of free and full communication with others. But conditions can occur wherein creative interchange breaks through the barriers of estrangement and opens the way to appreciative interchange. This work of divine grace results in salvation when salvation means restoration of the self in growing wholeness and the satisfaction of this unified self in the experience of continuous creative transformation.

The inability of men to give themselves completely to what saves and transforms can be called original sin. Here we have a term with many meanings which must be repudiated in order to make clear the one meaning intended. Original sin is not a condition of the newborn infant. But every newborn infant is helplessly in the nurturing care of human beings who are inwardly divided. On that account they interact with the child in such a way as to produce in him a divided self. This develops in the child a way of life in which evil is judged to be good when evil is what opposes the unification of the self but satisfies the partial self.

When a child developing under these conditions reaches the level where he can make choices and self-commitments by way of symbolized meanings he is unable to give himself to the greatest good which human life can ever have. This is the predicament which calls for divine grace. Divine grace comes by way of the fellowship of those committed to creative interchange and through whom this creativity reaches out to other persons.

The only way to keep evil in the realm of possibility and out of actuality is to be forever aware of it as a danger and by heroic and saintly action to guard against it. In a perfect world great art would still be required to set forth by works of imagination the contrast and the struggle between good and evil. In a world free of all actual evil this service of great art would be more urgently and imperatively needed than it is in our imperfect world because in no other way could evil in its true magnitude and in its true character be kept vividly and constantly in the minds of men. Without this awareness the world would automatically and inevitably sink into evil.

The pattern of coherence revealed to us in great art is not the coherence of the actualities of good and evil but it is the coherence of the awareness of good and the awareness of evil, presented in such form that we find in this coherence a profound satisfaction of the unified self. The self in such an experience is unified (relatively speaking) because in this experience it is not striving with hidden terror and other forms of anxiety to keep out of consciousness the reality of evil beating on the doors of awareness. Since evil is now allowed to enter consciousness, the self is relieved of this strain and inner conflict which divides the self into parts opposed to one another.

Thus it is no paradox to say that the awareness of evil is a great good second to none, while the actuality of evil is the extreme opposite of good. Furthermore the actuality of evil need not occur to keep men vividly aware of it. I am not suggesting that human life will ever be entirely free of the actuality of evil. But this condition can be approached indefinitely provided that the increase of good carries with it an increase of men's awareness of evil. If this does not occur, if the increase in men's awareness of evil does not increase along with human good, the increase of good will soon come to an end and the reverse process begin. There is no known limit to the increase of human good if these conditions be met.

In order to act intelligently in the struggle to make life better, it is necessary to clear away the confusion which now obscures the guide to greater good. It has been the intention of this chapter to point out some of the sources of this confusion. The next chapter will continue this endeavor by discussing the distinctions and connections between reason, faith, and freedom.

Chapter 7

REASON, FAITH, AND FREEDOM

THESE THREE, reason, faith, and freedom, all indispensable to the conduct of human living, are often interpreted and practiced in ways so diverse as to bring the three into conflict with one another. But human life suffers serious damage when reason, faith, and freedom do not support and magnify one another. Hence conflict between them would seem to indicate a mistaken interpretation. This error is, I believe, very common. Consequently there is need to examine the three in their relation to one another. Religious faith and theology, as frequently practiced, allegedly transcend the bounds of reason and reject its claims in certain areas. Freedom also is involved because, as we shall try to show, freedom is restricted when faith assumes the form of belief beyond the tests of reason. Since theology is the discipline chiefly responsible for interpreting faith in relation to reason and determining the form and limits of reason in matters of faith, perhaps the best approach to the problem is to ask certain questions of theology. Theology is not one but many. Different individuals and groups have different theologies which often contradict one another. Hence the answer which one theology gives may be contradicted by the answer of another.

The first point to consider is the way of access to truth which theology claims for itself. Is theology limited to the use of reason, even as science, common sense, and philosophy? Or does theology have another way of gaining knowledge which science, common sense, and philosophy do not have?

Science is distinguished from common sense not in the sense that the one uses reason and the other does not. Both use reason but in different areas and in different ways. Philosophy is distinguished from the practical arts, and both from science and common sense, not in the sense that some use reason and the others do not. All use reason; but they deal with different areas and problems, hence use reason in different ways.

Is theology distinguished in like manner, using reason and reason only for getting knowledge and solving problems, but applying reason to different problems and so using it in a different way? Or, on the other hand, does theology have a way of reaching knowledge of reality which is other than the way of reason? And does faith have a way of gaining access to reality which is other than the way of reason?

The last two questions bring out a distinction which, if ignored, leads to confusion. The distinction is between access to reality and access to knowledge of reality. The two are not at all the same. Breathing has access to reality and so does digesting and so does loving and so does faith. But the experience of reality had by these several ways does not necessarily yield knowledge. Loving, for instance, is an experience of reality, but he who has this experience may have a very mistaken idea of what it is he is experiencing. Life is made up in great part of noncognitive strivings which give us access to reality in many forms but without knowledge. The experience had by way of these noncognitive strivings such as breathing, digesting, loving, and having faith, do not yield knowledge until a proposition has arisen in the mind which meets the tests of reason. Not otherwise is knowledge to be had in any area whatsoever.

Of course breathing is no less of value even when it does not yield knowledge, and the same is true of loving and having faith. But as life becomes more complicated, these all need the guidance of knowledge and become dangerous when not so guided. When industry fills the air with poisonous fumes, breathing should be guided by knowledge. When conflicting forms of faith bring on wars which destroy the human race, faith should be guided by knowledge.

From all this we conclude that faith is not a form of knowledge; but faith like breathing or love may yield experiences from which reason may obtain knowledge not otherwise accessible. From this also we conclude that theology is mistaken when and if it claims to gain knowledge by way of faith or Bible or any other source allegedly transcending the tests of reason.

It is true that reason is not creative when we mean by "reason" nothing more than the tests by which we distinguish what statements are true and what are not. Breathing, digesting, loving, having faith, and many other noncognitive activities must generate the experiences, and creativity must generate the concepts and propositions, before the tests of reason can be applied. In that sense reason is not creative while noncognitive strivings and creativity are. But we do not have any reliable knowledge until after the tests of knowledge have been applied. In this sense there can be no knowledge which transcends reason, even though a great part of experienced reality does transcend both knowledge and reason.

The word "reason" has been used in different senses. To avoid confusion and ambiguity it is necessary to pin the meaning down to one and only one of these several different interpretations. If reason should be identified with creativity as creativity has been interpreted in this writing, it would be very different from reason identified with the tests distinguishing true from false statements. It is confusing to use the same word to refer to matters which have almost nothing in common. Therefore we shall be thinking of reason not as the creation of insights but as the methods and operations by which true statements are tested and distinguished from false statements, from dreams, aesthetic and artistic creations, fanciful imaginings, and much else of like sort.

But here again let us not introduce falsifying evaluations. Dreams have their own value and so do aesthetic and artistic creations and fanciful imagining. So do myths and legends, love and devotion, worship and ecstasy. To say that none of these can be identified with knowledge, except only that meager element in them made up of statements which have met the tests of reason, is not to disparage in any way the value of these creations and experiences. The good life includes much more than knowledge. But the good life cannot protect itself when it uses as though it were knowledge what is not knowledge. Myth, legend, love, devotion, worship, and ecstasy can themselves become evil in the sense of leading to confusion and error if the element of knowledge is not clearly distinguished from what is not knowledge. Only after the tests of reason have been applied can we know that a statement is true with some degree of probability, this probability itself being determined by these tests. A statement might be true before it has been tested, but we cannot know that it is true until after the tests, and in this sense knowledge cannot be had without reason.

Reason, as the word is here used, can be most simply defined as the method of analysis, observation, inference, prediction, experiment, and logical coherence. I shall not attempt to enter into all the subtleties and complexities of this method and all the many forms that it assumes in the different areas of knowledge with different kinds of problems. But through all these complexities and diverse forms these six are always present—analysis, inference, prediction, experiment, and logical coherence.

As said before, reason cannot itself produce the insight, the theory, the innovating idea, the hunch, the clue, or the suggestion to be tested. Reason is exclusively a method for distinguishing what is true and what is false in these insights or new ideas and showing how they should be applied or used, whether as descriptions or as ideals or as aesthetic fictions, or as rules of procedure or whatever they may be. Without this method of reason for distinguishing true from false, fact from fiction, systematizing formula from empirical description, moral ideal from phantasy, illusion from true perception, beliefs from rules of procedures, and all the other distinctions which must be made, we cannot know what a new idea really is. Therefore these distinctions and tests must be carried out by reason. But the new idea, the insight, the suggestion cannot be produced by reason. The new idea is the grist for the mill of reason but reason cannot create its own grist. Creativity produces that.

The new idea or insight which presents itself to reason for testing may come when reading the Bible or talking with another person or in the hour of meditation or in a thousand other ways. But every affirmation that enters the mind when reading the Bible is not necessarily true. Nor is every affirmation which emerges when talking with another person or when in meditation. We must have some way of testing these ideas which arise in the mind so as to allocate them each to its proper place and function in the conduct of human living. The performance of this task when properly done we call reason.

A very simple example of the way reason works appears when we try to understand what is in the mind of another person. The other person speaks and I hear him. Hearing is observing. Observing means apprehension by any of the senses. This hearing must generate in me some idea of what is in the mind of the other person. This is an insight, clue, or suggestion. But this idea I have of the other person may be mistaken. Even when partially correct, it is never the whole truth. Therefore it must be tested for error and for further interpretation by reason.

The method of reason in this case is to listen attentively to the further statements of the other person. This listening is further observation. These further statements made by the other person may either confirm or refute my first idea of his meaning. My attention to these further statements are further observations by which I test and correct, or further develop, my first idea of what was in the mind of the speaker.

My first idea of what the other person means to say involves the prediction that later statements made by him will confirm this original idea. Question and answer can be a kind of experiment. After the first statements have been made I have some idea of what the other person means. The questions and answers are experiments by which I gather evidence to show either that this first idea is correct or is not. Also these experiments may be conducted to elaborate and develop my understanding. In any case, they are in principle the same as any experiment with its accompanying observations, inferences, predictions, and logical coherences. Whenever doubt arises concerning what is in the mind of the other person, this is the common procedure and it is rightly called reason. Generally this procedure also includes observation of the posture of the other person, tone of voice, expression of face, the social and physical condition in which he speaks. The same words in one situation have a very different meaning from their use in another context. But all this is analysis, observation, experiment, and logical coherence. It is reason.

Note that in thus coming to understand another person two things are necessary—insight and reason. Either one without the other will get nowhere. If I do not have the insight in the form of an emerging new proposition to test, no amount of reason will enable me to understand the other person. On the other hand, if I have a first insight but refuse to test, correct, and develop it by listening attentively to further statements and making all the other observations, inferences, predictions, and observing the logical rule of noncontradiction, I shall not only misunderstand him. By holding to my first idea about the other person in this dogmatic manner, and refusing to modify, correct, and develop it by listening attentively to all the other things he says and observing all the other evidence, I shall be building a barrier of misunderstanding with all the attendant evils of conflict, suspicion, fear, and hate. By refusing to add reason to insight I shall be sinning against the God of love. Another name for insight is intuition. The two terms are equivalent. In the present context they refer to a statement which calls for the tests of reason.

It is true that two or more persons brought into interchange with one another under proper conditions can have floods of experience which they assume is shared with one another. With this fullness of shared experience they may act intuitively and by unchecked impulses in such a way as to sustain a total system of mutual support and rich experience. All this can occur without any tests of reason because nothing happens which suggests the need of verified statements. In such cases knowledge is not sought unless some affirmation or negation emerges in the mind which leads to some unwanted experience and which, on that account, requires to be tested, corrected, or exchanged for a more trustworthy affirmation or negation.

The depth and fulness of experience we have of another person is not knowledge. Only the statements we make to ourselves or to another about such experiences can be called knowledge if they have met the tests of reason. To reduce the depth and richness of experience to the abstractions of knowledge would deprive human living of almost everything which makes it good. That fulness of experience called communion of minds is one of the greatest goods of life, but it is not knowledge. Only tested statements about it can be knowledge. In a complex and changing society such knowledge about the communion of minds is indispensable to avoid disaster. No doubt the Nazi youth under the dominance of Hitler telling them that they shared the noble destiny of the Aryan race to rule the world of its own good had a very profound communion of minds which led to concerted action in which they joyously gave up their lives. We need to have knowledge about such experiences as well as the experiences themselves. He who refuses to use reason in such cases is likely to be the source of confusion, ill will, misunderstanding, conflict, and the builder of barriers of ill will, fear, suspicion, and hate between individuals and groups, peoples and cultures.

Let me take another example in which one might think at a superficial glance that reason in the sense of analysis, observation, prediction, experiment and logical coherence cannot be used, but where in truth they must be. I take the example of Radhakrishnan's philosophy. In a radio broadcast he set forth the form of Hindu philosophy which he is defending.[1] He says that the reality which concerns religion is invisible. It is the ultimate reality hidden in the depths of the being of all individuals, infinite and all-unifying, and the same for every person. First of all, I must understand what he means when he speaks in this way. To this end I must use reason in the way just indicated. Then I must find this reality in the depths of my own being. When and if I find it, or think I find it, some proposition about it must be available because otherwise I have no way of knowing if there is any such reality. This first proposition which comes to my mind of what I think I have found in the hidden depths of my individual existence is what I here call an insight, suggestion, clue, or theory. If such an insight does not arise in my mind, I can never know what Radhakrishnan is talking about. If it does, I must subject it to the tests of reason by making further observations. Otherwise I shall very likely be misunderstanding him and what I think I find will not be what he means at all. Radhakrishnan describes the experience thus:

> When the individual withdraws his soul from all outward events, gathers himself together inwardly, strives with concentration, there breaks upon him an experience, sacred, strange, wondrous, which quickens within him, lays hold on him, becomes his very being.[2]

If it is said that they who have this experience do not need to communicate nor exercise reason to understand what the other asserts because they have already been united in the experience of the One all-inclusive Being, I think the claim is unjustified. How do I know that I have experienced the One all-inclusive Being which the other has experienced? If I cannot by way of communication know what the other has experienced, how do I know that he and I are experiencing the same reality? I can believe it, of course, just as I can believe almost anything if I disregard the tests of reason. At times Radhakrishnan seems to agree that the experience he is considering yields no knowledge for he says further, "it is beyond the word of tongue or concept of mind." If there is no claim to knowledge then of course there is no argument, but in that case we cannot know what this experience is nor what the reality is which is experienced, nor can we make any claim concerning it other than the claim that some kind of experience occurred which is "beyond the word of tongue or concept of mind." In that case, I do not see how we can say that the reality experienced is the One Being which includes all or is divine or has any other character except only that the experience happened to be very delightful, supposing it was.

The point of these remarks is only to show that even the mystic and transcendentalist cannot escape the tests of analysis, observation, inference, prediction, experiment, and logical coherence if he is to assume any responsibility for the truth of his beliefs, for the instruction of his fellow men, and for doing anything to help others along the way.

I shall not discuss further the nature of reason. It is a vast subject. All I can do here is to define reason in one of the many uses of the word and illustrate how it works in test cases, especially cases where many seem to think that reason does not apply, namely, in understanding other minds and in mystical experience. Faith in the sense of commitment to creativity generates insight and insight is the material with which reason works. In this sense faith and reason are necessary to one another and work together. But just as soon as either one (or both) is interpreted and practiced independently of the other, it becomes an obstacle in the way of getting the knowledge. Faith must generate the insight; reason must discover what the insight truly signifies.

At this point someone may object that religious conversion cannot be accomplished by rational persuasion. That is true; but the way we know it to be true is by reason, that is, by observation, inference, prediction, experiment, and logical coherence. Religious conversion is not accomplished by reason. Surely not. Neither does the blood circulate by reason. Neither do the flowers bloom in the month of May by reason. Neither does reason cause people to love one another. The child does not grow to maturity by reason, although the ability to reason grows in the child when required conditions are present. Insights are not generated in the mind by reason. But reason has its proper work to do and every claim to knowledge which has not met the tests of reason is a false claim.

Given the insights, reason and only reason can discover the conditions which must be provided for the blood to circulate, the flowers to bloom in May, the child to grow to maturity, the sinner to undergo conversion, and love to increase among men. Only by reason can we discover what beliefs and affirmations about God are true and which ones are false.

In controversy with Professor Raphael Demos, Professor C. J. Ducasse discusses the claim that religion has a way of attaining knowledge beyond the reach of reason. Mr. Demos defends the claim that religious knowledge is of a different kind from that of common sense, science, and philosophy, therefore must be judged by different criteria. In reply Mr. Ducasse makes the following statements:

Now, Professor Demos's initial and most radical contention was, we noted, that the basic beliefs of science are, like those of religion, matters of pure faith. This contention, however, and all that he rests upon it, is, I submit, disposed of at one sweep by the fact, which the preceding remarks have made clear, namely, that what he calls the basic beliefs of science *are really not beliefs at all*, but are the rules of the game of pursuit of knowledge; and that it is only within this game, i.e., in terms of its rules, that the question whether a given belief is erroneous or true, groundless or well-grounded, valid or invalid, has any meaning at all.

This game, however, is the one which the theologian too intends and purports to be playing; but he cheats at it when he takes, as starting point for his inferences of fact, assertions merely *known to be contained in the Bible*, instead of —as the rules of that game require—assertions *known to be true* by observation, whether physical, psychological, sociological or other. The automatic consequence of such cheating is that the beliefs reached through it put into the hands of the cheater no verifiable power to predict events, nor any verifiable power to control them. . . . There is thus a radical difference between the scientific and the theological systems of belief. It is that difference which constitutes the first a system of knowledge, but the second a system only of faith, that is, according to Professor Demos's own definition, a system of beliefs "which rest on no evidence whatever." [3]

The substance of this quotation can be summarized briefly. Knowledge is the name we give to affirmations when they have been subjected to treatment by certain rules of procedure and organized accordingly. These rules of procedure we call reason. When affirmations have not been so treated they are not knowledge. Demos gives his case away when he says that so-called religious knowledge is not subject to these rules and must be judged by different criteria. When we use different criteria we are talking about something else and should use a different word. If we still insist on using the word "knowledge," we should recognize that we are referring to something totally different as when we use the word "high" to mean elevation in referring to a mountain and using it to mean superior when we speak of high religion.

I am sure that Professor Ducasse is mistaken if he thinks that theologians who use language in this ambiguous way are deliberately and consciously cheating, but I think he is correct when he says that they are practicing "the art of befuddling oneself methodically." [4]

Over against this claim made in behalf of reason, theologians frequently assert that the important religious truths cannot and must not be subjected to the tests of reason. Following is a statement typical of hundreds of others made by the same author and by many other religious leaders. The quoted statement is from the most influential religious thinker of our time in the United States.

. . . religious faith cannot be simply subordinate to reason or made to stand under its judgment. When this is done the reason which asks the question whether the God of religious faith is plausible has already implied a negative answer to the question because it has made itself God and naturally cannot tolerate another. [5]

The answer to this condemnation of reason is obvious. If reason makes itself God when exercised to distinguish between true and false religious beliefs, faith becomes demonic when it refuses to submit to these tests. Does the author mean to say that every instance of religious belief is true? He does not, because he criticizes many such beliefs. He himself uses reason in criticizing other religious beliefs but refuses to allow his own beliefs to be "subordinated to reason or made to stand under its judgment."

When the tests of reason are rejected, the only remaining ground for selecting religious beliefs is that pernicious kind of pragmatic test which chooses them for their utility in producing desired psychological effects. Religion practiced in this way becomes a tool to serve man in opposition to what in truth has the character and power to save man as he cannot save himself.

I think Professor Ducasse in the above quotation is mistaken when he says that knowledge must necessarily lead both to prediction and control. It should enable us to anticipate the future within the bounds of that order which the science has discovered but not necessarily to control what will happen. Knowledge of that organization of personality which distinguishes another person should enable me within limits to anticipate what he will do but not necessarily to control what he will think, feel, and do.[6]

While religion often fails to keep faith (in the sense of commitment to creativity) in right relation to reason, science and art do much better in this regard. Science and art both exemplify the close connection which should be maintained between creativity and reason.

Science like art is the exercise of imagination to discover ever more inclusive patterns of coherence. While alike in this respect, art and science are opposites in another respect. Art seeks ever more inclusive patterns of coherence whereby diverse qualities are brought into a unity of vivifying contrasts, including the contrasting qualities of justice and injustice and good and evil in all their diverse forms. Art seeks ever more inclusive patterns of coherence not in the sense that one work of art is better merely because it is more inclusive of diverse qualities than another, but in the sense that the development of art is the development of patterns of coherence bringing qualities into the unity of vivifying contrasts which previously could not be related in this way. To state the point in other words: A great original artist is one who produces shock, wonder, and sometimes ecstasy by bringing into a pattern of vivifying contrasts qualities never before related to one another in artistic form.

Science also seeks patterns of coherence, not of qualities but of structures relatively barren of quality. The coherence sought by the scientist is one which will enable him, by observing few happenings, to deduce the relation of many other happenings to one another and to those immediately under observation.

While the scientist must observe many happenings before the pattern of coherence can be created by which these happenings are related to one another and to many others which are never observed, the pattern of coherence itself, which is an implicative system of propositions, is beyond all possibility of observation. It is never observed but is created in the mind of the scientist even as aesthetic patterns are created in the mind of the artist. In neither case is the pattern created independently of prior observations but in both cases the pattern is a work of creative imagination. It emerges in the mind spontaneously beyond the control of the individual except in the sense that he can provide conditions favorable for its occurrence. Whether in science or in art or in interpersonal relations or in developing a social order and a total culture, the new patterns which emerge are the work of creativity. The new patterns may be innumerable microscopic creations emerging in the minds of millions of individuals through the centuries and brought together into a system more or less coherent by creative interchange between these many individuals. In this way a language, a social order, and a culture are created, although occasionally outstanding individuals may arise in whom creativity operates in a grand style.

The newly emergent pattern brought forth by creativity may not be fit to serve science. It may not be fit to serve art, nor develop a more adequate social order nor enrich the lore of myth and legend nor deepen friendship nor build a bridge. What the new creation emergent in the mind is fit to serve must be determined by reason. This shows how faith in the sense of commitment to creativity and reason should work together. When the new pattern brought forth by creativity is misapplied, resulting in error or other evil, the fault lies in failure to exercise reason to determine where and how it should be applied. The fault does not lie with creativity. A great wealth of imaginative constructions produced by creativity is the highest endowment of man. But these creations must be correctly applied, else great evils result. It is the responsibility of reason to determine where and how they should be applied.

Scientific inquiry is addicted to error by the faulty use of reason, but in science there is more readiness to recognize and correct error than in religion or in other walks of life. Besides the detection and correction of error, reason in science has other uses relative to faith in the sense of commitment to creativity. The scientist can often, perhaps always, develop more complex theories which will meet the tests of prediction just as well as the theory he finally chooses. The most famous example is the Ptolemaic theory versus the Copernican. The most simple pattern of coherence is chosen and the more complex rejected, other things being equal, because one can do far more with a simple theory.

A further choice must be made by reason between alternative theories even when the alternatives are equally fit to meet the tests of prediction. The most fertile theory is chosen, meaning the one from which other theories can be derived, reaching out into other areas of inquiry, thus opening up new fields of knowledge.

The full import should not be missed of this choice which reason makes in science in selecting alternative theories brought forth by creativity. It is profoundly significant and brings out a characteristic of scientific knowledge often ignored. It is this. Many different theories are equally true and equally correct as descriptions of the universe or any part of it. But only those theories are chosen at a given time which [1] happen to be most useful by reason of their simplicity; [2] are most fertile relative to the diverse problems which happen to engage the interest of scientists at the time; [3] are most appealing by reason of their elegance and aesthetic appeal. Still other choices are made by reason in science with other criteria besides the three mentioned, but I do not want to complicate the subject and only wish to illustrate the point, not exhaustively describe it.

The conclusion to be drawn from this is not that scientific knowledge is subjective but that the scientific view of the world at any given time is only one view made up of theories selected because they are more useful for purposes of scientific inquiry than other theories equally correct as descriptions. These other theories would give a very different view and this other view would not be false.

Science could never have made the advances which it has made if it had chosen complex instead of simple theories, theories which did not carry implications applicable to a great diversity of problems, and theories which were not elegant and thus incapable of inspiring the scientist with joy and satisfaction in the beauty of his discoveries.

This fact demonstrates that the truly divine thing in science is not the universe as viewed in the form of theories which scientists have chosen and tested at any given time. This view could be very different even now and still be equally true; and it certainly will be very different in a few years. But the truly divine thing is the creativity which produces in the human mind the theories which can meet the tests of prediction.

Creativity in science refers to the emergence in the mind of the scientist of patterns of coherence which lead to further knowledge. Creativity in art is the emergence in the mind of the artist of patterns of coherence which bring into a unity of vivifying contrasts qualities never before experienced in these relations. Creativity in aesthetic appreciation is the emergence in the individual of patterns of coherence which add to the beauty which he can experience. Creativity in interpersonal relations is the emergence of patterns of coherence which add to one's appreciative understanding of the unique individuality of the other person. Creativity in morals is the emergence of ideal patterns of conduct which add to the reach of moral aspiration. Creativity in religion is the emergence of patterns of coherence symbolized by myth and ritual by which a fellowship of individuals each in greater wholeness commits himself more completely to what saves and transforms.

The last mentioned, namely, a pattern of religious commitment, is not a theory leading to knowledge. But it is imperative that we gain knowledge about it because otherwise we cannot know if commitment delivers the self to what saves and transforms or not; nor can we know whether the new pattern of commitment gathers up the self in its wholeness more completely than some other pattern. Knowledge about these matters of religious commitment is religious knowledge and it depends upon the emergence of a new theory by way of creativity and the critical examination of the theory by reason. In this respect it is the same as scientific knowledge about anything.

The conclusion from all this can now be stated. What is divine in our experience, what is holy, what should command our religious faith, is not the knowledge we now have nor the vision derived from moral idealism or mystical experience. Neither is it the beauty we are now able to experience nor the love nor any virtue found in us. All these should be appreciated and enjoyed and cherished, but no human being has reached that completeness and finality of knowledge, nor that depth and variety of aesthetic experience, nor that perfection of moral idealism and religious commitment, nor that comprehensive and understanding love, such that he can point to his attainment and say that it is divine. On the contrary, what is divine in him and you and me is that creativity which can widen and correct our knowledge if we meet the required conditions; which can enrich and multiply the times and places where beauty greets us; which can deepen our religious commitment; which can magnify beyond any known limit the reach and understanding of our love.

All this creativity can do for us but only on one condition: reason must be applied relentlessly and persistently to every new pattern brought forth by creativity to learn where and how it should be applied to the conduct of our lives. If we refuse to do this, if we reject the tests of reason in defence of faith in any pattern of religious commitment or moral ideal or mystic vision, the very creativity which would save us will be our destruction because the new patterns emergent will be misapplied, misused, and wrongly selected.

This brings us to the third of the triad here under consideration, namely, freedom. How does freedom depend upon faith
and reason and how are all three related to creativity? That is
the question now to be answered.

Since freedom is sometimes thought to be uncaused thought,
feeling, or action, it is necessary to start with a definition of
causation. Cause is the aggregate of conditions under which
something dependently happens and effect is what dependably
happens under these conditions. If the aggregate of conditions
necessary to the choice of a course of action includes the delibera-
tions, insight, reason, and other resources of an individual, then
that course of action is caused by that individual. Certainly other
conditions must also be present because no human being can
think and choose without a sustaining environment. Also the individual in his wholeness has developed out of prior conditions.
But when we speak of freedom we are referring to one part of
the total aggregate of conditions, namely, the individual exercising his insight, his reason and all other resources relevant
to the decision. In this sense freedom is a form of causation but
different from every other kind of causation in that a cause acting on the individual brings into action all the resources of his
mind and personality to determine the further consequences of
that cause.

When a cause acting on an individual does not bring into
action all the resources of his mind and personality to determine
the further consequences of that cause, he lacks freedom to that
degree. Thus freedom of the individual is more or less, depending on the degree to which his personal resources are operative
in determining further consequences. When the cause produces
a conditioned reflex and nothing more, there is no freedom of the
individual. Under changing conditions the freedom we exercise
can vary from zero to a maximum. Perhaps no one exercises the
freedom he might have if his potentialities were fully realized.

Four mistaken ideas of freedom are prevalent.

1] Freedom is often identified with opportunity to do as you
like. But people often like to escape from freedom. They

like to be relieved of the exertion and responsibility of making decisions with the full exercise of personal resources. They prefer to accept the dictates of some authority or conform by conditioned reflexes to social convention without giving the matter any thought. Therefore if you say that freedom means to do as you like, you are saying that freedom means to be not free in such cases. We all seek to escape from freedom under some conditions and to some degree because we like not to be free. Consequently freedom cannot be identified with doing as you like. There is a kind of liking which leads to freedom; but many likings do not.

2] Another current idea of freedom calls for criticism. "Freedom to seek the truth" is not infrequently identified with constructing moral and religious beliefs to suit oneself. But this is generally a way of seeking illusions. Truth or, more accurately stated, knowledge which may approximate the truth, can be achieved only by the rigor and discipline of a method which detects the errors you cherish and requires you to accept statements supported by evidence whether they suit you or not. Nowhere is disciplined inquiry more difficult than in morals and religion. Nowhere is human desire and self-esteem and social bias more treacherous. The claim that each person can find the truth for himself in this area but cannot find it for himself in the exact sciences simply is not true. In both areas the majority of people get whatever reliable knowledge they have by accepting the authority of those who are trained, disciplined, and competent in the use of the methods for detecting error and correcting it. Regrettably no such method is widely recognized and used in morals and religion. Such being the case, it is perniciously misleading to speak of "freedom to accept new truth" when one is merely changing his beliefs without any reliable method for distinguishing the true from the false and without trained competence in the use of such a method.

When the moral and religious "liberal" without such a method and without the labor and discipline required for competence in its use, constructs his own religious beliefs, believe as you like. But this is not freedom.

Two kinds of authority should be distinguished. One is dogmatic. The other is authority of a reliable method for detecting error and gathering evidence when this method is used with competence acquired by rigorous discipline. Authority of the first kind is the foe of freedom but authority of the second kind is one necessary condition of freedom. This shows the connection between reason and freedom since the method for detecting error is reason. Illusion does not liberate because it impairs the ability of the whole self to control the consequences of a cause acting on the individual, and this control we have identified with freedom. Hence reason must be joined with freedom to save from the bondage imposed by illusion.

3] Still another mistaken idea about freedom calls for examination. It is the error of thinking that freedom requires tolerance without any clearly defined limit determining where tolerance must end.

No people can be free and tolerate enslavement. Neither can they keep their freedom if they tolerate what will lead to their enslavement. Freedom can tolerate everything except tyranny. Tyranny can tolerate everything except freedom. Tyranny can be as tolerant as freedom, but with the opposite principle defining the limits of tolerance. To associate freedom and tolerance without stating the principle distinguishing what can be tolerated and what cannot be, is to render freedom defenseless against tyranny. Tyranny can tolerate a great variety of persons and practices in the sense of a great variety of deceptions, frauds, and tricks by which a society is enslaved, a great diversity of subtle methods by

which a people is kept in bondage, a great diversity of
disguises by which the external forms of freedom are used
to conceal the actual presence of tyranny. A tyranny which
is intelligent, resourceful, and potent must be widely tolerant.
A free society which is intelligent, resourceful, and potent
must be widely tolerant. But no society whether enslaved or
free, can be intelligent, resourceful, and potent if it is not
very clear concerning the principle distinguishing what can
be tolerated and what cannot be.

All this does not lead to the conclusion that a free society
can be intolerant. A free society, I repeat, must tolerate
everything which makes for freedom but not tolerate anything which leads to tyranny.

One crucial problem for freedom is to formulate clearly
and enforce relentlessly the principle distinguishing what
can be tolerated from what cannot be. This principle must
be absolute, not in the sense that man's understanding of it
and formulation of it is infallible, but in the sense that
people will struggle, fight, and sacrifice for it. Freedom cannot stand if men are not fully committed to what is required
to save it. Without such a principle held inviolable, freedom will continue to be in the future what it has been in
the past, a rare and transitory accident in social developments.

4] Freedom is not uncaused choice and uncaused action. The
only kind of action anybody ever wants is action caused and
guided by knowledge of conditions leading to anticipated
consequences.

If action is not caused by knowledge of conditions and
anticipated consequences, one is just as likely to jump off a
high cliff as to jump off a six-inch platform; he is just as likely
to stab his dearest child to death as he is to give the child
a dish of ice cream; he is just as likely to betray his friend
to death as to save his life. Choice and action which are
free must be subject to causation if freedom is a great good
to seek and cherish. The form of causation which appears
in free choice and free action is different from other forms

partly because of the vast complexity of the operating mind and partly because of the complexity of causal conditions, these including knowledge and anticipation. But to represent freedom as opposed to causation is to give the name of freedom to something which would swiftly bring all human life to an end.

We have looked at four different ideas of freedom all of which are self-contradictory. They frustrate and mislead human striving. These four are the following: "freedom" to do as you like, "freedom" to believe as you like, "freedom" which tolerates without defined limits of tolerance, "freedom" to choose outside the chain of cause and effect.

The relation of freedom to causation calls for further consideration. Every human action and every human decision is a link in a chain of cause and effect. A causal chain leads up to the action and issues from it. The action is caused by preceding and consequent temporary sequences and is itself the cause of subsequent sequences. If this were not the case no one could trust anybody else, nor even trust himself.

Causation does not completely determine the future. The only sense in which we find causation anywhere is that one in which we find correlations which have some degree of reliability. Where causation prevails, the reliability of prediction can be increased as we gather more knowledge and develop what we know into a coherent system. One can judge with some degree of reliability that human beings will act, think, and feel in certain ways under certain specifiable conditions. Such judgments are not infallible but they have some degree of reliability else we could not live at all. Some reliability in judging the future course of events is the only kind of causation we ever actually experience. Even the judgment that the sun will rise tomorrow is not infallible except in a very special sense.

When a coherent and comprehensive system of statements about a given matter has been verified we can predict with certainty only in the sense that if the prediction does not come true we say that the matter under consideration has ceased to exist as it has been defined by the system of verified statements. For example, if the sun should not rise, we would say the solar system has ceased to exist, being resolved into something else. In that case the prediction has not failed because it was about the solar system and not about anything else.

Causation is necessary for freedom because the whole self in action with all its resources cannot get what it seeks if prediction is impossible. But freedom is the ability of the whole self in action with all its resources to get what it seeks. The denial of any such ability is the denial of freedom. Since reason is necessary for prediction and since faith or commitment is necessary to bring the whole self into action, we see again why reason, faith, and freedom are inseparable.

When the human mind is one link in the chain of cause and effect, causation assumes a form very different from what we find in things less complex and not endowed with such a range of knowledge and foresight as the human mind possesses. A causal process passing through a stone is very different from a causal process passing through a tree because, for one thing, a tree controls the consequences of a blow by healing the wound. Passing through a dog the causal process assumes still a different form because the dog can control the consequences of a blow not only by healing but by defensive action. The human mind, in contrast to these, can use linguistic and other symbols to achieve knowledge of self, of other minds, and of comprehensive systems of causal connections. This gives it not only more control but a different kind of control over the consequences of any cause acting on the mind. This is freedom.

For example, when a man is hit in the face he may act under the control of an unthinking impulse to strike back, or grovel at the feet of the man who struck him, or flee in terror. In all such cases he has minimum freedom because his whole mind is not caused to act but only a part, perhaps only a set of conditioned reflexes. On the other hand, when a person is hit in the face his whole mind with all its resources might be caused to come into action by the blow. The most effective resource available to any human mind is appreciative understanding of the minds of other persons. In this case it would be appreciative understanding of the mind of the man who struck the blow together with understanding of the other minds involved in the situation. A man with this understanding would exercise greatest mastery and thereby have most freedom, provided his whole mind with all its resources was caused to come into action by the blow.

With these resources at his command, the man who was hit might act in such a way that he would change the mind of the man who hit him from a condition of hate or rage or fear into one of goodwill, respect, and co-operation. When this appreciative understanding of other minds is magnified, freedom is magnified because it enables each to draw upon the knowledge, skill, and wisdom of all the others. It enables each to control the others not by exercising authority over them but by reason of the concern of each for the needs and interests of the others. This is mutual control as over against authoritarian control. It is freedom as over against the opposite of freedom.

One way to be assured that the whole self with all its resources will operate under causation is to keep the whole self with all its resources in readiness for action. This is accomplished so far as it can be by the continuous practice of religious commitment to creative interchange. Since religious commitment is commitment of the whole self and creative interchange is the greatest resource for wise and masterful action, religious commitment of this kind is a way to greatest freedom.

The less freedom one has, the less free he is to seek more freedom. The more freedom he has, the more free he is to increase his freedom. An objector might say, "Cannot a person increase his freedom if he will it with his whole self?" The answer is, "Yes, but . . ." a person who wills with his whole self already has maximum freedom because that is precisely what freedom is. But he who lacks this wholeness of the self, hence to that degree lacks freedom, cannot gain this wholeness in action by his own efforts. He cannot because he has an internal block which prevents him from willing anything with his whole self, including the will to be free. A part of himself is always willing not to be free and this keeps him from becoming free. A man can increase his freedom to some degree but the degree depends upon how much freedom and integrity he already has.

The problem of freedom is to release the individual from those inner constraints which prevent the whole self with all its resources from coming into action when a cause effects him. These constraints arise at two levels. They arise out of the failure of associated individuals to seek and achieve appreciative understanding of the unique individuality of one another. At a deeper level they arise out of the failure of individuals to commit themselves completely to the kind of interchange which creates this appreciative understanding along with mutual enrichment and mutual empowering. Therefore the constraints which limit freedom are best overcome by way of fellowship with those who practice ultimate commitment to this creativity. Such a fellowship is one of religious faith practicing the disciplines of commitment. Such a fellowship is the driving wedge which opens the way of increasing freedom for all. It is necessary to sustain a free society.

In a fellowship of faith of the kind described, the native wholeness and the true individuality of the unfree man begins to rise up and gather itself together. He begins to come alive with his total capacity to feel and appreciate, with his total capacity to know and exercise control over the consequences of any cause acting upon him. Thus his freedom grows. He becomes increasingly able to understand appreciatively the individuality of others and to be understood by them. He learns to live under the power of mutual control rather than authoritarian control.

Individualism is often associated with freedom. But two kinds of individualism should be distinguished. One kind diminishes freedom while the other kind increases it. The kind of individualism opposed to freedom is the kind in which the individual is dominated by a single ideal which rules his life. But no abstract ideal can comprehend the richness and fulness of experience which is the potentiality of every human being. No matter how noble the ideal and no matter how devoted to it one may be, one lacks integrity under such domination because no ideal can obtain the wholeness of his being. With the individualism which is defined by devotion to an ideal one can develop only that part of himself which the ideal can compass and that is always fragmentary.

There is nothing wrong with ideals in their proper place. Every-one should have them. The question is not whether we should have ideals. The question is rather this: What is the organizing agency which creatively develops individuality in such a way as to have freedom? Is it ideals or is it the actual process of inter-change with persons when this interchange creates appreciative understanding with mutual learning and mutual enrichment? Ideals must be cast off and outgrown as the individual develops from childhood to youth to maturity and on through the years. Therefore something else than ideals must be the creative or-ganizer of the developing individuality. This something else is the interchange which magnifies freedom when one is committed to it.

This brings us to individualism of the second kind. It is repre-sented by the person who develops most fully the potentiality of his own individuality by commitment to the kind of interchange just mentioned. Individualism of the first kind gives us a person cramped and constrained by the effort to force his unique in-dividuality into the accepted pattern of his ideal. Individualism of the second kind gives us a person who has ideals, but they are the servants of a higher authority and are shaped and changed to meet its demands. This higher authority is the creativity we are describing.

Here we have two kinds of individualism. One is opposed to freedom, the other essential to it. The Western democracies in-cluding the United States have not adequately distinguished these two kinds of individualism in fostering freedom. We have come to the time when this distinction along with many others must be made with care and the whole idea of freedom cleared of the confusions which have prevented us from developing it, extending it, and protecting it as we now must do.

If freedom is to be saved amid the dangers now threatening it and if it is to be magnified beyond the bounds thus far con-fining it, it must be sought by way of ultimate commitment to what liberates the total self from the fear and hate, the vanity and self-concern which restrict and suppress large portions of one's capacity to appreciate and love, to know and exercise control, to sustain others and to be sustained by others.

We seem to be entering a period in the history of the world when the greatest struggle for freedom will occur which ever engaged human kind. The chief threat to freedom is not any ideology or group of conspirators or social system or men addicted to tyranny. It arises from the compact unity into which all peoples of the earth are being drawn by modern technology and mass production. It arises out of the problem of living together in such a unity when people are so diverse in their ways of life and when the individual, to be free, must be able to develop and express his own individuality.

The loss of freedom is not inevitable when diverse peoples must live together in the kind of world now emerging. If freedom is sought and guarded aright this close association of diverse peoples may open the way for a richer, fuller, and more creative freedom than was ever before possible. But if freedom is sought by way of the older individualism which prevailed in the nineteenth century it will surely be lost because the new conditions of this world community will not permit freedom in that form and by that route. If we are to have any large measure of freedom it must be freedom in creative community; it cannot be freedom in the form of individual independence of the community.

PART TWO

Institutions under Commitment

Chapter 8

THE CHURCH
UNDER COMMITMENT

PERSONAL commitment without institutional help in a society complex, powerful, and tightly interdependent is not very effective. Therefore we shall examine the major institutions and see what bearing they have upon our problem.

The major institutions might be listed as church, school, industry, government, and home. The home is so very much a matter of the private lives of a few intimates, except in those respects where it is dependent upon the other institutions of society, that almost everything which might be said about it is covered either in Part One or in the discussion of the other institutions now to be considered. Hence no separate chapter is devoted to it.

Each of the major institutions has a primary responsibility peculiar to itself; but the activities and way of life served by each institution extend far beyond its bounds. The government, for example, provides certain services but the actual conduct of the government in the form of activities and a way of life is carried out and upheld by all the citizens. Even the kind of government called a dictatorship requires that the majority of the citizens carry on the government and not alone the officials. This is demonstrated, for example, by the tremendous amount of effort devoted to propaganda in every dictatorship. In case of a democracy this responsibility resting on every citizen for the maintenance of the government is even more obvious and widespread.

What is said about the institution of the government applies also to the school. If no education occurred throughout society except among people attending school, education would fail and the school would be futile. The same applies to industry. If no one did any productive work except those working for the huge corporations, the huge corporations themselves could not survive.

No institution can be effective unless the majority of the people in the society served by the institution embody in their lives and in their daily practices what the institution seeks to promote. An institution which fails in this respect becomes relatively ineffective. The church largely fails in this respect and on that account is relatively ineffective. The majority of the members of the society do not embody in their daily lives and carry out in their activities what the church seeks to promote.

Devotees of the church often insist that what the church attempts to do is of such a character that its responsibility for the entire society cannot be compared to that of the other institutions. The church, say these devotees, is not designed and should not attempt to uphold any society as a whole. Rather its mission is, say they, to call out from the society a select minority and this small minority is supposed to uphold a way of life opposed to the way of life followed by the rest of humanity.

This interpretation of the mission of the church arose in the first centuries of the Christian era when Christians were a small minority within the prevailing society and had no responsibility for the society as a whole. Furthermore, they were, for the most part, what Arnold Toynbee calls an "internal proletariate" who had repudiated the society of their time. In any case they could not have exercised responsibility for the society in which they lived, no matter how much they might have wished to do so. After these first centuries, the church became one of the major institutions upholding the way of life which distinguishes the Western world and it continued to do so until recent centuries.

I shall try to demonstrate that the church will cease to serve any high purpose in our lives if it continues to interpret its mission as that of upholding a way of life which is by intent and profession alien to the life of the great majority. If the church continues to profess and practice its mission in this manner, some other agency, either the school or the government or some other, will assume responsibility for proclaiming, spreading, and deepening the ultimate commitment by which all men must live and without which the human level of existence may not long continue. Some institution must assume this responsibility because the interdependence of man with man, group with group, people with people has become far greater than ever before and is enforced with tremendous power, while the destruction resulting from failure to share a common commitment of life has reached devastating proportions. For these reasons some agency must assume responsibility not only for the ultimate commitment of a select few, but for the commitment which guides the social process itself. If the church does not do it or cannot, some other agency must, if civilization is to continue. The very survival of the human race may depend upon some institution assuming responsibility for the ultimate commitment of man and not alone for a chosen few, which latter is what the church is now doing.

The church can assume this larger responsibility if the school, the government, and industry co-operate to promote in general this same way of life. The need for this kind of co-operation is not peculiar to the church. It applies to every one of the major institutions. The school cannot do what it is supposed to do without the co-operation of government, industry, home, and church. The government cannot govern without the co-operation of school, industry, church, and home. Industry cannot produce without the co-operation of government, school, home, and church.

The point is that every major institution, including the church, can do its proper work only with the co-operation of the other major institutions. Therefore, after discussing what is required of the church, we shall go on to state what is required of the school, industry, and government in the common cause. The ineffectiveness of the church has arisen from a widening cleavage between it and the other major institutions. Government, industry, and school all work together, more or less, but the church stands to one side and works in relative isolation and independence of the others. If that continues the church will commit suicide even though something called a church might continue in the form of clubs where people gather who happen to be congenial. Many churches approach dangerously near to that condition even now.

There may be times when the church can do nothing more than repudiate the social drift of its time and demand only that it be free of the demands laid upon the rest of society. This is what some members of the church did under the Nazi regime in Germany. But this condition of the church in Germany was in part the consequence of a prior refusal to assume responsibility for the whole of society. Even more it was the consequence of an intellectual and devotional structure of religious commitment which could not be applied directly to the secular problems and institutional activities of society. We are rapidly developing a society in which the enormous power of control exercised by man over the direction of social development combined with the close and coercive interdependence of all parts of society make it imperative that the ultimate religious commitment be interpreted in such a way that it obviously and directly applies to the entire process of social living.

Whether or not the ultimate commitment of religion as interpreted on these pages has this practical relevance to the entire movement of society and also opens the way for continuous and searching inquiry, at least it illustrates what such an interpretation of the religious problem might be. To demonstrate this may I restate the ultimate religious commitment as here set forth. It is dual in character. One part demands that I seek above all things to provide in every situation the conditions most favorable for appreciative understanding between myself and the other persons concerned, and to yield myself to whatever transformation must occur in myself to achieve this appreciative understanding of others. Only in this way can I search more deeply into the basic problems of human existence and at the same time deal constructively with the most urgent social problems of our time.

The second part of the dual commitment is required because of the fallibility and other limitations of the human mind. Beyond all we know or think we know and beyond all the errors in our cherished beliefs stands the reality which sustains, saves, and transforms, no matter how different may be its character from my present beliefs about it. This second part of the dual commitment is a self-giving to this reality which in its mystery lies beyond the reach of my present knowledge and my present errors.

This outreach of faith into the realm of mystery is needed in part because we actually are encompassed with mystery. It is also needed to save from bigotry, dogmatism, and incorrigible ignorance and to keep the mind open, receptive, inquiring, and outreaching. It is needed further to provide a source of hope, renewal, and recovery when we find that we have been mistaken in the beliefs which guide the first part of the dual commitment. With this outer reach into mystery we can always know that beyond our errors, failures, and defeats is the reality to which we have given ourselves in our ignorance. With this outer reach of faith the very defeats which we encounter and the errors we discover in our beliefs can throw us more completely into the keeping of what ultimately sustains us beyond the limits of our definite knowledge. With such a commitment we can always rise again out of every disillusionment with zest and striving unabated.

There is no escape from idolatry and no escape from spiritual arrogance except by recognizing the possibility of error when one burns his bridges behind him as he must do in making his ultimate commitment. Having passed beyond the point of no return such a one will be tempted to affirm dogmatically the finality of his beliefs. But this is sin. No appeal to divine revelation can save any man from the imperative need to utter continuously the plea to be corrected, because his human mind claiming to be the recipient of divine revelation is always fallible. No appeal to the authority of Church or Bible or religious tradition, no appeal to reason or science or inner conviction, no claim to have undergone the divine encounter nor to be continuously in the I-Thou relation with God, can deliver one from presumptuous arrogance in making the ultimate commitment of his life if he seek not to have the structure of his life destroyed when it is wrongly constructed and when this destruction will help reveal the way in which man should live.

The dual commitment has two arms, so to speak. With one arm it reaches after the best knowledge attainable concerning what sustains, saves, and transforms. With the other arm it reaches out to the mystery of that reality which can never be completely comprehended.

With this understanding of religious commitment, the ministry and mission of the church can be examined.

The mission of the church is to evangelize in the sense of winning men to this kind of dual commitment; and it is also to cultivate, deepen, and empower this dual commitment in those who have already been won to it. Other institutions do the practical constructive work demanded by this commitment. But the mission and responsibility of the church is to spread and deepen the commitment itself. To this end the church should lead men to practice both in private and in public assembly those rituals and the use of those symbols and all other methods which may serve to win more men to this dual commitment and also serve to renew and deepen it among those who have already attained it. Without an institution specially designed and devoted to this service, men in our society where interdependence, power, and complexity are increasing so rapidly cannot be faithful to any commitment whatsoever.

Men cannot be saved in our society when and if they refuse to sacrifice whatever must be sacrificed for creative interchange to occur with fulness and power. Also they cannot be saved without the second part of the dual commitment which opens the way to further knowledge of the saving entity and which provides recovery and renewal when efforts fail and when creative interchange itself proves ineffectual.

Men in our society cannot be saved when and if they refuse to use their science and technology to seek out and build up and defend the conditions which must be present for creative inter-change to occur as widely and fully as possible and, when they fail in this, to find the further resource in the second part of their commitment.

Men in our society cannot be saved when and if they refuse to conduct education with the one supreme and sovereign purpose of promoting this kind of interchange with the added resource of the second part of the commitment which keeps the mind open and inquiring concerning the best way for men to live.

Men in our society cannot be saved if they refuse to organize industry and government in a way to promote this kind of inter-change and to live after the manner indicated. Neither can we be saved if art is not devoted to this same end.

When creative interchange is restricted by reason of failure of the agencies just listed to provide conditions favorable for its occurrence, men lose the capacity to recognize and appreciate this process by which the individual person is progressively in-tegrated in a way to experience more richly the qualities of life, and by which appreciative understanding between individuals is deepened. Being unable to recognize and appreciate in their own lives the good of this creativity, men unintentionally do things and build conditions which reduce this interchange still further with ever-increasing decline of appreciative understand-ing between people and a corresponding increase of fear, hate, suspicion, and resentment both consciously recognized and un-acknowledged.

In this way self-destruction begins to hover over the life of man, darkening his vision, blinding him to the way of salvation. Meanwhile men do not understand what has gone wrong, and either curse fate or blame some person, group, or people which happens at the time to be an object of safe attack. All this in-creases fear and hostility, thereby reducing appreciative under-standing of one another still further. So the vicious circle rolls on toward the end unless it is stopped by an awakening of the ulti-mate commitment to creative interchange.

The church is especially responsible for showing men the kind of ultimate commitment which saves from these evils, for leading them to make this commitment and for promoting the practices by which this commitment can be deepened and empowered.

The distinctive mission of the church appears when we see the difference between doing the many practical things sustained by other institutions under this commitment, on the one hand, and on the other, practicing the rituals and symbols, the self-examination and assemblies, and receiving the exhortation and instruction necessary to keep the organization of the personality in alignment with the commitment. Many influences tend to dull the sensitivities and distract the attention from the demands of creative interchange and impair the readiness of the personality to engage in this kind of interaction with others. To get the viewpoint of the other person appreciatively and profoundly and reconcile it with his own so far as possible is the supreme achievement of man and his highest vocation. The personality must be kept in a state of fitness for it and its abilities cultivated and developed to this high end. The practices by which this is done include prayer and worship and much else. The responsibility of the church is to carry on these practices which help to establish, conserve, and deepen the habits, attitudes, and dispositions required for achieving appreciative understanding and personal integration in dealing with every kind of person.

There is no known limit to what might be done to make individuals more fit for living in this way. The actual doing of all that is required in this way of living is under the supervision of the other institutions. But the spiritual exercises by which the personality is fitted for this doing are the prime responsibility of the church.

To meet this responsibility the church should build progressively a system of religious thought and religious practice not only out of the religious traditions but also out of the findings of those sciences which explore the depth of human personality, which seek out what human personality needs to develop its potentialities, which seek out also what causes human personality to become self-destructive and socially destructive and what the human personality must have to attain its highest possibilities.

Discoveries concerning personality in all the respects listed are fast accumulating. The saints and sages of the Christian tradition and of other religious traditions have much to teach us. Some of their teachings are only now becoming more clearly understood and appreciated because of what the psychology of personality and the study of different cultures are revealing. All these findings from all these sources, both traditional and scientific, should be gathered together. They need to be integrated, formulated, interpreted, and put into such form that the church can use them to help individuals and groups develop to the utmost the capacity for appreciative understanding and personal integration in dealing with all sorts of people.

These findings need to be lifted out of the technical and specialized and scattered formulations in which many of them are embedded. The men engaged in specialized, technical, compartmentalized research, in whose keeping much of this needed information now lies, cannot integrate and interpret and apply their findings to the problems of religious commitment. They cannot in the first place because they are prevented by their specialized training and the code prescribing the rules of conduct for scientific research. They cannot in the second place because they do not understand the problems of an ultimate commitment, many of them are not interested in it and some are hostile to any such undertaking. Some men of specialized research can co-operate magnificently. But the leadership should be taken by men trained in the problems of religion, meaning the problem of man's self giving to what saves and transforms.

A religious faith guided and informed by these findings about the nature and needs of human personality in interpersonal relations can be more intelligent and more powerfully operative in shaping and directing human life toward the best that man can attain than any other form of religion in our time. Furthermore, it is precisely this kind of religion which our times need to save both the individual person and society from disintegration and self-destruction and to open the way to the possibilities which our civilization contains when combined with this kind of commitment. A religion not equipped with this knowledge about human personality can scarcely meet the needs of men at the level of a highly complex and highly advanced civilization such as ours.

The ways in which institutionalized religion, whether in Christianity or elsewhere, spread and deepen the ultimate commitment in dual form can be listed under four heads, namely, [1] the use of rituals and symbols; [2] searching self-examination to guard against and repudiate unfaithfulness to the commitment, this repudiation called confession and repentance of sin in the Christian tradition; [3] assembly for social re-enforcement and that deepening and contagion of the commitment which results from people practicing together a common devotion; [4] inquiry and instruction concerning the nature and demands of the commitment and concerning the entity which commands the commitment.

1] Rituals and symbols of personal commitment and group commitment are necessary if habits, impulses, sensitivities, focus of attention, and all the resources of personality are to be organized and directed under the control of what sustains, saves, and transforms toward the best that man can become.

All too frequently rituals and symbols become a mere matter of form or a means to aesthetic enjoyment. In a decadent religion this generally happens. Hence to see the real importance of ritual and symbol let us look at it in other walks of life and especially when it is done unconsciously. For in truth it is impossible to be faithful to anything unless one practices the rituals and symbols of commitment. Take the instance of a mother and her baby. Quite impulsively as she passes the cradle she will coo at the baby. She kisses and fondles it. These are rituals of commitment by which her personality is ordered and directed in devoted care of the infant.

Football practice is a way of developing required skills, but the daily practice serves also as a ritual to organize and focus the resources of the personality upon the game. Or, again, take a married couple. They constantly practice rituals of commitment to one another. As one goes from home or returns, they kiss. There are many kinds of kisses but along with

the other kinds married people have ceremonial kisses, ceremonial caresses, and ceremonial terms of endearment. These
are indispensable rituals of commitment to their life together.
The point of all this is not to suggest that these rituals are
religious. They are not. I am only trying to show that the practice of the rituals and symbols of commitment, when sincerely
and rightly done, is necessary to keep the resources of personality organized and devoted to the end sought. They are
necessary not only in groups but also in private. Without such
practices there can be no institutional religion when religion
is defined as commitment. A church which does not induce its
people to practice these rituals sincerely and effectively is not
a religious institution, no matter how large the crowds that
assemble to be entertained by brilliant lectures and aesthetic
performances.

2] Self-examination to discover wherein one has been unfaithful
to the commitment is a further practice for which the church
is responsible. This also is indispensable. Unfaithfulness or
evil in any form is not fatal if it is freely and objectively and
correctly acknowledged and repudiated. The evil which drags
a person down like an undertow to his ruin is the evil not
confessed and repented. When sin is defined as unfaithfulness or deviation from the demands of the religious commitment, genuine religion is impossible without confession and
repentance of sin. One may not want to use the word sin, as
he may not want to use the word God, because of the many
meanings attached to these words which may be false and
misleading. But regardless of words, the facts are that men are
always more or less unfaithful and deviate more or less from
their ultimate commitment, and this unfaithfulness and deviation call for confession and repentance else the commitment
is not genuine and becomes a source of corruption because of
the self-deception generated by it. The repression which results from refusal to confess and repent leads to conduct destructive of the personality and of social relations, as psychology of personality makes plain.

3] Assembly of those who practice commitment to the same end is necessary to sustain and deepen the commitment and keep one true to the way of life arising out of it. Human personality is created by social interaction and cannot be sustained apart from interaction with others, indispensable as periods of solitude may be to interpret the experiences derived from interchange with people and situations. But private meditation can be no substitute for the re-enforcement, mutual criticism, correction, and powerful shaping of the mind to be gained from assembly with those who practice the same commitment in company with one another.

The weakness of liberal religion is due in no small part to the inability of liberals to agree on what is supremely important and the consequent inability to unite in a common commitment. Until they can agree there can be no great power in their faith. The influence upon the individual of great numbers when they are all swayed with the same ruling devotion, gives a power and a courage that enables one to live and die devotedly. This, of course, can be directed to evil ends as well as to good. Hitler was a master at using it with giant crowds for Nazi goals. But this way of empowering the religious commitment is of prime importance. The weakness of community and the weakness of any ruling devotion in present day society is due in no small part to the unreconciled diversity of minds concerning what should command the ultimate commitment of man. When and if some degree of unanimity can be attained on this matter, the power of assembly and the power of faith will rise again. A great gathering of many people expressing their shared and supreme devotion is mystical in its power to lift the individual to the heights of a transfiguring devotion.

4] Inquiry and instruction the better to understand what commands our last commitment and what it demands of us is the fourth practice which enters into religion. This is in part what preaching is supposed to do. It is also done by groups gathered for study and discussion. This need is so obvious and has received so much emphasis to the point of overshadowing the other ways of spreading and cultivating commitment, that further examination of it at this point seems unnecessary.

5] Action to shape conditions in the way demanded by the commitment is certainly one necessary part of a dedicated life. But action of this kind takes us beyond the bounds of the church to the areas of life more directly under the supervision of the other major institutions and so may be left for treatment when we consider them.

There can be no genuine religion, certainly none with power, unless the participants practice commitment in these several ways, namely, by ritual and symbol, by self-examination, by inquiry, by assembly, and by action to change or sustain conditions in a way to conform to the demands of the commitment. It is scarcely possible to find language strong enough to denounce that form of alleged "religion" which consists of nothing more than a world view or a metaphysical system or a set of doctrines or a vision of what one would most enjoy or a glorious ideal and dream. All these have their place, to be sure, but when there is no discipline and rigor of commitment, giving the whole personality without reservation to an actual power known to exist which transforms human life toward the best it can become, there is no religion worth having.

Prayer and worship remain to be considered as part of the work of the church. The two words are variously interpreted. We shall here understand worship to be the practice of commitment by ritual, symbol, self-examination, and assembly as above described. Prayer is petition added to worship. Petition even when directed to a divine being is not properly prayer unless combined with the practice of commitment in the form of worship.

It is sometimes thought that prayer is meaningless unless directed to a supernatural person. But this is a naive form of thought which cannot defend itself when critically examined. Prayer certainly is meaningless unless God responds to prayer in a way to answer it. It is impossible to show how a supernatural person could answer prayer in this natural world but it is quite possible to show how the creativity present in creative interchange can answer prayer.

Prayer is an attitude of sensitivity and responsiveness to God combined with a seeking for some specific outcome. When God is identified with the creativity just mentioned, the efficacy of this sensitivity and responsiveness combined with focus of attention upon achieving some outcome become quite intelligible. This attitude of sensitivity and responsiveness and this focusing of attention are not, of course, limited to the time and place when the prayer is uttered or silently expressed. If the prayer is genuine and combined with worship as it must be if it is truly prayer, this attitude and this focus of attention become established as persistent dispositions of the personality. As subconscious states of sensitivity and readiness they are most effective. When the prayer is thus established as a continuing condition of the personality, the subtle and complex interplay between the individual and other persons is brought into service of the petition which is the prayer.

The sensitivity to creativity established by the prayer opens the way for interacting individuals to undergo transformation by acquiring thoughts, feelings, and perceptions from one another and integrating these with the resources already possessed by each individual. This transforms the minds of all concerned so that there is more sensitive and effective co-operation between them. Also each is thus able to perceive and feel what he could not previously perceive and feel because each learns from the others and each integrates what is learned with what he was previously able to perceive and feel and know. Thus his world acquires a depth and expanse it did not have before. Since one can perceive and feel as he could not do before, and in consequence interacts with the physical world as he could not do before, the physical world is transformed relative to the mind. New resources are discovered in what is going on round about. As stated in Chapter One, in this way miracles are performed if by miracle one means happenings which could not possibly occur prior to the transformation of the mind and the world relative to one another but which do occur after the transformation.

In many cases the most important part of this transformation is not in consciousness but in the sensitivity and organization and focusing of the subconscious levels of the personality, so that individuals in association do things and attain ends previously impossible and in ways which may seem astonishing to the consciousness of the individuals concerned. In this way outcomes may be achieved through prayer which could never be attained without it.

At this point a common misunderstanding should be corrected. Some will say that I have just described the work of the subconscious mind. That is incorrect. To be sure a reordering and refocusing of the subconscious sensitivities and responses are an essential part of the transformation which brings about the answer to the prayer. Rather this reordering and refocusing of subconscious sensitivities is the prayer. This is the meaning of the phrase "the heart's sincere desire, unuttered or expressed." But equally essential is the transformation of the minds of associates and transformation of the physical environment due to a different way of interacting with them. In sum, what answers prayer is not the subconscious mind; what answers prayer is the creative interchange between all factors involved, thus producing the outcome sought in the prayer.

The creative transformation which answers the prayer may transform the prayer itself so that one comes to seek and find what he did not seek by way of the prayer in the beginning. If what is sought in the initial prayer runs counter to the demands of creative transformation moving in the direction of the kingdom of love, then the prayer will be changed by the creativity which answers it, so that in the end one seeks and receives what is much better than the original petition.

This understanding of prayer in relation to creativity shows again that God interpreted as creativity meets religious need much better than God represented to be a supernatural and almighty power. The ways of a supernatural and almighty power are entirely beyond our understanding. Hence it would be presumptuous to try to show how such a being might answer prayer. Consequently it is impossible to gather any evidence or justify in any way the claim that such a being produces any particular outcome in answer to anybody's prayer. Since we cannot know the ways of such a being, we cannot know that any one outcome was his special doing more than another. Therefore it is impossible to establish any intelligible or defensible ground for saying that such a Being answers prayer. But when God is identified with creativity we can see very well how God answers prayer as well as doing the other things which the religious person seeks and finds within the bounds of actual experience. To be sure, the speculative answers to questions about the beginning and ending of the world and all such matters lying beyond the reach of human knowledge and verification cannot be found in creativity. But these alleged answers to speculative questions are not relevant to the deep personal need of the religious man. His need is for salvation and transformation, for deep communion and appreciative understanding, for answered prayer, and for the kingdom of love. These are the essential religious needs. It can be demonstrated how creativity meets these needs; it cannot be demonstrated how a supernatural person and almighty power does so.

What is said about prayer applies also to religious conversion and evangelism. Men will not voluntarily turn to God until after the initial stages of this turning have been accomplished within them by creative interchange with those who are committed to God. Thus creative interchange is the power which brings about religious conversion. The church exercises the power of evangelism by creative interchange. This power of God working through the church to save the world becomes intelligible when God is identified with this creativity.

If we are to trust the findings of recent psychological and other anthropological studies of man which also seem to be corroborated by some of the teachings in the great religions, we can point out that cause of evil-doing which must be corrected to the end of sanctification. Very briefly stated this chief cause of man's self-destructive and evil propensities is his inability to allow to come fully to consciousness the anxiety generated by his failure to find what his nature most imperatively needs. This most imperative need we have repeatedly described as appreciative understanding found in creative interchange. When this need is not adequately satisfied it generates anxiety and a sense of meaninglessness in all we do and are. It generates what the existentialists call the sense of nothingness or emptiness and may mount to anguish. But men cannot ordinarily endure this sense of anxiety or anguish or meaninglessness or frustration when it comes fully to consciousness. So, to keep it out of consciousness, they do all manner of foolish things, destructive things, and also at times constructive things. Many of the great works of civilization have been reared under the compelling drive to try to satisfy this imperative need, but in ways which cannot satisfy.

When the constructions of civilization are reared and sustained by a striving to satisfy what is not satisfied by these constructions, except in the sense that the striving helps to keep the unendurable anxiety out of consciousness, and when the tearing down of these constructions of civilization can serve just as well as their construction to keep this anxiety out of consciousness, and when many men turn to the destructive striving as others to the constructive, it is plain that the constructions of civilization are precariously reared and sustained. The story of the civilizations of the world support this claim.

The same ambivalence of human striving is seen in the more intimate affairs of daily living. Love of mate or child or home, ethical striving and serving the church, making money and supporting the family, or doing any of the works of daily living may be practiced primarily as a device to keep this anxiety and unsatisfied need out of consciousness. But when these ostensibly worthy activities assume the form of devices to deceive oneself and evade the truth, they are corrupted. Also, when they fail to keep the anxiety out of consciousness and thus fail to serve the real end sought by means of them, the opposite striving will arise in which case hate or indifference may supplant the love, malice take the place of moral effort, and all the opposites of constructive effort arise. This is the ambivalence which corrupts the virtues of man.

According to this interpretation, one cause of man's demonic propensities is the refusal or inability to allow the anxiety deeply wrought into his nature to come to consciousness and accept it as the mark of his highest destiny. This anxiety is deeply wrought into man's nature and is the mark of his highest destiny because it indicates his insatiable hunger and need to be transformed to greater appreciative understanding between associates, which is to say greater love and truth; and to greater appreciative understanding of all the qualities of the world, which is to say beauty and truth. Sanctification occurs when a man is able to recognize this anxiety as his chief glory and to accept it as the sign that creativity has broken free in him from the limitations and constraints elsewhere imposed and will, if man commits himself to it, transform the world so that it will embody more or less continuously increasing ranges and depths of love and beauty and truth.

The responsibility of the church is to awaken in men this sense of their destiny and lead them to give themselves over to this creativity with full acceptance in consciousness of their anxiety because this anxiety indicates man's capacity to be transformed in the direction of love and beauty and truth. The suffering of this anxiety is the sign of man's greatness, not because it is good to suffer, but because this particular kind of suffering is the obverse side of potentialities unfulfilled. As hunger is a suffering which indicates the need for food, so this anxiety is a suffering which indicates the need for more love, beauty, and understanding. As hunger is a suffering which shows that man is made for food, so this anxiety is a suffering which shows that man is made for a depth and height and fulness of love and beauty and understanding far beyond anything he has ever yet attained. This anxiety shows that man is the child of God if God is this creativity. This creativity in man has now broken free from the limitations imposed upon it in all the rest of the world. Thus liberated in the nature of man it can transfigure the world. But, if man refuses to commit himself to it, it will destroy man and all his works.

The mission of the church is to lead men to the full and free acceptance of human destiny with its hazards, its suffering, and its glory; also it must lead him to strive to shape social institutions and the conduct of personal life in such a way that creativity can operate more effectively through the entire range of human existence.

The man in the pulpit has a peculiar responsibility although the mission and responsibility just described belongs to the church as a fellowship and not merely to the man in the pulpit. The religious leader should be especially trained and fitted to quicken the religious fellowship with a sense of this mission and responsibility. Also he should awaken in each individual this vision, this sense of destiny, and this acceptance into consciousness of the anxiety which properly pertains to the individual by reason of his potentialities.

This responsibility of the man in the pulpit does not require that he have infallible knowledge concerning man's destiny and concerning what in human life has the character and power to transform man in that direction. The preacher's ideas on these matters may be deeply infected with error as are the ideas of us all when we undertake these most profound problems pertaining to man's existence. There is nothing about the pulpit which renders a man infallible; and no matter how infallible the Christian Bible might be—assuming for the moment that it is—the mind of the man in the pulpit is just as fallible as any other mind when he undertakes to deliver any message from the Bible. The infallibility of the Bible, if it is infallible, does not impart infallibility to the preacher when he tells what the Bible allegedly teaches. But the task of the religious leader still remains, provided he freely admits his fallibility. This task is to awaken in the minds of men the awareness of man's destiny and the saving and transforming power by which it is accomplished.

One part of the primary task of the church is to arouse inquiry into the problem of man's existence. The mission of the church is not to declare the final truth but to induce a dual commitment to a reality which may be more than any set of propositions can comprehend. The commitment which does not inquire is not a saving but a damning commitment.

While the church should awaken the mind to inquire concerning the way of life for man, the church is not itself equipped to conduct inquiry very effectively. The schools, above all the institutions of higher learning, should do this. The church has its own work to do as we have tried to indicate. This proper work of the church would be seriously impaired if it tried to turn itself into an educational institution.

Certainly the church should engage in teaching. So does every other institution. Industry, government, the home, all devote much time and effort to providing the information and developing the skill, focus of attention, and organization of personality required of participants if they are to be effective in what concerns the institution. For that matter contract bridge, prize fighting, and the Olympic games engage highly trained teachers devoting their entire lives with high salaries and considerable equipment all devoted to education of a sort. Perhaps the church should give as much time and effort and money to education and research as the big industrial organizations do in conducting their enterprises.

But all these institutions including the church have a prior responsibility and this special interest confines the scope and limits the freedom of instruction and inquiry. Consequently the education conducted by these institutions cannot search out the errors and generate the insights which might run counter to their interests or would be irrelevant to their primary responsibility. For this reason industry, government, the home must be served, corrected, criticized, and informed by institutional education unconfined and free of the bias of the special interests of these institutions. Indeed our entire educational system is set up in no small part to do this very thing for industry, government, the home, and for all the other institutions and interests of our society *excepting religion and the church.* Where in our universities can we find men who without trying to serve the special interests of the church have devoted their lives to the basic problem which concerns religion, seeking out the errors in religious belief and criticizing and developing the insights generated by this kind of free inquiry into the religious problem? "Free inquiry" does not mean inquiry without religious commitment but it does mean inquiry without commitment to the special interests of any institution.

The other major institutions are served by this kind of inquiry and instruction; religion and the church are not. The theological seminaries and schools of religion are servants of the church and are analogous to the sort of schools set up by industry to train men to serve the industrial institution. No doubt these are needed.

But that is not the kind of education here under consideration. It cannot provide the kind of free inquiry which every major institutional interest must have to keep fit for the work required of it in a society undergoing continuous and radical reconstruction and demanding of those responsible for the work of the major institutions an ever wider and deeper self-identification with the basic problems of human existence. In this respect religion is sadly lacking because the universities have not assumed responsibility for religion in the way they have done for the other essential interests of humanity.

If the educational institutions do not assume responsibility for inquiry into the problems of human life which concern the church, the church is as much frustrated as any of the other major institutions would be if higher education did not undertake disciplined research into the problems which concern them. This holds whether or not the leaders of the churches and the schools of religion recognize the relative frustration and futility of their efforts due to this deficiency.

The church can awaken the commitment which inquires only if the schools provide opportunity for free inquiry in matters of religious concern and spread abroad throughout society the attitude of inquiry concerning these matters. Today exactly the opposite attitude prevails. With the exception of a few individuals, no group is devoted continuously to the study of the basic religious problem of human life apart from the special interests of the institutional church and the schools which serve these special institutional interests. Anyone who has tried with members of a university faculty to institute a study-group devoted to the problem of religion independently of the special interests of the church will recognize the truth of this claim. People either accept the doctrines of some church or ignore the problem or struggle futilely with it because they cannot find the stimulus, guidance, and suggestion which widespread association with other inquirers would give them. Especially when the religious institutions frown upon such inquiry does such an individual find himself frustrated. The greatest evil infecting the church is moral and spiritual arrogance. This is always a danger involved in worship. Members of the worshipping group may feel that their access to God gives divine authority to their judgments of right and wrong. They may claim that their lives are endowed with a righteousness and love which are only to be found in God (or Christ) and in themselves. What they do, God does. What they condemn, God condemns. They may claim that their virtue is so far superior to other men that their existence in our midst would be impossible without the special intervention of God in their behalf.

When this claim is made by simple-minded people it is not a great danger, perhaps. But it is not limited to that level. It is found also among sophisticated people and even in the divinity schools of the great universities. One outstanding religious leader expressed it in a sermon entitled "The Impossible Existence," meaning that the members of the church are called to a life so far superior to other people that their existence would be impossible without God's protective care extended to them in a very special way. Following are quotations which indicate the substance of the sermon.

> The church of Christ lives a life in this world which—according to reason and experience—is actually impossible. . . . Jesus defies the generally acknowledged standards of human existence and coexistence in this world. . . . We are meant to lead this same impossible sort of life as Christ did, obeying God rather than man and loving our enemy rather than trying to destroy him . . . we enter into a world where people believe that only the death of their enemies can save them . . . the whole world is raging with hatred and enmity. . . . The church is called to obey and live and to survive even the threat of the "gates of hell." Looking to the Master, she will not sink or die. . . . Here possibly our doubts may begin if we listen to our own reason and experience; yet "the things which are impossible with men are possible with God." Reason and experience could not be of any help; and the temptation was great to fix our eyes on the risks and dangers instead of the Lord, whom we wanted to obey, in bringing the message of his forgiving and renewing love right into the heart of the world caught in hatred and despair.[1]

People who claim to love with a love like unto that of God and thus superior to all others, yet refuse to be guided by reason and experience, cannot be informed of the actual needs and condition of the persons they "love." Such "love" unguided by reason and experience may not be "trying to destroy," but what it does is very likely to be destructive, nevertheless. Love without intelligence can do little good and can do great harm.

A church which claims to be guided by God while repudiating reason and experience is incapable of learning anything because learning can only come by reason and experience. It is incapable of criticizing itself and incapable of accepting the criticism of others. Its ideas about what God would have it do, being human ideas, are subject to error. But these errors cannot be corrected or even admitted when reason and experience are repudiated.

A church which conceives of its mission in this way cannot work with other institutions. It cannot because these other institutions are the world and the world is so evil compared to the assumed virtue of the church that the worshippers maintaining an impossible existence and looking only to the Lord can have nothing in common with these worldly institutions.

This brings us to an examination of these other institutions so far as they can have some part in man's ultimate commitment. Education is of such a character that it can be closely allied to the commitment by which human life is transformed toward the greater good. Hence the next chapter will consider the responsibility of the school for the problems which concern religious living.

Chapter 9

EDUCATION

UNDER COMMITMENT

T H E R E is much talk these days about putting moral and spiritual values into education.[1] But any values which seem to be added on to education rather than being essential and intrinsic to what the school seeks to accomplish are bound to be ineffective. Spiritual values in our tradition are identified with certain theological doctrines and these doctrines have been excluded from the public schools. They were excluded in the first place because parents and churchmen could not agree on what doctrines should be taught and the doctrines were of such character that the controversy could not be adjudicated as many others can be by rational and empirical evidence. For example, many parents object to having their children taught belief in God when "God" carries the conventional idea of Deity. Still others passionately reject belief in God because this belief so frequently is used as a device for giving divine authority to the personal projects and private notions about right and wrong held by the "believers." The cruel moral arrogance resulting from this has led these parents to reject on moral grounds religious instruction in the schools.

Despite these difficulties and objections there is a powerful movement to revive some of these theological doctrines as part of the content of general education. This movement arises from the need to make moral and spiritual values the central concern demands and intrinsic to the nature of learning and teaching.

This dilemma in which public education finds itself is a striking manifestation of the chief difficulty and dangerous weakness threatening our entire culture. This danger can be briefly stated. The doctrines allegedly affirming the commitment of faith by which our culture and social existence are shaped and guided do not in truth express this faith for the people. But a culture and a society which do not have a central, unifying, motivating, and guiding faith suffer from a dangerous weakness which will in time be fatal if not corrected. The American people and Western culture and perhaps all other cultures when they reach the level of a complex civilization have a latent, unformulated, and unclarified faith which would be central, unifying, and sustaining if it could be clearly formulated, effectively symbolized, and made central to all education. But it cannot so long as various conflicting theological doctrines are accepted as expressing this faith when in fact they do not.

This strange condition of having doctrines which stand for the faith sustaining our civilization but which in truth do not is the source of confusion and the obstacle which prevents any living faith from becoming articulate and rising to serve as a guiding unity and central motivation for society as a whole. Furthermore, such a faith cannot become articulate and effective until it is made the central concern of education. When the theological doctrines which allegedly express our faith cannot be made the focal center of general education, we know that these doctrines do not express this faith in the form in which the people as a body accept it.

It would be fantastic and unbelievable if it were not a familiar fact that the public schools cannot make the ruling faith which sustains our society their central concern. This anomolous condition does actually prevail. The reason for it has been stated.

It is this: Exclusion from the schools of what is mistakenly thought to be the faith sustaining and guiding our social life makes it impossible to put into the schools the real faith needed to sustain our civilization. Since this real faith is mistakenly identified with the institutional form of faith which must be excluded, it is thought that this real faith must be excluded also. From this predicament of confusion we must be delivered if our civilization is to survive and its great potential value realized. This is the problem of education so far as concerns the ultimate commitment upon which depends the creative transformation of man made possible by the rise of civilization.

In a complex and diversified society equipped with great power to act, it is necessary to have an agency able to give to the rising generation some unity and direction in its development and in its strivings and aspirations. Consequently institutional education is necessary in such a society. To this end it prepares the minds of students for knowledge and appreciation of literature and history, the other arts and the sciences. But if it does not promote a unifying and directing commitment of faith, the school cannot accomplish for the society what it is set up to accomplish. Yet this is the predicament of our educational system. More important, it is the dangerous predicament of our society.

The statement just made must not be misunderstood. It is not asserted that the school alone can impart to the people the unifying and directing faith which the society must have to survive and realize its potential values. This the school cannot do. This must be done by the daily interchange going on in society. But the school is needed to interpret to the youth the sustaining faith and direction of life which are implicit in the complexities of the social process. If the school does not lift out and make explicit this faith and direction of life, the rising generation will not find them nor follow them amid the great complexity and diversity and power of our society. Not to find them and not to follow them will lead to disintegration of the developing personality of the individual and the social system itself. But if the school is to serve this indispensable function it must have as central to its entire undertaking a commitment of faith which gives unity and

direction to the developing mind of the individual and to the entire social process.

If the school is to assume responsibility for nourishing a common faith to sustain our society it must be done in such a way as
not to conflict with the essential nature and aims of education, on
the one hand, nor with the nature and aims of the church on the
other. Therefore the first step in dealing with this problem is to
search and find in the essential nature and purpose of education
an implicit commitment of faith of the kind we need. There is
such an implicit faith within education. It is so essential to education that teaching and learning become not only ineffective but
even pernicious without it.

No teacher can teach effectively, and no student can learn profoundly, unless teacher and student together give themselves in
commitment to creative interchange. In no other way is it possible
to teach or to learn with the whole self. To teach and learn only
with the conscious mind and not with the whole self has serious
consequences.

When the whole mind does not undergo creative transformation in education, only the top surface of the mind is educated,
so to speak. When the student learns in this way he gets from
the school at best a utility and at worst an incapacitating inner
conflict. He does not get an educated mind and in that sense
a transformed self. When only the top surface of the mind is
educated, the driving power and passion of the total self is not
engaged in what the educated part of the mind thinks and says
and does. Such a person at the educated level lacks conviction,
purpose, and integrity. "Education" has made him into a con-
formist, repeating all the proper things which "educated" people
are supposed to say.

One consequence of this kind of "education" is cynicism. It
is quite common in "educated" circles. Nothing has great value
for such a person; nothing is very important. Everything serious,
every glowing aspiration, every great admiration and devotion
is ridiculed or criticized and rejected or ignored. In some cases
the sentiment of great admiration may be imitated but not truly
felt. Such an "educated" person with his pose of sophistication

stands on the side lines to watch the spectacle of "fools" pass by. "Educated" people of this kind repudiate social responsibility and have no power of commitment to anything. They are "liberals" in the worst sense of that word.

Since this kind of "education" is not what we want and not what the school intends but is the kind which results when commitment of the whole self to creative interchange is lacking, it is plain that this kind of commitment is essential to good education. Therefore commitment of the whole self to creative interchange is a faith implicit in education and essential to its nature and purpose.

"Education" without this ultimate commitment produces in some persons another consequence even more destructive than the cynicism just described. Conflict between what a man learns and must accept at the superficial level of the conscious mind, and what his own true individuality demands and must seek with passion and power, causes him in some cases to rebel against the whole social structure and hate all the authorities by which it is imposed. In some this rebellion and hate may remain hidden and latent until some leader comes along who expresses it with force. Then all who are thus afflicted join with him in fanatic zeal to express the hate and rebellion now at last permitted to come forth under strong leadership.

Still other evil consequences result from "education" without an ultimate commitment of faith in what sustains society, but no further description of them will be attempted. The social sciences are now making them known in many publications and lectures. But it is important to see what these facts indicate. They indicate that education lacking commitment to the creative interchange by which the whole self learns is a kind of education producing people who are unable to sustain with passion and power the society which educates them and in some cases people who turn upon that society to tear it down.

If education is not to produce futile conformists, cynics, fanatics, rebels, subversives, and destroyers, it must establish as central to its entire undertaking this commitment of faith. This commitment is a rudimentary kind of religion. It is not a fully developed religion. A fully developed religion requires all the practices of commitment, the rituals and symbols and assemblies, the instruction, and the philosophy or theology with which to cultivate, evangelize, instruct, deepen, and empower the ruling commitment. All this the school cannot do. All this is the responsibility of church and home. But this rudimentary form of religion should be the central concern of education if the school is to be constructive and not destructive to the mind of the individual and to the social order.

When the whole self is engaged in the creative interchange of learning and teaching, education enables the individual to find himself. His potentialities are awakened; they come alive. The individual becomes able to act, think, and feel constructively with the whole self. Instead of enthusiasm dying as it does with the other kind of "education," enthusiasm is deepened and at the same time made more intelligent and effective in thought and action and appreciation. Life becomes real instead of becoming a kind of pretense as it does when the educated part of the mind suppresses instead of releasing the individual's full capacity to think, feel, act, and appreciate.

So far we have been discussing the need which education has for religion of a rudimentary kind. Now we shall reverse the picture and look at the other side, namely, the need which religion has for education when education is conducted with personal commitment. We have been looking at the need of every human person and the need of our entire civilization for the kind of education which carries the ultimate commitment of man. But in providing education of this kind the school must have the help of other institutions and without their aid can do little. In developing the form of faith which our society needs, the church must co-operate. A fully developed religion is needed and this requires the church as well as the school.

Here it is important to distinguish between what the school can do for religion and what the church or some other distinctively religious institution must do if we are to have a fully developed and fully effective faith. The primary responsibility of the church was described in the previous chapter.

To see clearly the service of the school in contrast to the service of the church in respect to religion, it is necessary to distinguish rather sharply between two things which enter into religion. One of these two is a problem to be solved; the other is some proposed and practiced solution of the problem. The religious problem is never completely and perfectly solved any more than the problem of government or education or industry is ever completely and perfectly solved. Therefore these problems should always be in process of being solved. But in the meantime religion and government and education and industry must be practiced. People cannot merely inquire; they must live. They must think; but they must also act. Hence in all these cases there is both a problem to be solved and also a proposed and practiced solution to the problem.

This distinction is often obscured, especially in case of government and religion and most of all in religion. It is obscured because the proposed and practiced solution of the problem is so often taken to be the final and perfect solution. So important is religion, engaging so fully the passions of life, that it is difficult in many cases to keep this distinction clear. Yet the distinction is of utmost importance when society becomes increasingly complex, when interdependence and power are magnified, and when social change is accelerated. In primitive and agrarian culture this distinction may fade from recognition without great danger. But in a complex and dynamic civilization it should not fade because the changing conditions, the increasing complexity, power, and interdependence render earlier solutions of the problem unfit for the new demands made upon the sustaining faith. Consequently at the advanced levels of civilization the problem to be solved in religion should engage the resources of devoted inquiry even when at the same time a proposed solution is being practiced.

This distinction between the problem to be solved and a proposed solution being practiced marks out the distinction between the service rendered to religion by the school and the service rendered by the church. The school should prepare the mind for inquiry in this field of religious search while the church should conduct the practices of religious commitment according to the best proposed solution of the problem as achieved to date.

Of course there can be no absolute division between seeking and practicing. Life cannot be divided into exclusive departments. Research in science and the practical application of the findings of science cannot be separated. Yet we have different institutions which assume primary responsibility for the research on the one hand and the practical application on the other. So it is with political science and the practice of government. So it is with schools of business administration and the conduct of business. So it is with home economics and the conduct of a household. So it should be with religion.

First of all we must be clear on just what is the religious problem which calls for inquiry. We have stated it before but since there is much obscurity on this point, it must be stated again in marking out the distinctive services of school and church respectively. The most important question calling for answer in the field of religion is this: What in truth has such character and power that man must commit himself to it to be transformed as he cannot transform himself to the end of being saved from self-destruction and to the end of being transformed into the best he can ever become? This is the question for which there are many proposed answers. These answers have been accepted and are practiced as the sustaining and saving faith in the various forms of religion.

When this distinction is made between the faith which inquires and the faith which practices, many will confuse the issue by claiming that the answer has already been found for this question which underlies all religion. This claim can be accepted and still the distinction remains. In truth the answer has been found. It has been found in the form of a faith which has been found. But such practice should not exclude further inquiry. In the Christian tradition the accepted answer to this question is often stated with a single name: Jesus Christ. Let us not dispute this answer. But Jesus Christ is a name interpreted religiously in ways utterly diverse from each other and often one interpretation contradicts everything asserted by another. It would require the history of Christendom to make a list of all the different ways in which devoted Christians have interpreted Jesus Christ as the answer to the religious question. Obviously, then, merely to utter the name Jesus Christ gives no intelligible answer and leaves the basic problem of religion unsolved.

The same applies to all the other apparently brief and simple answers to the religious question. The teachings of Gautama may call for the ultimate commitment of man but these teachings are diversely interpreted by different advocates. Confucius might answer the religious question by referring to the mandate of heaven. Communists answer it by pointing to the economic determinism of history, the Nazis by proclaiming the destiny of the Aryan race.

It is the primary responsibility of church and home to practice a form of religious commitment based upon the acceptance of some proposed solution of the religious problem. But it is difficult to combine the practice of a commitment based upon the assumption of a problem solved and at the same time look at the problem as one to solve. For this reason church and home cannot assume responsibility for guiding religious inquiry. They ought to inspire the kind of commitment which does not close the mind against further searching. The commitment they practice should be dual in character as previously described. They should arouse the mind to seek beyond any proposed answer which may be practiced in the rituals of worship. But the inquiry itself is the responsibility of the school, especially at the higher levels of education.

Some who feel that answers have already been given beyond which no human mind can go, may object to this proposal by saying: Why should the individual be led to struggle with a problem when the problem has been solved? It will only disturb and weaken his faith.

Even if we assume that answers have been given beyond which no human mind can go, still there are good and sufficient reasons for inducing religious inquiry in the mind of the student.

The first of these reasons should be obvious to any educator. No one ever understands the solution of a problem until he

understands the problem to be solved. One must first understand the question before he can understand the answer to it.
It has long been established as a fundamental principle of
teaching that no student can understand the subject matter in
any field until he understands the problems and learns to solve
some of them for himself. One will never learn to understand
what it is all about if he merely looks up the answers in the back
of the book and commits them to memory. Yet a very large part
of religious instruction and religious practice in church and
home is like that. The answers are given and commitment is
practiced without much struggling with the problem. To say this
is not to criticize the religious instruction and practice in church
and home. This is what they should do. This is their function.
But this religious function of church and home shows the imperative need of another religious function, namely, that of the
school.

Small children are not able to deal effectively with the basic
religious question which underlies all religious practice and this
problem should not be forced upon them. In church and home
they should be taught the answers which guide religious commitment and give it meaning. But when the student reaches high
school and college he is ready to undertake this religious question for himself. In any case, he will ordinarily take it on whether
or not he gets any help. Therefore at this stage he needs help
most urgently, for there is no question more difficult and none
more important than this.

The schools must take over the religious question if for no
other reason than to enable the student to understand and appreciate the real significance of the answers in the back of the
book, given to him in church and home. However, I think most
will agree that even if the ultimate answers are in the keeping of
the Bible, church, and home, there is a vast amount yet to learn
which is relevant to the religious question underlying the whole
of human life.

The religious answer will never be a living and driving force,
and the inquiring mind will not grow in its understanding of the
answer, until the individual understands and appreciates the full

significance of the religious question. He should be led to feel its tremendous importance, its urgent demand, its character as pervading the whole of human conduct and experience. This is the first reason for saying that the school should teach the problem that underlies religion.

The second reason appears when we note the three alternatives open to the student in high school and college when he begins to question the religious answers given to him in childhood. One of these alternatives is that he will reject the answers and along with them all religious faith. The second is that he will quench all doubt, silence the questioning mind, accept the religious answer as part of the routine of daily living, and devote his active attention and searching mind to other matters. The third alternative is that he will struggle with the problem, seek to improve his understanding of the answers taught him in childhood, and thus make religion an active, growing and pervasive concern of his life.

Surely the third alternative is the best. But scarcely can one take this third path unless he is led to understand religion not only as a set of answers but also as a question or problem wrought inextricably into the fabric of all human living and one from which the individual cannot escape even though he may reject all the answers so far given to him. It is the great opportunity, the high responsibility, and the imperative task of the school to present religion to the student as a problem to be solved, a question to be answered and one that is inescapable, imperative, destiny-determining.

To teach religion as a problem without final answers is to teach it as every other subject is taught. Excepting mathematics, there is no final answer to the questions considered in the classroom. Religion may have its final answers but it is not the business of the school to teach them. Every subject taught in the school deals with some problem or other. Successful teaching should arouse the interest of the student in the problem so that he will be deeply concerned, sometimes passionately concerned, to find the best possible answer. This applies to religion as to every other important subject taught in the schools.

This raises the question of objectivity in dealing with any subject matter and most especially with religion. It is claimed, and rightly so, that the teacher must be as objective in dealing with religion as with any other subject. But confusion often arises at this point. To be objective does not preclude the most passionate interest in a problem. The greatest scientists and the most objective have sometimes been so completely committed to the problems of their science that all their lives were given to research to the point of utmost sacrifice. Objectivity imposes no constraint on the passionate concern one has for the problem. Objectivity means to accept no proposed solution except to the measure that evidence supports it, and to be very critical of the evidence. It means, furthermore, to reject any solution that may have been accepted and adopt another when the latter is supported by greater weight of evidence. It means, still further, that one will recognize that every accepted solution based on empirical evidence is incomplete and subject to revision. But all this can be combined with the uttermost self-giving in faith to the importance of the problem when faith means commitment to a problem and not the final acceptance of any proposed answer. Furthermore, all this can be combined with the acceptance of an answer as the best working solution found to date and living by it until a better is attained.

Everything said in the previous paragraph applies to every field of instruction and learning whether it be the interpretation of a period in history, the interpretation of any great work of literature, or philosophy or any part of science. It applies to everything one does in business, home, and politics. It also applies to religion in exactly the same way.

Apologists for certain religious answers say that religion cannot be approached objectively as other problems. Religion is an existential problem they say; it involves the person so deeply that he cannot be objective. Such a statement reveals a confusion about objectivity. Certainly religion is an existential problem involving the person so deeply that he cannot approach it religiously without committing himself very completely, even passionately. But such a commitment does not exclude objectivity if one practices the dual commitment. The more important the problem the more concerned should one be to get the best possible answer; and the more insistent that every proposed answer meet the most rigorous and objective tests. Even after accepting an answer by these tests as the best working answer found so far, he will hold it subject to revision when further evidence demands it.

If this is a correct understanding of objectivity, whether in religion or elsewhere, some of the wrong ways of trying to be objective in teaching religion should be examined.

One of the wrong ways is to assume a beaming attitude toward all the great religions and try to show that they all have much the same truth disguised though this truth may be. This is not the kind of objectivity needed because it is not interpreting the religious question and appraising answers and seeking better answers where possible. Furthermore, it reveals a lack of true concern with the problem because he who has that concern will not be satisfied with any answer except as the best possible working answer he can find. One who has this kind of concern will be highly critical of answers, perhaps including the answer he himself has adopted as the best known to him at the time. But he will not try to make diverse answers appear to be equally acceptable.

In the classroom the student will be informed of some of the widely accepted answers, but they will always be presented, including the Christian answer, in the form of questions. The purpose will always be not to show that any of these answers when put in the form of a set of propositions are final and complete, although one may be much better than the others and adopted on that account. But the purpose will always be to help the student understand the question, its magnitude, and its supreme and imperative importance. Each of the great religions, and every form of Christianity from Unitarians to Nazarenes, has its own answer to this question. Every practicing form of religion must have an answer because religious faith is commitment to what one believes to be—often quite mistakenly—of such character and power more than human that man must commit himself to it for salvation. Every student must adopt some answer if he is truly religious, even though he may accept it as something less than final and complete. So must every very teacher if he is a religious man. But the questioning and the searching for a better and more complete answer need never end.

There is a second mistaken way of trying to be objective in the teaching of religion. It is to substitute passionate commitment to scholarship in place of commitment to the religious problem. Of course scholarship in the academic world is always to be praised. But one can be very competent in his mastery of all the facts pertaining to the religions of the world, including all the answers offered to the religious question, and still have very little understanding and appreciation of the religious question itself. It is another case of learning all the answers in the back of the book without having struggled personally with the problem to the point where one can appreciate the real significance of these answers. Students subjected to that kind of scholarship and motivated to study with that kind of leadership may become very facile in their mastery of all the factual material about religion and yet miss the whole point of instruction in this field.

Another mistaken attempt at being objective appears when the Christian Bible is made the subject of study in courses of religion. The Bible can be taught in three different ways: as a book of answers to the religious question, as literature, or as a book of inquiry which seeks an ever better answer.

As used devotionally in church and home the Bible is a book of answers. People read it, study it, pray with it because they believe that they find in it the only final and reliable answers. But the Bible cannot be taught in the school as a book of answers involving the theological doctrines because these are excluded from general education. There is often some unintentional dishonesty in trying to teach the Bible without involvement in these doctrines when the teachers by reason of past training cannot look upon the Bible as other than a book of answers.

The Bible can be taught as literature. But the Bible is primarily a religious book and should be taught religiously if the course is in religion and not in literature. Furthermore, to teach it as literature is to impair its religious significance. Here again dishonesty is likely to creep in when the announced form of instruction is to teach the book as literature although the real motive is religious. But if the motive is religious, there is the other kind of dishonesty also, namely, clandestine teaching of religious doctrines that have no place in the school.

Thirdly, the Bible can be taught as a book of inquiry. In such case it is taught as the history of the religious search of a religiously gifted (or chosen) people. But if truly taught in this fashion, the answers found in the Bible must be treated as incomplete and subject to correction. Such treatment of the Bible runs counter to the demands of its usage in church and home as a book of answers. In many cases it outrages the religious sensibilities of people devoted to the Bible. The conflict between these two ways of using the Bible, namely, as a book of answers and as a book of inquiry, may be concealed for a time. But it will be present in the minds of the students and in the minds of parents and churchmen. Students in time may learn to use the Bible as a book of inquiry and not as a book of final and complete answers. But to make this shift constructively, supposing that it is desired, requires that the student first understand the religious question and be rather well grounded in its true character, its indestructible and vital significance, and the unlimited scope of inquiry which it demands.

There is still another objection to using the Christian Bible as the subject of instruction in religion if the purpose of instruction is to acquaint the student with the religious question in all its force and magnitude and to incite inquiry for the best possible answers by seeking for them in all the subject matter of school instruction. The use of the Bible tends to channel all religious inquiry upon itself to the exclusion of free and penetrating search in other areas. This it does as consequence of the way it has been used for centuries in the Christian tradition. It may contain the final answers that guide religious commitment but such use of it should be reserved to church and home for reasons that have been reiterated. The purpose of introducing religion into the school is to enable general education to assume responsibility for the transmission and development of spiritual values by way of the total body of instruction. But this purpose is prevented if the total body of instruction cannot be the area of religious inquiry relevant to the religious question. When the Bible monopolizes the religious concern of the student, it automatically diminishes the religious significance of all instruction outside the Bible. This runs counter to the whole purpose of bringing religion into the school.

For all these reasons it seems unwise to use the Bible as the subject of study in any course in religion in the school. When used it either stirs up theological controversy which cannot be permitted in the school, or else is taught in a way which impairs its true religious significance. Also it concentrates religious interest upon itself, thus preventing that spread of religious interest to the whole body of instruction which must be achieved to enable the school to be the transmitter and promoter of spiritual values.

While the controversy over the Bible should be avoided by not using it as a text in the school, there is another kind of controversy which almost surely will arise and this one must be taken on and carried through to a finish. It is controversy caused by those who insist that basic religious inquiry cannot be permitted except when directed to learning the religious answers laid down in the dogma of the church. Basic religious inquiry means seeking a more complete answer to the question underlying all religion: What in truth calls for man's ultimate commitment? Learning the final answers as laid down in dogma may be practiced in church and home. But such teaching and such learning have no place in the school. Therefore, if all religious inquiry in the school is forced to take the form of learning the final answers contained in dogma, no religious inquiry at all can be permitted in the school. But we have seen that our salvation depends upon the school's assuming responsibility for moral and spiritual values. Therefore opposition to free religious inquiry in the school must not be allowed to prevail. The school, the government, and the American people must not yield on this issue. The good of our society and of humanity and the outcome of the present critical moment in human history are at stake.

The religious question is too important, profound, and fateful to allow any group to take away from the school this religious responsibility.

Another error due to religious zeal should be prevented. It is to expect teachers to deal with this religious question who are not deeply concerned about it. Men and women teaching the various subjects of the curriculum should not be asked nor expected to point out the religious significance of what they teach. Certainly when they are spontaneously inclined to do this, it should be welcomed, provided that they themselves understand the religious question and are true inquirers and not dogmatists. But there is something artificial if not a bit nauseating in always pointing out the religious significance of what one is teaching unless it comes naturally and spontaneously.

On the other hand, if the school is to assume responsibility for spiritual values along with church and home, all teachers should know what the legitimate and profound problem of religion is. This should be a required part of the equipment of every teacher, just as every teacher is supposed to have some awareness of the problems in all the other areas of instruction although not necessarily to know any of the answers. Not only should all the teachers know what this religious question is, but they should appreciate its validity and importance, no matter how completely they reject any or all of the traditional answers. This holds for the same reason that no teacher has a place in a school who has no appreciation and no respect for the other subjects taught there. That much co-operation in any school is required. An English teacher who did not recognize the importance of mathematics, or vice versa, would be an unacceptable member of the faculty because the student must not be subjected to instruction where one teacher tears down what the other tries to do. Teachers may well criticize, attack, and reject the proposed answers to questions championed by one another. They may not even know the correct answers to the problems in other fields than their own. But it is scarcely permissible for any member of the faculty to deny legitimacy or significance to questions and problems of instruction outside of his own field. On the other hand, to ask the English teacher to be concerned always to point out the contribution which literature might make to mathematics, or the reverse, is to impair the work of all concerned. The same applies to religion in its relation to the other areas of instruction. I am not suggesting that the study of the problem of religion in the schools will bring about a great religious awakening. There are many reasons for denying that any such thing would happen. For one thing, the schools cannot attempt to indoctrinate with any specific form of religion beyond inducing commitment to the learning process of creative interchange. It is here contended that any form of religion meeting our need must include this; but a fully developed religion must include much more and this much more cannot be provided by the school.

One thing, however, the school can do to prepare the way for a great religious awakening. After people have studied the basic religious question in the school they might be able to see that the destiny of man hangs on finding the best answer to this question. Also, after study of the religious question, they might be able to distinguish what answers move in the direction of truth as over against those which are plainly wrong. They might be able to distinguish the answers which are worthy of serious consideration as over against religious proclamations which are trivial or pernicious. An understanding of the religious question should equip people for making these evaluations.

The birth of a powerful and profound religion fit to save man in the midst of a complex civilization and able to realize the creative transformation of man which our civilization makes possible, waits on prophetic leadership. But the people must be ready to receive the prophet. At present the vast majority of people do not understand the religious question. They have not studied it nor had opportunity to study it sufficiently to distinguish a false from a true answer, nor what is trivial from what is profound, nor what is destructive from what is saving and creative. If this continues, false prophets will arise and lead the people into wild and evil ways. Many such false and misleading religions are rising in our time because the people feel the need of a faith fit to cope with the problems of a complex and powerful civilization. They feel the need but do not understand the religious question well enough to judge wisely. So they are led astray. Naziism and communism are examples of recently developed faiths. If the people continue to lack standards for judging the worth of proposed answers to the religious question, the fanaticism, conflict, and confusion of false faiths will increase. Hence the need to study the religious problem in the schools.

The human race cannot go on magnifying the power to destroy at the same time increasing the interdependence of diverse peoples and casting off the controlling and moulding power of old traditions unless within the next fifty years or so the guiding power of a sovereign and saving and constructive faith lays hold upon the hearts of men. Such a faith will arise if the way is prepared by study and understanding of the religious question. Here, then, is the place of the school, especially the college and university, in the service of religion. Gradually the teachers, the methods, and the materials for this undertaking should be acquired and developed. It cannot be done quickly and easily but it can be done.

The school cannot do this without the support of other major institutions. But certain developments in industry and certain developments in government call for the service of the school along these lines. With this support the school should be able to undertake this task. How and why this support can come from industry and government will be examined in the next two chapters.

Chapter 10

INDUSTRY UNDER COMMITMENT

T HE ECONOMIC system can be viewed in two different ways. In one way it is viewed in its autonomy, as though it were independent of all human problems except those concerned with the production and distribution of goods and services. This is the view of the economist or other expert. In the other way it is viewed as one part of the total problem of meeting the needs of the human person and conducting human life in a way to make the best of it. This is the view of the humanist or moralist or man of religious concern.

The first view looks at the economy from the inside, so to speak, and does not look beyond it. The other view looks at it from the outside, to see how it helps or hurts the other major concerns of human living. The first view appraises the economic system in terms of its efficiency as a producer and distributor, and tries to point out how it might be improved in this respect. The second view appraises the economic system in terms of the good or ill it does to the human person, and tries to point out how it might be improved to this end.

The second of these two approaches to industry and business is the one here adopted. But this humanistic, moral, or religious approach can get nowhere if it ignores the problems of efficiency and all those rules of the game by which industry and business are conducted. These rules, internal to the economic system, may be at times in opposition to the rules by which the good life is conducted as these rules are interpreted by the one who takes the moral and religious view.

This opposition between the internal demands of efficiency within a given organization and the external demands of the more comprehensive needs of life applies not only to the economic order. It applies to church, school, home, government, and every organization which serves the needs of the human person. It is often the case that what is required to maintain a special form of service will run counter to the needs of human personality, when these needs are viewed in their wholeness. But this opposition must often be tolerated because if the special form of service lacks efficiency, the consequent evil may be greater than the evil caused by opposition between the demands of efficiency within a given organization and the more comprehensive needs of life. On this account the humanist is often in error in condemning what is done in business, industry, government, church, or school because the practices and rules of action in these special organizations conflict with the larger ideals of the good life. Certainly these conflicts should be removed when possible, but to condemn the practices of a special organization without understanding the internal problems of its practical operation is to indulge in error. For this reason we must glance at some of the internal demands of efficiency in industry before we look at the relation of the economy to the more comprehensive concerns of human living.

One of the internal demands of the economy goes by the name of the profit motive. The striving to increase profit to the maximum is often condemned. But profit, in one of its many meanings, is nothing else than what must be fed back into the productive and distributive system to keep it going and to increase its productive power. Profit in this sense, namely, the surplus reinvested to increase production, is sought as avidly in the socialist state as it is in the United States. No possible kind of industrialized economy can dispense with it.

This feed-back or profit must be sufficient not only to maintain the level of production but also to increase it, because greater demands are constantly being made upon the economy. The population is growing, the needs of individuals are multiplying, all the major institutions are drawing more heavily every year upon the production of goods and services. The whole world is looking to the United States for economic aid and trade. Hence to oppose profit is to misunderstand the source of productive power.

On the other hand the ability to buy the products of industry is just as essential to economic stability and increasing production as profits and investments. There is some optimum balance between investments, profits, prices, and wages. What this optimum is and how the wealth should be distributed to achieve it is a controversial problem among the experts. Where they disagree the amateur cannot judge. In any case industry under commitment to the creativity which is the source of all human good must seek this optimum and not any "equal distribution of the wealth." Persons bearing chief responsibility for industrial production must have command of far more wealth than other people because they cannot otherwise do what their responsibility requires of them.

Without great productive power and ever-increasing production the creative transformation of the human mind cannot be carried very far by way of education and religion, art and science, home life and neighborhood, government and politics, love and friendship, and by the work within the industrial plant itself. This last, we shall try to show, can be very creative. Therefore any proposal for the distribution of wealth which limits production is an error and hurts the spiritual life of man as much as the material. Of course maximum production can do evil as well as good, depending on how it is done. The organization by which wealth is produced can be degrading but it can also be ennobling. But the cure of evils cannot be had by diminishing the power to produce and create markets. These are the distinctive functions of business and can be as creatively transforming as anything else.

We shall try to show that certain recent developments in the economic order make it possible to increase productive power continuously and also to order and direct industry in a way to serve creative interchange and the spiritual values of life more effectively than any other economic system. One of these developments is the rise of the manager taking the place of the owner in the control of industry. Another is the size of the modern corporation and its intimate connection with all areas of social life. A third is automation. These all are not necessarily good but they open up possibilities for creativity beyond any other economy which ever existed.

Another feature of modern industry and economic exchange should be left to the experts although it profoundly determines the good and evil of human life in all areas, reaching out into every part of society. It has moral and religious consequences of utmost importance and yet it has technical complications calling for specialized competence. It is the problem of inflation and deflation, depression and unemployment, boom and bust. From my reading in the field I understand that we have methods for avoiding extreme depressions and periods of excessive unemployment, provided that the interested parties who exercise control can be persuaded to apply them at the right time and to the right measure. This is a matter about which one who adopts the humanist approach to the economy should be deeply concerned. But the economist whose attention is focused on the internal problems of the economy is no less concerned. Perhaps nothing absorbs the attention of experts so much as this problem of finding a way to stabilize production, distribution, consumption, and investment. In any case it is not a matter about which an outsider can make a recommendation; and to bewail and condemn without making a constructive suggestion is futile.

I shall not further discuss the problems internal to the economy which require mastery of the technical complexities, except as these are involved in the more inclusive needs of the human person. These more inclusive needs cannot be ignored in the conduct of industry and the experts are coming increasingly to recognize them and work upon them. The production and distribution of goods and services must be done by human beings, all working together, each person with his individual needs and interests, personal problems and difficulties, hopes and fears.

Under highly industrialized conditions all the people must be served by the economy and not only a favored few if the business is to prosper. Furthermore this service must promote creative transformation of minds as well as provide material goods if there is to be a market for the quantity and quality of goods produced by the huge corporations in a society so intricately and widely interdependent as industrialized society. The more industry produces above the bare necessities, and the higher the standard of living, the more dependent does the economy become upon states of mind prevailing throughout the society which it serves and upon high cultural standards generally. Not otherwise can industry at an advanced level have the science and the scientists, the technology and the art, the imagination and resourcefulness of workers and managers, the variegated demand for goods, and the expanding range of needs which must be present in any society upon which it depends and which it serves.

As an example of this, take the case of producing workers fit to operate the economy when machines control machines as in automation and when all work reducible to routine and repetition is done by machines. Men who design and construct such machines in ever-increasing quantity and diversity and with great changes constantly demanded by new inventions must be imaginative and resourceful, versatile and cultured. Automation will create many new kinds of work in industry and commerce but it will not be routine work. Machines will do that. It will be work which requires a rather high level of mental ability and moral development. As Peter Drucker so well demonstrates, in the new industry now emerging all the workers must have the "managerial vision." [1]

The managerial vision means an understanding of the product or outcome of the enterprise and how the special kind of work which the individual does will contribute to this product. Each individual worker must be aware of the comprehensive objective of the corporation and the part his work plays in it. Also he must have a definite idea of what his work should be and a method for measuring the excellence of his own performance. All this was not required when the mass of workers were engaged in routine operations. It is required in the new kind of industry.

Still another feature of the new industry should be noted which shows that the economic process must promote creative transformation of the mind if it is to sustain itself. In other days the worker was driven to his job by fear of hunger and other deprivation. But in a society rich enough to provide subsistence even to the unemployed, fear has lost its motivating power. How then can men be induced to work? Obviously only by a positive motivation to take the place of fear. Positive motivation must be gained by creative interchange and personal development found in the work itself. The new demands of the economy and the new possibilities which it offers for developing the potentialities distinctive of the human being have not been so widely recognized as they should be. The developments have come so recently that recognition has not kept pace with it. But the most successful of the large corporations have recognized this coalescence of demand and possibility and have acted accordingly to organize the corporation to serve creative transformation of the mind in the work which is done. The International Business Machines Corporation, Sears, Roebuck, Western Electric, General Motors, Standard Oil, and others are moving strongly in this direction.[2]

No attempt can here be made to enter into the complex problems of modern industry. We wish to say no more than to defend the claim that industry and commerce are developing in such a way that it is not at all fantastic to suggest that they can be committed to that creative interchange which is here set forth as calling for man's ultimate commitment.

Potent in forcing our economy to participate more widely and deeply in all the concerns of human living is the complex interdependence of all the parts of the total organization required to produce and distribute economic goods. Education and religion, science and art, politics and government, sex and child care, home life and neighborhood, morality and good will, all these are conspicuous and powerful component parts in the production, distribution, and consumption of economic goods; and the part these ostensibly non-economic concerns of human living play in determining the stability and efficiency of the economic process increases constantly. There was a time when industry could develop by working women and children twelve hours a day, keeping wages to the level barely sufficient for muscular exertion, and allowing the mass of workers to live in slums which degraded the mind and character. Today the whole economic system would break down if such practices became widely prevalent.

It is important to emphasize that this concern for the well-being of all men has become an economic necessity. Modern industry cannot operate without highly developed cultural resources widespread so that producers and consumers alike and the great majority of all members of the society have the minds and the resources, the interests and the imagination to consume as well as to produce as the economy requires. This has its dangers to be sure, but it also opens the way to magnificent possibilities. Increasingly our entire culture shapes and influences what occurs in the industrial plant, in the market place, and in finance; and what occurs in these areas is increasingly influential in shaping our entire culture. Therefore if the economic system runs counter to the demands of the extra-economic part of the social system, it will, like a blind Samson, drag down the whole house and destroy itself along with all others depending on the social order. But the opposite course is also open. If the leaders of industry recognize, as increasing numbers are beginning to do, that the economy itself demands universal development of the human mind and human character, the creative transformation of man can move forward to a new level, provided religion, education, and government co-operate to the same end.

This is not a rosy prediction. It is not a prediction at all. It is only pointing to an opportunity and an opening which is now with us. Whether we follow the path of this opportunity or go in the opposite direction no man can predict. All any man can do is to point out and define the alternatives and some of the conditions which must be met. Also it should be emphasized that the creative transformation of man which our economy is now able to promote cannot be accomplished by industry alone. The responsibility laid upon religion, education, and government must not be forgotten when examining the part to be played by the economic order. These all are being tied more closely together in the total enterprise of human living. The weaving of the web of our advancing civilization is doing this regardless of human intention and desire. But industry has the greatest power to influence men directly and its power relative to the other agencies is rapidly increasing.

The significant development of our economy bearing upon the opportunity just mentioned can be summarized. The chief problem of industrial development has come to be the minds of men and their relations to one another. Machinery, technology, and finance are important but the stability and productive power of industry depend far more upon the way men think and feel toward one another, toward the major institutions and social developments than upon anything else. The managers of industry and others responsible for industrial production are coming to recognize this and devote themselves to this problem. What the responsible persons do in this regard may bring disaster but the opportunity is open to the industrialists along with the leaders in education, religion, and government to provide conditions permitting the creativity in human life to realize more fully than was possible in the past the constructive potentialities of man. This opportunity is open in a peculiar way to industrial management and labor leaders partly because of the enormous power they exercise, partly because their own economic interests point in that direction since the stability and power of the economy are so largely determined by the morale, goodwill, satisfaction, loyalty, and co-operative attitude not only among workers in the plant but throughout society.

A further feature should be noted which is driving the men responsible for the conduct of industry to be concerned about creative transformation of the mind and the prevalence of creative interchange throughout society. It is the huge investment embodied in the big corporation. To pay for such an investment the books must show on the average a profitable balance over a long stretch of years. When long periods of time are not required to pay back the investment and where the corporation is small enough so that social conditions are not dependent on its own behavior, larger profits can be made in a short time without much regard for the effect upon society of what the business does nor even great regard for the reputation it may acquire and the goodwill of the general public toward it. But when a corporation is very large it must depend [1] upon profits continuing for many decades if not generations, [2] upon social conditions favorable to its operations when these conditions depend upon its own conduct, [3] upon a reputation and goodwill in the public mind acquired after many years of good behavior, [4] upon the intelligence, loyalty, imagination, and energy of its own plant community built up through many decades, [5] upon the co-operation of powerful labor unions where distrust and resent-ment can grow into powerful opposition if labor is not well treated.

Perhaps the most significant fact about the giant corporations is that the condition of society is so largely determined by their own behavior. Therefore if profits depend upon a buying public with a rising standard of living, upon an intelligent and imagina-tive public able to consume the products and also to provide industry with the kind of government and schools it needs and with the kind of workers and managers, scientists and artists, raw materials and inventions it must have, the corporation must exercise its great power to sustain and build such a society.

This does not mean, of course, that industrialists will always do this. A powerful tradition in business points in the opposite direction. Larger profits can often be made by reducing taxes when the method used is to get men on school boards who will block expansion of much needed school facilities. This is only one of many devious ways to help increase profits. Perhaps the greatest danger of all is the one previously mentioned and well described by David Riesman in *The Lonely Crowd*, by Erich Fromm in *Escape from Freedom* and *Man for Himself*, and in other current writings. It is the danger of developing a mass of human beings content with a surfeit of material goods, with leisure and entertainment, and with social and personal devices which make life smooth and easy but shallow and irresponsible, without integrity, without great love, without great hate, without aspiration.

While these evils and dangers must be recognized it is equally important to recognize the promise of our time and what might be done for developing conditions to promote the creative transformation of the human race.

I have mentioned one of the recent developments in our economy which carries both the promise and danger, namely, the size and character of the big corporation requiring for its own success and profitability a good society with human capacities highly cultivated, and with power residing in the corporation itself to play a major part in creating such a society.

A further feature of modern industry previously mentioned drives in the same direction. It is the shift of control from the owner to the manager. This is a change of momentous importance the implications and potentialities of which are only beginning to reach the minds of students in this field. The manager is not merely the top executive. In the large corporations there are hundreds of managers. More than that, as previously stated, the managerial function is reaching down into all the different kinds of work done by human minds in the industrial enterprise. Furthermore we are rapidly moving into the time when all work must be done by minds and not merely by hands.

This shift of control from owner to manager is misunderstood if it is thought that the manager merely takes over the work once done by the owner. It is not the same kind of work; and management in control of industry is a new kind of being in human society. This new agency with its new kind of work is not merely an expression of benevolence but is being forced by the requirements of success in the conduct of business.

The chief task of the manager at all levels from foreman to chief executive is to communicate and motivate. Even the individual worker under the foreman who works in a team with a small group will find that his success depends pre-eminently on his ability to communicate with his associates, learn from them, to be motivated by them, and to motivate them. To be sure the manager at all levels must do much more than this or rather do it in certain specific ways. He sets the objectives for the work to be done. He determines what the goals of achievement should be for each kind of work and what is required to achieve these goals. But these objectives, these goals, and these supplies and services must be communicated to others, not only to subordinates but also to superiors with interchange of suggestions and with appreciative understanding between all concerned.

The manager at all levels organizes. He must make a unity of mutually sustaining parts out of all the activities under his control. Also this unity must be integrated with other unities under the control of others and this progressively on and up to the unity of the entire enterprise. But if this is to be achieved effectively it must be through the appreciative understanding by each party of what he has to do in relation to the whole undertaking and his willing co-operation to that end. So this again comes back to creative interchange between all parties concerned.

The manager must devise methods for measuring performance and these yardsticks for judging the excellence of what is done should be communicated to those whose work is thereby judged so that each can judge and measure his own performance by some objective standard. This makes possible self-control by each in relation to the others and hence freedom or democracy. Also it inspires the individual to do his best. When the individual can judge his own performance and see clearly what he should do to achieve excellence, he has an inspiration and freedom which releases creative potentialities. Under such control he does not feel dominated and so is not likely to feel resentment or lose interest in his own work because under such conditions his work offers opportunity for initiative and self-development.

All this can be summed up by saying that the work of the manager at all levels is pre-eminently the work of developing the potentialities of individuals by providing conditions under which they can learn most abundantly from one another and from the work which they do, this learning to include not merely knowledge and skill but all the other forms of development which pertain to the human being. As Drucker says in books above cited, the successful manager in industry is one who can impart vision and develop people. He gives to others vision and ability to perform. His task is above all educational.

The impact upon society of decisions made by industrial management is perhaps greater than the decisions made by any other group of individuals in a free society. Even the decisions of government must be modified to sustain the massive flow of industrial production. No government can retain power if it does not do this because the power of any society in our time depends more upon industrial production than upon anything else.

This power of industrial management over the well-being of society has come so swiftly and is increasing so rapidly that management itself has scarcely awakened to a realization of its own power and responsibility. Since it has this power, the fate of future social development and individual attainment will depend very much upon the policies and decisions of industrial management. If, for example, business is not conducted by management in a way to sustain employment and abundance, if it does not motivate men to work with loyalty and high competence, if it does not organize and direct by giving objectives which each can adopt for himself and thus judge and control himself, if it does not thus promote the democratic way of life, if it acts irresponsibly in a way to antagonize large sections of the public, it is very likely that government will take over the power of control and our society will change into a monolithic, centralized organization which stifles initiative and creative interchange.

Any agency with so much power and carrying so great a load of responsibility for the social order is required not only to recognize the identity of its interest with the public good; it must act in such a way that the public generally will recognize this identity by the way the business is conducted. Also to retain its place and function in our society it must anticipate the demands which society will make upon industry and manage to meet these demands in a way which will not hurt but will help the business. Drucker gives several examples showing how management in some cases has done this and in other cases has not, with the kind of consequences which follow when one or the other course is pursued.

The first of these examples is the matter of pensions and the care for employees beyond the age of retirement. This example and others to follow are presented to illustrate a general principle and not to make a special plea for the specific measures considered.

Some managements faced the problem of pensions and work for the aged employees years ago and developed a method which strengthened the industry and helped the worker at the same time. But many refused to recognize that this would become an irresistible demand of society. Consequently when government and labor union forced them to adopt a plan they had to accept a program which management itself had not planned and which was unduly costly for the enterprise and not so very beneficial for the employee. The problem is not merely to pay a pension but also to provide work for older men who are able and willing to do it, while at the same time planning this work in a way which will not block the promotion of younger men. Work for the aged becomes increasingly important as the proportion of older men increases as it is doing. Without such work for older men the load of sustaining them in idleness can in time become oppressive and restrictive for all. The managers who undertook the problem voluntarily before labor unions and government forced a program upon them have been able to do it constructively in a way to serve all concerned. But those who delayed action until compelled to accept a plan not of their own designing find it costly and restrictive. Neither does the coerced program serve so well the interests of the employees as the programs developed by managers before pressure was put upon them.

Another example is the matter of providing stability of income and employment. This demand will have to be met sooner or later. Currents of growing power are moving in that direction. If management does not take care of it in a way to improve and strengthen the enterprise, increase its productivity, and raise its over-all profits, it will be saddled with a guaranteed annual wage forced by labor unions and government. This will restrict the elasticity which industry must have to do its work and will not meet a real social need so well as a better plan might do if carefully designed by management.[3]

These illustrations might be multiplied. They show, first, the enormous power and responsibility of industrial management for the well-being of all members of society and, second, the two ways in which this power may be exercised and this responsibility met. Industrial management may carry this power and responsibility constructively with vision, foresight, social concern, and long range planning. If it does, we shall continue to have a free society with creative transformation of the human mind extending to more people and reaching higher levels of attainment. On the other hand, this power and responsibility may be carried blindly by management without recognizing the ever-increasing interdependence of business success and social responsibility. Both kinds of management, those with vision and those who are blind, are now in operation. The blindness in some cases is the result of social developments so rapid that men in high position are not aware of the new demands and responsibilities laid upon them. But the fate of our society and the course of history for years to come may be largely determined by the way industrial management exercises its power and meets its responsibility. If the blind leaders prevail, the coercions and control of government will increase until freedom and creative transformation are reduced to a minimum.

This enormous power in the hands of industrialists and labor unions is considered dangerous by many. Power in human hands is always dangerous; but what other agency is fitted to direct the power generated by our civilization in a way which will be less dangerous and more beneficent for all? It is impossible to have an advanced civilization such as ours without great power under human control. Advancing civilization means increasing power exercised by men. Furthermore great power cannot be directed by masses of people. It must always be controlled by groups sufficiently small to enable individuals working together to make decisions and to plan co-operatively with high competence.

There never has been an organization for the exercise of great power which distributed it so widely and so fruitfully as does the system of industrial management now developing. As said before, this widest possible distribution of power and responsibility and its fruitful use in the service of creative interchange and human development has become a necessity imposed by the working of the system itself. The big corporation cannot operate successfully without giving power and responsibility to many individuals each responsible for his own division and function within the enterprise.

Not only is this great power exercised by management distributed within each large industrial enterprise; it is also distributed between the many different branches of industry. Despite the outcry about monopoly there is intense competition and countervailing power between these different forms of industry. The corporation must buy from another big organization and sell to another. Also if prices, services, and form of management within a given corporation become unsatisfactory, some new invention outside the corporation will be produced and developed to supplant the goods and services of the first corporation. Railroads must compete with buses, trucks and airplanes; coal with oil and gas and electricity; copper with aluminum. If any of these fail to satisfy the market something else will be brought forth by scientific research to take its place and compel the negligent corporation either to improve or pass from the scene.

This tremendous dynamism, innovation and new invention of methods, kinds of organization and machines is another feature which makes our economy different from that of any other time. This continuous innovation compels management to serve creativity. Any corporation will fall behind and either fail or merge with a stronger organization if it does not provide conditions favorable for creative interchange and the creative transformation of the human mind. It must do this to keep up with what is going on in the world. The point is not that industry must undergo continuous change; the point is that it must undergo creative change. Otherwise stated, every corporation must undergo change either in the form of disintegration or in the form of progressive integration. To succeed, management must serve creativity. This creativity going on throughout industry makes it impossible for any corporation to maintain a monopoly, although a combination of corporations might do so.

Three checks have been noted which prevent arbitrary exercise of power by management of industry despite the great power under its control. These three are the competition and distribution of power within every big corporation, imposed by the necessities of successful enterprise; the competition and distribution of power between the different forms of industry; and, third, the dynamic, innovating character of modern industry which compels management to serve creativity rather than dominate and channel it.

There are three other checks to arbitrary power by management. One is the countervailing power of organized labor. Another has been mentioned repeatedly, namely, the peculiar dependence of modern industry upon the stability and well-being of human life generally. Industry cannot create the markets it must have nor recruit the managers, scientists for research, the technicians and other workers required without the kind of government, education, art, science, religion, and morality capable of bringing human minds to a high level of development with considerable initiative and independence. A further check to the power of management in private enterprise is government. So long as government stands over against industry and does not itself try to manage all production and distribution, supreme and all-dominating power cannot be gathered into the hands of a single ruling group. Industry checks the power of government and government checks the power of industry.

For all these reasons there is little justification for the outcry against the mounting power in the hands of industrial management. The danger is that this power will be taken over by a monolithic government. So long as it can be kept in the hands of industrial management, the danger is at a minimum. To repeat, power is always dangerous and the greater the power the more danger, other things being equal. But we cannot dispense with power. We must have it and have it increasingly because every great good as well as every great evil depends upon it. Consequently only two alternatives remain: A more dangerous and a less dangerous way of exercising power, a more constructive and a more destructive way of using it. The least dangerous and the most constructive kind of organization for the exercise of power seems to be the kind of industrial system which is now developing. This is no ground for complacency. Great evils abound which should be corrected and great evils as yet unforeseen will arise. But it would be a tragic error to turn away from that course of development which carries least danger and greatest promise and adopt some other way of using power which would be much worse.

The potentialities for the development of an industry committed to the creative transformation of the human mind are with us. We must not cast them aside but develop them. The system of industrial management now developing is better fitted to this end than any conceivable form of the political state and immeasurably better than the old-fashioned capitalism of the nineteenth century. This does not guarantee that the power channeled through the managerial system of industry will be used constructively but there is no better way to channel it. No other economy and no other organization for the exercise by men of supreme power was ever subject to internal demands of successful operation which coincided so fully with the demands of human development throughout society.

Civilization is always dangerous because of the increasing power which it puts into human hands. But criticism and pessimism and concentration on the evils to be corrected, important as such criticism truly is, become misdirected and fatal when they cause us to turn away from the most hopeful path because we see so many evils actual and possible along the way. There is danger that the critics and pessimists during the difficult times ahead will cause the American people to turn aside from the way of their salvation or develop a critical attitude which saps the energy and devotion needed to follow the best way now open to them.

Before leaving the subject, two growing evils in our industrial system should be mentioned. A more competent student in this field might mention others which are worse. These evils arise from the fact repeatedly mentioned that the chief problem in industry is the developing of minds and personalities. This can take the form of moulding men and women into efficiently functioning machines glamorized and sociable, intelligent and persuasive, efficient in administration and highly communicative, but without time, energy, interest, or capacity to gain any appreciative understanding of the human individual in depth nor to cultivate one's own original experience which is the true self beneath the metallic surface of efficient action.

The other evil is also a case of shaping minds. It is the coercive drive of suggestion promoted by every conceivable device to induce everyone to consume more and more of everything which can be put on the market. This can have a disintegrating effect upon the human personality. Buying and using these utilities and earning money to buy more can absorb the attention so completely and take so much time and energy, that nothing is left for the most important concerns of human living. All the great values to be attained in human living may be lost in this way and all capacity to appreciate them atrophied. Life itself can be consumed in the striving to consume what industry can produce so that no other end in life is ever attained.

Other evils and growing dangers might be mentioned. But the intention of this writing has not been to examine these evils. That is an important task, but it is not the task here undertaken. Rather I have tried to point out a possibility which might be pursued by industry in support of man's ultimate commitment.

Industry in our society is closely related to government and connections between the two are likely to increase. These two major institutions are highly sensitive and responsive to changes in one another. Also the two in close relation exercise more control over the lives of men throughout society than any other human agency. So our next task will be to examine the place of government in dealing with the creative transformation of the human mind.

Chapter 11

GOVERNMENT
UNDER COMMITMENT

GOVERNMENT is the organization traditionally equipped to exercise more power of control over the lives of men than any other kind of social device. The actual exercise of power may be very narrowly limited by the constitution of the society when constitution is understood to be not merely a written document but the habits, customs, institutions, and other organizations which make up the constituent parts of the social order under jurisdiction of the government in question. The actual course of social development may be shaped more powerfully by Big Business than it is by government. Nevertheless the government must be able to exercise supreme control when there is call for it. For this reason it has the legal right to use violence, to kill, and to demand that the citizens shall die in its service on the battlefield. Without this authority no government can govern because without it no government can control all other organizations and forms of collective action in a way to uphold the social order and protect the peace.

The only source of this power exercised by government is the willingness of the people to obey its commands. This willingness may be motivated by expected rewards and benefits, by fear, by loyalty and devotion. Most of all, perhaps, it is motivated by habit and custom. For the most part people obey the commands of government because it never occurs to them to do anything else. Such obedience has been wrought into the organization of personality from infancy.

When custom, habit, and established organization of personality fail to sustain the government, when obedience must be calculated by estimate of rewards and punishments, the power of control exercised by government is likely to decline very swiftly. When this happens coercions must be increased to enforce obedience and this often leads to tyranny and dictatorship. For this reason every government established after a social revolution is a dictatorship if it retains power of control because custom, habit, and established organization of personality to sustain a government can be developed only after a considerable period of time.

The function of government is to regulate behavior and reconcile differences at those points where the automatic, voluntary, and local regulators are not sufficient. Regulate to what end? The answer to this question is highly controversial. Also it can be answered in two very different ways. It may be answered in terms of what ought to be the end sought. That is one kind of answer. But it may also be answered in terms purely descriptive, stating the ends which historic governments seem actually to have sought by their regulatory devices.

Glancing at some of the descriptive answers it seems that in early Asiatic empires in some cases the government sought primarily to collect taxes and other forms of tribute for the benefit of a small ruling class. While this may have been the conscious purpose of some or of all in power, other ends must also have been served if the government was stable and retained its power of control. These other ends necessarily include a measure of internal peace, social order, and enough economic well-being and other satisfactions sufficient to command the resources of the society and the obedience of the people.

In ancient Egypt under Cheops the government seems to have been chiefly occupied in building a tomb for the emperor in the form of the biggest pyramid ever erected. Under Hitler and his associates the end of government seems to have been to fulfil the destiny of the Aryan race as this destiny was portrayed by the myth and endowed with the mystique of the German people at that time.[1]

This mystique of the nation-state is not peculiar to Germany under Hitler. Since the American and French revolutions the domination of the nation-state over the mind of the individual has been inordinate.[2] Men have identified themselves with the nation-state to find a sense of glory, pride, and power in their lives not otherwise accessible to them. In not a few cases this has transformed nationalism into a form of religion commanding a devotion which overrules all others. Even when Christianity or some other faith is professed, actual practice seems to indicate that national interest is the real content of the faith. God or Christ or some other Being may be constantly invoked but the actual reality which determines what this Being shall demand and the form this Being shall assume is the national interest. This of course is not true of all who profess the Christian faith in the nation-state of our time, but it does happen. When this occurs the traditional religion, whatever may be its name, becomes a disguise for the religion of nationalism. So far as concerns politics and government this is perhaps the most dangerous development in the modern world.

We have seen that very extensive changes are now occurring in the conduct of industry because it is impossible to succeed in business without them. The changes are coerced by new conditions which have arisen. So it is with government. Changes will be made in the methods and goals of government when it becomes impossible to govern successfully without making them. Government will not change markedly until compelled by new conditions. But the coercions must be internal to government itself in the sense that the changes must be made in order to sustain the government in being just as the coercions forcing change in industry are internal to the economy. Such conditions are now developing which will compel government to undergo change in form and purpose. In government, however, these changes have scarcely yet gathered much momentum while in industry they have already come a long way. Perhaps the economy is always more quickly responsive to changed conditions than is government. Government lags behind the economy and religion lags even more. In general this is true although the opposite may occur when emergencies arise.

In case of government as in case of the economy, developing conditions are demanding more creative interchange. This demand is irresistible in the sense that a government which does not provide for more extensive interchange will either break down or become subordinate to some government which does make the required changes.

The period of change which brought to maturity the nation-state and democratic form of government we now have was the eighteenth century. England had been hammering out such a system of government for centuries. The American Revolution, the French Revolution, and various developments in England and Europe brought these changes to fulfilment. For one hundred and fifty years, roughly speaking, the nation-state with our kind of democracy has prevailed. We have now come to another time of change when a different form of government with somewhat different purposes will dominate. We hope this new form and purpose of government will protect the privacy and freedom of the individual. But this hope will be futile if we resist making the necessary changes and do not give priority to those purposes which must be given first place if freedom is to be secured and the unique potentialities of individuality developed to a high level. As stated in the last chapter, what happens in industry will be one powerful factor in determining whether government in the future will provide freedom for the individual or the reverse.

If freedom is to prevail, government in the future must aim more definitely than it has done in the past at providing conditions most favorable for creative interchange between individuals and peoples; and this purpose must be given priority over other purposes of government to a degree greater than in the past.

Government has always provided for this kind of interchange because no society is possible without it. Peace, order, and security have human value primarily because they are conditions under which it is possible for the infant to acquire a human mind by way of creative interchange and to develop a character which will sustain the social order in association with others.

Every government in the past has provided for creative inter-change within limits because it would not otherwise have a society to govern nor enough social cohesion to sustain it. But this purpose of government has not been clearly defined and professed nor has this purpose been deliberately selected for priority over other purposes. Also governments in the past as well as governments now in being have done this in a very re-stricted way. They have done it by developing a character in their people which sustained the social order and the govern-ment of a given region but *in opposition to the order and govern-ment of other regions*. Indeed one of the most common devices used by governments to win support from the people and weld them into a unity has been the use of conflict with other gov-ernments and peoples. Hate and fear of the way of life of other peoples have been in no small part the unifying bond, and gov-ernments have deliberately cultivated such hate and fear to this end.

This opposition and exclusiveness in the social order and the social character of individuals under different governments has been magnified by the mystique of nationalism described by Cassirer and others to whom reference has already been made. Every individual needs to identify himself with a larger whole which has more power than he in isolation can have and which magnifies his own power when he identifies with it, which has a grandeur and nobility greater than his own isolated self but giv-ing to him grandeur and nobility when he identifies with it. The nation-state has met this need for thousands and in this way has acquired a mystical quality reaching in many cases to the level of a religion. But this religion of nationalism has been nourished by conflict and opposition against other peoples. Until recent date war and the symbols of war and martial pomp and cere-mony have been the chief inspirers of this mysticism.

In the past these practices and this spirit have been a source of strength for governments. If in the future successful government could be conducted in this way, these practices would continue no matter what the cost in suffering and bloodshed. But if and when these practices become a source of weakness in government, they will cease to prevail because strong governments will dominate weak governments. If the strong governments cannot be achieved in this way, then other methods will be practiced by strong governments. Hence these other methods will prevail.

The thesis of this chapter can now be stated. It is this: World-wide conditions are developing of such sort that no government and people can stand and grow strong without close connection and mutual support with other governments and peoples. While in the past a government could grow strong by promoting creative interchange among its own people to the exclusion of other peoples and in opposition to them, in the future this practice will be a source of weakness.

This statement must not be misunderstood. Every social group will always develop a social character different from other groups. This applies all the way from the family, the neighborhood, the fraternity, the plant-community of a corporation, a geographical region, and a national state. This difference between groups along with the uniqueness of individuals will never disappear and their preservation and development should be one of the responsibilities of government. But this uniqueness of the individual and this coherence of the culture of the group can be exclusive, building barriers of hate and fear or indifference toward others. On the other hand, it is possible for a region or a people to have a unique character and coherence which grows more strong and rich by opening channels of interchange with other societies very different from their own.

We have come to a time when individuals and peoples must achieve appreciative understanding of one another and be able to learn from one another beyond the confines of the various traditions and beyond the limits which governments and econ-omies have generally laid down. This innovation requires a re-versal in the order of domination as between creative inter-change on the one hand and the government and economy on the other. Creative interchange must be made sovereign over government in the sense that government will give priority to the demands of interchange rather than confining and channeling the development of minds in a way to serve the ulterior ends of government.

This reversal in order of domination has become an internal demand of government as well as being necessary for the survival of civilization. For example, no government can protect the people under its jurisdiction any longer except by promoting interchange and appreciative understanding between its own people and the peoples under opposing governments. This is so because war fought with atomic weapons will no longer protect any people. Either the different peoples of the world support one another or they destroy one another. There is no third alternative.

Another change has occurred in the source of power exercised by any government. The power of government has always been derived from the willingness of its own people to obey its demands and co-operate in carrying out its policies. Today, however, the power of any government is measured not only by the loyalty of its own people but also and increasingly by the number of different people beyond its own jurisdiction who are willing to co-operate with it. The wider the orbit of this co-operation and the more complete the response of the people of the world to the announced and practiced policies of any government, the greater the power of that government. No government today can stand against the world or any large part of the world, partly because of the intricate interdependence of peoples, partly because of the enormous destructive power now available. Many Americans seem to think that the United States can conserve its power by keeping its wealth to itself, and by following policies of its own making in disregard of the wishes of other peoples. It is amazing that such blindness to our own national interest should prevail.

Still another reason supports the claim that a government cannot survive and grow strong unless it gives priority to creative interchange among all peoples. Power in our time depends upon industrial production, invention, science, and technology.

But these cannot be constantly and rapidly improved unless persons responsible for their development have access to theories and discoveries wherever they emerge. The intricate network of discovery and invention now necessary to advance the complicated technology of our time requires interchange with Fermi in Italy, Niels Bohr in Denmark, and others in all parts of the civilized world. It is true that Fermi and Bohr came to this country because of peculiar conditions of their time and they would not have come under normal conditions. In any case the point should be obvious. No country can keep to the forefront without this kind of interchange between scientists and technicians in all parts of the world.

Still another condition is compelling government to give priority to creative interchange between all peoples in order to develop the kind of minds which are able to build and hold power. We cannot win the goodwill and co-operation of England if we cannot see problems more or less from the standpoint of the English people; and the same applies to the German people, the French people, the Italian, and all others. Our government has been compelled to revise disastrous errors because of failure to see how a given course of action effects another people.

To exercise world leadership not only the leaders but the people who follow them must understand the needs of other peoples and have some sense for the problems of society both national and international. But all this requires creative interchange wide and free and full between all societies under all governments.

These are facts about the modern world all of which point to one conclusion. While government heretofore has generally channeled and confined creative interchange to serve its own ends to the exclusion of the need and interest of other societies under other governments, this cannot continue without undermining the power and authority of any government which practices it. Governments which open the channels of interchange most freely will be the governments which dominate the world community hereafter. Those who persist in the practice of exclusion and opposition between their own society and others will decline in power and authority both with their own people and in the council of nations.

This reversal in the order of domination between government and creative interchange has thus become an imperative in terms of power, authority, and protection as well as a moral and religious imperative. The tides of social change will beat down any government which resists this demand.

The consequences of this reversal in the order of domination between government and creative interchange is demonstrated in Jewish history. The Jews as a people have had no government of their own throughout most of their history. As a people they have survived solely by the creative transformation of the minds of each generation through transmitting to each generation the Jewish tradition. At the same time many individuals inheriting this tradition have been open to interchange with other traditions round about them. Having no government of their own and no nation dominated and controlled by such a government, the political barriers confining this interchange have not been present for them. There have been other barriers to be sure, sometimes even more coercive and confining. But in those instances where individuals of the Jewish tradition have been liberated from these other barriers as well as freed from the confinements imposed by a government of their own, the consequence has been startling. This relative freedom of interchange has enabled Jews throughout three thousand years of their history to produce many of the most influential minds which have ever appeared among men. Isaiah, Jeremiah, Jesus, and Paul in the ancient world, Marx, Freud, and Einstein in our own time are examples, to mention only a few out of many.

Jewish history points the way which must be followed henceforth by the history of the entire human race, not in the sense of discarding government, but in the sense of subordinating government to creative interchange between all persons and all societies. It has become the only way of salvation for mankind. The creativity which rears the human mind to its full dimensions when required conditions are present must be released from bondage to any one government and to any one economy. All governments and all economies must be shaped to provide the conditions under which creative transformation of the human mind can spread throughout humanity with as little restriction as is possible.

The consequence of this reversal in the order of domination will not be, of course, the rearing of a spiritual giant in each individual. Perhaps millions will not rise much above the level they have now reached. But more men having the native endowment will be able to develop their potentialities. If this does not occur, civilization will destroy itself and possibly bring human existence to an end because the complexity of the problems and the antagonisms between peoples in our time cannot be mastered without minds developed in this way. To deal competently with the problems of a global society, minds must be developed by interchange among all societies and not confined to interchange within one society in opposition to the others.

What has been said of national governments applies also to any world government which may arise as in time it surely will if we endure. A world government which confines and suppresses creative interchange will become a vast and cumbersome bureaucracy imposing intolerable tyranny. On the other hand if national governments do not submit to the control of world government they will develop antagonisms which, if they do not lead to devastating war, will force each national government to assume the form of dictatorship to protect itself from the wiles directed against it by opposing governments and from internal subversion instigated by its enemies. Obviously these two alternatives are both disastrous. But there is a third alternative. World government and national governments together in co-operation with the economy, the school, and religious institutions might subordinate other ends sought to the one end of opening the channels and providing conditions for creative interchange. In that case disaster would be avoided and the creative transformation of the human mind might reach dimensions not otherwise possible.

This brings us to another political problem which seems to overshadow all others at the present time. It is the conflict between the United States and Russia.

The first step in dealing with any problem is to locate the chief source of trouble. Only when the problem is correctly analyzed and understood can effort be directed to correct the difficulty and solve the problem so far as it can be solved. So it is with this problem of conflict between the United States and Russia. What is the source of trouble which is of such character that, if it is corrected, the conflict will be resolved so far as it can be?

Some say that the source of trouble is the aggressive designs of Russia seeking to dominate the world and in a sense that is true; but that source of trouble is not the one which can be corrected by concentrating directly upon it. The aggressive designs and spreading power of Russia may be the source of trouble in the sense that water spreading over the floor is the source of trouble when a faucet is running. But if one tries to correct the trouble by sweeping out the water without turning off the faucet, he will only make matters worse. One must find that source of trouble which can be corrected in such a way as to stop the other troubles arising out of it.

Others say the source of trouble is communism and the Communists, not only in Russia but all over the world wherever Communists may be found with their ideology, with their methods, and with their evil minds. But here again we have an evil which cannot be corrected by direct attack upon it. Fighting communism is another case of trying to sweep up the water without turning off the faucet.

The real cause in the sense of what can cure the trouble when corrected is something different from Russian aggression and communism. Examination of the conditions which have brought on this conflict between Russia and the United States will reveal this cause.

The power of Soviet Russia since the revolution of 1917 has mounted and spread with a speed and magnitude which is astounding. Yet from the very beginning the Western powers have tried to stop this rising and spreading power. We all sent armies into Russia shortly after the Revolution in the attempt to overcome it, but failed. Even during the Second World War when the West was allied with Russia many outstanding repre-

sentatives of the Western powers expressed the hope in one form
or another that Germany and Russia might "bleed one another
white." Winston Churchill was ready to arm the Germans near
the end of the war and turn them against Russia if the Russian
army had continued to advance. So he himself has declared.
Many today would say that anyone who did not then and does
not now strive for the utter destruction of the social order prevailing in Russia is a Communist sympathizer if not a fellow
traveler and on that account unworthy to be trusted in high
position. For a number of years now it has been our announced
policy to do everything in our power to stop Russia and the
spread of communism by direct opposition at every point where
it was possible to oppose them.

Yet after all these years and with all this concentration of
effort Russia has continued to increase its power and communism
to spread. Never was the power of Russia so great nor the people under Communist control so numerous as today. Why is
this? Is it because the Communists and the leaders of Russia are
more intelligent and more competent than all those who oppose
them? Surely not. Why then has the great power of the most
highly developed civilizations of the West been unable to stop
what it has been fighting?

There would seem to be only one answer to that question. It is
that the Western powers have not correctly analyzed the problem. They have not located the open faucet and concentrated on
the effort to control it.

The open faucet is the struggle of all the peoples of the world
to acquire for themselves the instruments of political power and
economic production which have been developed so magnificently in the West.

The Soviet government could never have risen so swiftly after
the Revolution if it had not concentrated all efforts on acquiring
the science, the technology, and the methods of organization
developed in the West, fitting these to her own use and applying them in her own way. The leaders of Soviet Russia could
never have developed these political and economic instruments
of power if the people of Russia had not been eager to have these

benefits of economic production and political power. The same is true of the people of China and throughout Asia, Africa, and South America. All these peoples may not want communism and certainly they do not want to be dominated by Russia. But what they do want is political power and economic abundance. If Russian leadership and Communist practice seem to offer the quickest road to these ends, they will be inclined to follow that road.

So we come back to the initial question: What is the real cause of the conflict between Russia and the United States and what is the real cause of the spreading control of communism, when "real cause" is defined as we have defined it? It is the eager reaching out of the peoples of the world for political power and economic production. Russian power and Communist control spread when they seem to offer these peoples what the people want and are unable to get in any other way.

If this understanding of the problem is correct, the Western powers will continue to be driven back step by step until they learn to concentrate on the real cause of the trouble. To shut off the faucet we must concentrate on helping the peoples of the world to get what they are so passionately seeking. Doing this is no simple matter to be sure. Very serious difficulties stand in the way. We cannot here examine these difficulties because our central theme is not this conflict between Russia and the United States and between the East and West. Our central theme is the guiding commitment and ruling concern which any government in our time must follow if it protects its own people by its power and authority among the peoples of the world. The only way any government today can retain such power and authority is by serving all humanity and not alone its own people. Indeed, since all peoples are now bound together in close interdependence no government can serve its own people successfully without serving all humanity. This is the imperative laid upon every government by the social development occurring over all the earth at the present time.

To serve all humanity just now means to help the economically undeveloped peoples to gain the instruments of political power and economic production which the Western world has brought forth beyond any other people. But this in itself alone is not enough. Political power and economic production are indispensable; but they are instruments only to the end of finding the satisfaction which alone can meet the need of man. This satisfaction must be found in that which enables one to experience the abundance of aesthetic quality in all things, to understand appreciatively other minds, and to be understood by them in like manner. This can only be accomplished by creative interchange between associated individuals. This kind of interchange should, then, take priority over all else in the conduct of government both at home and abroad. But this interchange cannot occur unless political power and economic well-being are carried along with it.

The creativity which saves the world by reconciling differences and widening and deepening appreciative understanding cannot penetrate the walls of hate and fear which have been built up between the Communist and non-Communist parts of humanity. Our government must, therefore, to the end of protecting its own people as well as performing its other functions, seek above all things to tear down these walls. This it cannot do if it extends political and economic help only to people outside the Communist orbit and only on condition that people receiving such help shall join with us in hating and fighting the spread of communism. The spread of communism cannot be stopped in that way. It can be stopped or, better stated, it will cease to be a deadly threat, when the power of government is devoted to extending economic aid and opening the channels of communication among all peoples regardless of their political bent. Until the governments of the world, and most especially the government of the United States, make this their major concern they will be going contrary to the moral and religious imperative which is wrought into the nature of man and which is the meaning of history.[3]

The following statement by Barbara Ward expresses the point we are making so clearly and forcibly that I shall quote it in full.

Thus the backward areas of the world must look to the West to help them in the two main tasks of maintaining Western standards—the creation of capital and the training needed to diversify the social structure. There are, naturally, many people in Britain and America who feel that this is no part of the responsibility of Western peoples. Responsibility ends at national frontiers. If underdeveloped countries choose independence, then they must accept its full implications.

Yet one reflection alone is perhaps enough to undermine the argument. The poorer lands of the world in Asia and Africa are bent on modernization by one means or another. If Western support and assistance fail, then the Communist solution is ruthlessly adapted to "solve" their two main problems. Under total dictatorship, the accumulation of capital is straightforward for, even if standards are low, saving can be enforced by starving the marginal people. Russian "kulaks" yesterday, Chinese peasants today, have been taught to pay with their lives for the progress of industrialization. Communist techniques of mass training and education likewise turn out in a very short time the flow of technicians needed for a modern economy. True, the result is not an organic, diversified society, but a rigid utilization of all manner of men as the obedient instruments of state power. But modernization is achieved. The methods are there. This fact constitutes perhaps the chief attraction of communism to backward peoples everywhere.

In the Western world today the attitude is all too often one of complacency when Western forms and institutions are adopted and almost blindness to the economic and social preconditions which will make the enduring preservation of those forms even a possibility. Without capital, without trained and responsible middle classes, without the steady help and contact of the West, these forms and traditions of freedom will wither.

The Western world will then be left to face the question whether a policy of capital assistance coupled with a new missionary effort in the provision of Western technical and educational experts might not have prevented segment after segment of the still free world from slipping under Communist control. But by then, it will be too late to give the answer.[4]

This quotation from Barbara Ward together with the entire discussion up to this point brings us to the problem of democracy. The United Nations Educational, Scientific, and Cultural Organization has made an extensive study of the problem of democracy by getting representative persons from all over the world to participate in a discussion on this subject. After study of all papers submitted the committee in charge made this significant statement:

> Finally, the committee was struck by the fact that there were no replies adverse to democracy. Probably for the first time in history "democracy" is claimed as the proper ideal description of all systems of political and social organization advocated by influential proponents.[5]

It is true that this agreement on the word "democracy" covered great disagreement on how the word should be understood. But with all the differences agreement seemed to be universal that society should be so organized and government so conducted as to release and develop the potentialities of individuals by adjusting their relations to one another in such a way that this development can occur.

Disagreement over the word "democracy" centered around the distinction between political democracy and social democracy. Some went so far as to say that "social democracy" is so confusing and vague a term that it should not be used if one wished to be intelligible. Democracy properly is a political term and has no clear meaning when used in any other sense. Such is the contention of one group, while the others claimed that political democracy has no value apart from the social.

Most of the discussants seemed to agree that political democracy is a way of making the decisions which determine social policy. Democratic government is always a matter of degree but a government is democratic to the measure that all the citizens exercise effective influence in making the important decisions which are undertaken by the government. This influence is exercised in many ways besides the vote although voting seems to be one of the indispensable instruments to this end. Other ways of exercising influence on decisions made by the government are discussion both in private and public, pronouncements by outstanding leaders, and all the means of publicity, the testing of opinion by polls, and many other devices. In many ways this influence on government is exerted by the people.

While "social democracy" may have so many different meanings or be so vague in its designation as to be useless, yet it would seem obvious that the social order determines the degree to which the government can be democratic. A society can be so ordered as to prevent the great majority of individuals from developing the capacity to understand the decisions which the government must make or even to understand their own needs sufficiently to express them.

Many defenders of social democracy seem to define it as the widest possible distribution of economic opportunity and economic well-being. It is true that economic opportunity and wealth are indispensable conditions for the development of capacity to understand the needs of one's own person, the needs of the group to which one belongs, and the needs common to any great number of people. But if social democracy is defined solely in economic terms, the definition does not indicate the kind of society which is required to sustain a democratic government.

People cannot influence the government to serve their common needs if they do not know what those needs are. But to discover the needs common to many people which are of such a character the needs common to many people which are of such a character that they can be satisfied by political action and are also of such character that when satisfied they will not frustrate other needs equally significant is one of the most difficult problems in human life. To think that economic abundance widely distributed will automatically enable people to understand the needs of human life in this way is surely mistaken. Indeed, it is quite possible that a wide distribution of economic wealth easily acquired by all might prevent that development of the mind by which the human person comes to know the needs of his own person and those of his fellow men sufficiently to exercise intelligent influence upon the decisions made by the government.

This understanding of the needs of human life is not merely an economic and political problem. It runs far deeper. Ultimately it is a religious problem in the sense that men will never understand what is needed to develop the human mind and personality constructively unless they commit themselves to what does in truth develop this understanding. Philosophy, psychology, and all the social sciences can provide knowledge to this end if they direct inquiry to this problem of human life which, by the way, is not their most common practice. But all knowledge given in the form of verbal statements can only be an aid to insight. Lacking the insight one will not acquire the kind of understanding which is called wisdom when this word means to know what are those needs underlying other needs in the sense that they must be satisfied in order that the other needs dependent upon them may also be satisfied without falling into inner conflict and mutual frustration. This kind of insight is not likely to occur unless one is committed to what develops the mind in the way to produce such insight. Insights must be tested against the knowledge acquired by philosophy and the sciences, hence such inquiry is indispensable. But the kind of religious commitment just indicated is also necessary.

It would seem nonsensical to claim that individuals can discover their common needs without expressing themselves to one another freely and fully. People cannot do this if they have psychological obstructions which prevent them from so doing. Such psychological obstructions, in turn, are the result of interpersonal relations and a social order of such sort that people cannot trust one another and are on that account driven to resort to the deceptive, manipulative, and other kinds of interchange previously described.

All this amounts to saying that while democracy cannot command religious commitment without disastrous consequences, democratic government can never be developed with power and sustained with stability without the kind of religion which directs commitment to what transforms the human mind in a way to realize its constructive potentialities and generate insight into the common basic needs of human life.

In this sense and in this way government must be brought under religious commitment if ever we are to have good government.

One last problem concerning government must be considered. There has been much excitement over the increase in juvenile delinquency and adult crime in our society. Extensive studies have been made of this problem.⁶ The conclusion reached to date would seem to be rather obvious in any case. It is that a rising tide of delinquency and crime points to an over-all condition of society as its cause.

When there is neither a coherent tradition nor a ruling devotion to give unity and direction to the impact of the social process upon individuals as they mature, such individuals will not live in ways which are mutually sustaining. Delinquency and crime are the names we give to acts which arise when individuals live in ways which are not mutually sustaining. Our society does not have one single, coherent, and dominant tradition. It is made up of many diverse traditions, and the interpenetration of all the traditions and cultures of the world will make this increasingly the condition not only of our society but of all societies.

We have gloried in our diversity and in the kind of freedom which permits individuals to go each his own way. But diversity can be of two kinds. It can be the kind which disintegrates the personality and the society or it can be the kind which enriches the mind of the individual and empowers the society. Diversity of the first kind can bring great evils including the increase of delinquency and crime.

This is not merely a problem of morals although morals are certainly included. It is not merely a problem of family or or in-stitutional education or industry or government or religion. It is all of these combined. It is the problem of the way of life which prevails in a society. If crime and delinquency are not to increase, this way of life must be unified by a prevailing commitment which draws the individual into a common life of mutual support, giving to each a sense of personal worth while at the same time helping and encouraging each to develop his own unique capacity for appreciation and constructive action. The only kind of social process which can do this effectively is the kind here described as creative interchange producing appreciative understanding in each of the unique individuality of the other.

"Dignity of the individual" is a phrase in danger of being endowed with magic potency without understanding of what is required to uphold such dignity. Dignity attributed to the individual without appreciative understanding of his individuality by his associates, and without providing conditions under which such understanding can be obtained, will result in much indignity enacted in the name of this slogan.

Obviously government has its place along with religion, education, and industry in shaping the life of a people. If this way of life is to be sustaining, enriching, and creative, these several institutions must work together under a common commitment. What this commitment is and the place of government in its service we have tried to indicate. After the study of these institutions taken up individually we shall now look at the drift of the whole social process as seen through the eyes of social scientists in such a work as *The Challenge of Man's Future* by Harrison Brown. After that, in the final chapters, we shall examine the movement of history in relation to this interpretation of the saving and transforming commitment.

Chapter 12

ORGANIZATION
UNDER COMMITMENT

WE HAVE looked at organization as it appears in the major institutions of society. Now we shall examine it as a major problem of industrial civilization. By no means can organization alone solve the problems of human life. The entire argument of this book is plainly opposed to any such notion. But neither can the difficulties and dangers of our industrial civilization be overcome without extending the organization and control of human activities far beyond their present limits. As society becomes more highly industrialized, less attention and effort are given to the daily acquisition of food and other supplies, while ever more thought and action must be given to the adjustment of activities and developments to one another in a way to reduce conflict, promote co-operation, and control conditions. International organization must be added to national; the output of local industries is connected with the output of other industries all over the earth; what the individual does in the industrial plant is controlled relative to millions of activities and processes over which he has no power; even the number of births call for regulation relative to food supply and the number of deaths; the use of soil, of vegetation, of metals, oil, coal, and other raw materials require regulation to avoid their exhaustion. Gigantic cities must be fed and serviced by complex systems of control. The increasing number of specialists and specializations requires co-ordination if they are to serve the common good. Industrial centers must be connected with raw materials and markets by elaborate systems of transportation. The intricate process of supply and demand must be regulated since the free market no longer regulates it satisfactorily, supposing it ever did. International rivalries and hostilities must be controlled in a way to avoid total war with atomic weapons.

For these and other reasons industrial civilization cannot be sustained without a vast expansion of organization with regulators and integrators devised by men. This presents a serious problem. Organization can reduce human life to a regimented form of existence in which men become robots and all values distinctively human are lost. This consequence is not inevitable. The extension of organization does not necessarily mechanize life and deprive the individual of the most valuable form of freedom. It can do exactly the opposite. But to avoid the evil results of expanded organization the problem should be recognized and treated with understanding of the issues involved.

It is fatal to resist the increase of organization as though it were intrinsically and necessarily an evil because such an attitude makes impossible the constructive treatment of this expansion. Since this increase of organization cannot be stopped under highly industrialized conditions, this negative attitude toward it renders men helpless in dealing with it. It is like one cowering before the onrush of a huge wave until he is overwhelmed instead of diving through it and swimming beyond it. When organization and centralized control develop without any far-reaching plan and purpose, they are constructed to meet one emergency after another, but not fashioned to provide conditions favorable for that creative transformation to occur which enriches life and liberates the individual. When parts are added to the comprehensive system of organization without an over-all plan to protect freedom and creativity, these added parts of the organization afford opportunity for little dictators to step in and devise controls which enable them to dominate their fellow men. Tyranny is avoided not by resisting the extension of organization and control when these are needed but by making the extensions under the guidance of a plan which protects and promotes creative interchange between individuals.

Roderick Seidenberg in his book *Posthistoric Man* claims that the social order now being developed leads to the complete collectivization of humanity, reducing men to automatons and eradicating in them the capacity to seek and appreciate human values.[1] Seidenberg believes that this will be the future course of social development. Certainly that is a direction in which our society seems at times to be moving and, if the direction is not changed, the outcome may be as predicted. But the direction can be changed. It can be changed if, instead of allowing the extension of organization to creep over us unawares or against our resistance, we make it serve the ends of human living.

The conflict now raging between the United States and Russia produces a state of mind which increases the danger that we shall be blind to the imperative need to expand the organization of human life in a way to serve the greater good. This state of mind arises as a consequence of defining the conflict between the two countries as one between freedom and slavery. Slavery is then identified with a vastly expanded organization which regulates the life of the individual. In opposition to this, freedom is identified with the least possible organization. This view of the matter has caused the passions of hate and fear, pride and hostility, patriotism and loyalty to turn against the increase of centralized control and expanded organization because these are thought to be what we are fighting. On the other hand, we are being forced by the complexities of our society and by the need of collective action to increase the power of centralized control and to expand regulative organization very greatly. Hence the urgent need to recognize the problem and develop the commitment which will enable us to build a system of organized control in which a better life can be lived than is possible with less control.

The problem of organization involves another problem which is more intimately personal. The one cannot be treated constructively without full awareness of the other. It is the problem of human personality. Human beings are more or less enslaved to inner, unconscious compulsions and to the degree that they are they cannot live creatively and freely under any sort of social regime. Release of the individual from his own inner enslavement and the development of a liberating social organization are two sides of the same problem and need to be worked out together.

Perhaps the best approach to this psychological problem of the individual is to quote an authority. Lawrence S. Kubie, M.D., Clinical Professor of Psychiatry in the School of Medicine at Yale University and member of the faculty of the New York Psychoanalytic Institute, speaks of this internal enslavement of human personality in relation to our culture. He is discussing the responsibility of education for liberating the individual from this condition. But he makes plain that this task is also the responsibility of every branch of our culture. Also he asserts that ours is a "Culture of Doom" if we do not take measures to free the individual psyche from these inner compulsions. This internal liberation of the individual, says Dr. Kubie, has never been accomplished in sufficient measure, and in numbers sufficiently large, to save past civilizations from self-destruction when power and complex interdependence became great enough to bring forth the destructive consequences of this condition of the human person. Following is Dr. Kubie's statement of the matter.

> This automaticity of conduct which is governed predominantly by our unconscious psychological mechanisms is dependent directly upon their remaining inaccessible. Therefore, if 'self-knowledge in depth' ever becomes the goal of a new concept of education, and if it becomes a part of the equipment which education brings to the cultured man, it will make it possible for man to attain freedom from his ancient slavery to those repetitive psychological processes over which at present he has no control. . . . The next goal of education is nothing less than a progressive freeing of man—not merely from external tyrannies of nature and of other men, but from internal enslavement by his own unconscious automatic mech-

anisms. Therefore, all of education and all of art and culture must contribute to this. It has long been recognized that in spite of technological progress, and in spite of art, literature, religion and scholarly learning, the heart of man has not changed. This is both a challenge and a rebuke to our complacent acceptance of this bitter and devastating commentary on culture. My answer is based on the conviction that it is possible to break through the sonic barrier between conscious and unconscious processes, and thereby to bring to man for the first time in human history the opportunity to evolve beyond his enslaved past. . . .

Toward this goal a first step will be a deeper study of those early crises in human development, when the symbolic process begins to splinter into conscious, preconscious, and unconscious systems. The purpose of such study of infancy would be to illuminate the origins of the repressive processes which produce these cleavages, since it is these which must be guided and controlled. As its second goal such a study would aim at the reintegration of unconscious and conscious processes: something which has to be done not merely once, but repeatedly throughout the entire process of growth, from infancy through childhood, puberty, adolescence, and on into adult years.[2]

The central thought of this quotation has been the theme running through all the previous chapters of this book. What the author calls "symbolic process" is the use of signs and symbols, pre-eminently language, to convey meaning from one person to another. Also it is the process of thinking. Creative communication as interpreted in previous chapters is that practice of the symbolic process which does *not* cause a repression into the unconscious of the urges, propensities, thoughts, and feelings of the individual, but rather releases and develops them integratively so that a cleavage does not arise between the conscious and preconscious on the one hand, the unconscious on the other. To be sure, creative interchange is never perfect. There is always repression but, as Dr. Kubie states, there can be less repression, less cleavage, more progressive integration, more preservation of the wholeness of the individual person, so that he can in larger measure think, feel, act, respond, appreciate with this total self and with all his personal resources.

Here we have the purpose which should guide in constructing the organizations and controls which of necessity must be greatly increased in our society. The guiding purpose is to develop the organization and controls in such a way as to provide the conditions under which human beings will engage in the symbolic process without causing so much repression. This is not impossible, as Dr. Kubie states, but it will require personal commitment on the one hand and guiding directives for education, art, government, industry, and religion on the other.

With this understanding of the problem of human personality underlying the problem of social organization we are prepared to look into certain persistent problems of our industrial civilization.

Certain developments which do not require control by deliberate social policy and plan in an agrarian culture do require them in a highly industrialized society. So far as concerns these particular developments in an agrarian society, the balance required to sustain life in that form of the social order is maintained by certain controls which operate automatically without anybody giving thought to them. These controls cease to operate automatically when power and complexity increase with the machines and processes of advanced industry. Consequently these developments must be controlled and kept in balance by deliberate social policy when industrial civilization arises.

Three of these developments which do not destroy agrarian and primitive cultures because of automatic controls but do destroy industrialized society if not controlled by organizations deliberately planned for that purpose are the following:

1] War becoming ever more destructive with the advance of industrialization. Prior to industrial civilization wars could do much damage and cause great suffering to individuals and localities, but they could scarcely destroy agrarian culture all over the earth.

2] Overpopulation or underreproduction. In agrarian and primitive culture starvation, disease, pestilence, war keep the population within the limits of the food supply without destroying all agrarian life. But when and if industrial civilization prevents starvation, war, and pestilence and greatly reduces disease, either of two things will almost surely happen if adequate controls are not imposed. One is an increase of population to the point where it is impossible to live a free and rich human life. The other danger is a decline in the birth rate, such as many cities display, which would in time bring the human race to extinction or at least underpopulate the earth. This decline of the birth rate does not occur in primitive and agrarian culture. It does sometimes occur under highly industrialized conditions. The point is that births and deaths and food supply under industrialized conditions do not regulate one another as they do in agrarian culture. Consequently population is always likely either to increase too rapidly or decline too far. For this reason births should be regulated by deliberate policy, if great dangers are to be averted.

3] Exhaustion of resources such as fertility of the soil, vegetation, coal, oil, hydroelectric power, atomic and solar energy. Solar energy cannot be exhausted but the cost and the labor of constructing the equipment required to get enough of it could become prohibitive. The enormous and rapid increase of productive power brought on by industrialization consumes natural resources at a rate which accelerates year by year. The acceleration with which sources of energy are consumed is due to two causes, one, the rapid increase of production, and the second, the increased cost of tapping more difficult sources of energy. This second cause of the accelerated rate of consumption of energy can be illustrated by the case of coal. The amount of coal consumed in the process of mining coal is not nearly so great as the amount of coal or its equivalent consumed in the process of getting usable energy out of uranium and other sources of atomic energy. Not only is more energy consumed when industrialization reaches a high level, but more energy is consumed in getting energy. In these two ways the rate of consumption is accelerated.

This account of the long range problems of industrial civilization here listed as war, population, and exhaustion of resources,
is taken from the book of Harrison Brown, *The Challenge of
Man's Future*.[3] These problems indicate the need of organizational controls in an industrial civilization when the automatic
controls operating in agrarian culture without human plan and
purpose no longer suffice. As Brown puts it, industrial civilization is unstable whereas agrarian and primitive cultures are
stable, meaning that in the latter the balance required for continued life restores itself after disturbance, but in industrial
civilization this does not happen without undermining industrial
society and reducing human life again to the level of agrarian
culture.

These three, war, variation of population, and exhaustion of
resources, will not inevitably destroy industrial civilization if
they are controlled by proper organization. But if not controlled
they will either destroy machine society or bring on such misery,
corruption, and degradation as to dehumanize the life of man.
If these developments should bring on the disintegration of our
society by reason of not being controlled, Brown believes that
man will never again be able to rise above agrarian culture. His
argument defending this claim will be stated a little later.

Most people seem to recognize the destructive potentialities
of total war in our civilization but many do not seem to recognize
that nothing can prevent it short of a world government. Brown
shows why world government is necessary and the case is even
more conclusively argued in F. L. Schumann's standard work on
International Politics. Here then is the first imperative demanding
a very great extension of social organization.

The danger of overpopulation or underreproduction is not so
widely recognized in the Western world as the danger of war
because the Western peoples for the past three hundred years
have lived during one of those rare times in history when food
supply could increase more rapidly than the population. Also
until recent times there was not enough knowledge of the number
of births and deaths and their relation to productive powers of
industry and agriculture to demonstrate the reality of this danger.

Now we know that if the number of births should fall only a little below the level required to maintain the population, the cumulative effects in a few generations would lead to the extinction of the class or people concerned. On the other hand, if the births exceed the number which can be sustained by proportionate increase in supplies, then misery, degradation, corruption, starvation, disease, and savage animal ferocity alternating with animal stupor begin their dehumanizing work.

Harrison Brown shows how births relative to food supply and deaths can be regulated in a way to maintain a form of life that is free and enriching. Such regulation, however, will require very extensive organization and control in a form which might seem intolerable to people of the Western world. But the beneficial consequences would far exceed the disabilities. Furthermore, controls of this kind are largely a matter of conditioning. Every civilized man freely and comfortably submits to regulations which no man in primitive society would tolerate even as the latter submits to restrictions which the civilized man cannot endure. There are kinds of restrictions which we can never permit because they hinder the creative transformation of the human mind and personality, but many other restrictions are required to make possible this creative transformation.

It is not my purpose to discuss these problems of war, regulation of population, and exhaustion of resources and the measures required to deal with them except to demonstrate the inevitability of a vastly expanded organized control of human life if industrialized civilization is to continue; and this I wish to do to show how the ultimate commitment which is the theme of this book bears upon this problem. The problems of war, population, and natural resources are incidental to what concerns us here, but some of these incidental problems must be understood in their relation to our subject if the significance of the latter is to be appreciated. All too frequently the ultimate questions pertaining to man's destiny are discussed in a way so far removed from the practical concerns of life that their bearing upon these cannot be detected. This separation of the more obvious practical problems from the ultimate problems of commitment I wish to avoid.

The following quotation from the work of Harrison Brown presents the problem of population so effectively that, before we leave the subject, it should be examined. In reading this, one should bear in mind that the present population of the earth is approximately two and a half billion.

> If we were willing to be crowded together closely enough, to eat foods which would bear little resemblance to the foods we eat today, and to be deprived of simple but satisfying luxuries such as fireplaces, gardens and lawns, a world population of 50 billion persons would not be out of the question. And if we really put our minds to the problem we could construct floating islands where people might live and where algae farms could function, and perhaps 100 billion persons could be provided for. If we set strict limits to physical activities so that caloric requirements could be kept at very low levels, perhaps we could provide for 200 billion persons.
>
> At this point the reader is probably saying to himself that he would have little desire to live in such a world, and he can rest assured that the author is thinking exactly the same thing. But a substantial fraction of humanity today is behaving as it would like to create such a world. It is behaving as if it were engaged in a contest to test nature's willingness to support humanity and, if it had its way, it would not rest content until the earth is covered completely and to considerable depth with a writhing mass of human beings, much as a dead cow is covered with a pulsating mass of maggots.[4]

With the progressive powers of industry and science an abundance can be obtained sufficient to support a great increase in the population of this planet. But there is a limit beyond which degradation begins; and there is an optimum with which alone the best possibilities of human life can be attained. If this optimum is to be approached and this point of degradation escaped, population must be controlled. Today we have, as no other civilization ever had, an understanding of the problem of population together with the knowledge, skill, and resources to deal with it effectively. But will we undertake the kind of planning required and tolerate the measure of organizational control which must be imposed? We shall not undertake the planning nor tolerate the control nor live with the organization in a way to derive good and not evil from it unless the kind of ultimate commitment becomes sufficiently prevalent which can produce this willingness and adaptiveness to the demands of creative transformation.

Here is where the problem of organization connects with commitment to creative interchange. The degree of control required to master the three threats to industrial civilization will indeed be intolerable without this kind of commitment. Organization ceases to be oppressive and confining when it is made to serve creative interchange by providing conditions favorable for mutual understanding, sensitive personal concern for one another, and appreciative response of the whole person to the total need of the other so far as human limitations make this possible. With a commitment producing interpersonal relations of this kind, the demands of organized control cease to be irritants and become aids to richer living. Also when this commitment generates a vision of what creativity can do for man as a consequence of proper organization, men are willing to undertake the labor and care of the planning and of the elaborate organization for the sake of values to be attained. But commitment to creative interchange must spread farther and reach deeper into the lives of men than is now the case, if all this is to happen.

The problems of organization can be further studied in such works as the following: *The Organizational Revolution* by Kenneth E. Boulding, *A Free Society: An Evaluation of Contemporary Democracy* by Mark M. Heald, *The New Society* by Peter Drucker, *The Annals of the American Academy of Political and Social Science* of March, 1954, this issue devoted to "Bureaucracy and Democratic Government." Here we only wish to show that the creativity in human life, which we have been examining, now in the twentieth century encounters certain barriers rising up in its way. If these barriers can be removed, our industrial civilization combined with the ultimate commitment can release this creativity of life to attain a greater richness in human living. If these barriers are not surmounted, it is likely that creativity will be confined to levels even lower than have been forced upon it in the grim past.

Besides the long range problems which we have been considering there is a barrier to be surmounted which stands directly in front of us. It is the extension of industrialized civilization to Asia, the Middle East, Africa, and South America or else the desperate struggle to do it, ending in a war or a series of wars which will destroy our civilization. On this point also we are following Harrison Brown in the book mentioned.

The people in other areas of the world have seen the vast quantities of material possession in the hands of the people of Western Europe and the United States. They will not rest until they have similiar possessions for themselves or fail in the attempt. There are two ways, and only two, by which these parts of the world can be industrialized. One way is by internal revolution, dispossession of the wealthy, coerced labor, and coerced starvation until the capital equipment has been produced which makes possible an industrialized society. The other more peaceful, democratic way requires the investment of some 500 billion dollars over a period of 50 years, half of this coming from the countries already highly industrialized, among which the United States is chief.

> The annual average investment would then be somewhat over 10 billion dollars, of which perhaps one half could be furnished over the entire period by the underdeveloped regions. . . . On this basis, foreign investments averaging about 5 billion dollars annually over the 50 year period would be required. . . . If the industrialized area of the world were to join in recognizing the overwhelming importance of the problem, and would agree to take common action to speed the industrialization of the underdeveloped areas, the problems of financing would not be prohibitive. Largely because of the risk involved and the uncertain profits to be gained, it is difficult to visualize large amounts of private capital from Western nations contributing substantially to the development program. For this reason it seems likely that the greater

part of the outside funds, at least during the initial stages, must be public funds.[5]

The present conflict between the United States and Russia is caused by the struggle to industrialize the world. The opposed ideologies and ways of life would not generate the fear and hate and danger of war which now prevail if the underdeveloped regions were not striving to escape misery and impoverishment by increasing the productivity of agriculture and the industrialization which is required along with it. The connection between this striving of the underdeveloped regions to escape poverty and the conflict between the United States and Russia is not always clearly discerned. But the connection is direct and compelling. Russia could not reach out to dominate the world as she is doing were it not for this struggle of Asia, Africa, and South America to industrialize and improve their agriculture. This struggle of the impoverished peoples opens the way to Russia's expansion of power and this in turn leads to the conflict between the United States and Russia. The connection is also seen when we note the two alternative ways to extend industrialization. Russia does it by internal revolution, dispossession of the wealthy, coerced labor, and coerced starvation when these are necessary to accomplish her ends.

There is nothing to indicate that Russia seeks military conquest. She has nothing to gain and everything to lose in that way. On the other hand she has everything to gain by industrializing the underdeveloped regions in her way. This expanding power of Russia accomplished by extending her way of industrializing the world cannot be stopped by war. War cannot stop it because, if any civilization remains after such a war, it will be controlled by a world-wide dictatorship and so will be won by the Russian system even though Russia should be the defeated party.

These are the reasons for saying that the barrier which stands most directly in front of us is the difficulty of industrializing the world. If the potential greatness of man by way of creative transformation is not to be rendered unattainable, this barrier must be surmounted by extending industrialization and scientific agriculture in the second of the two ways so far as this is possible. Doubt-less armaments must be maintained until some workable agree-ment to reduce armaments can be achieved. But war has no place whatsoever in this undertaking except to set up an insuperable barrier across the path of human destiny. The only effective way of dealing constructively with the present conflict with Russia is by devoting all powers, all talents, all devotion, and all available resources to the first of the two ways of extending the benefits of productive agriculture and industry, resorting in some degree to the second way when that is the only possible means to the im-provement of conditions.

Some may think that the extension of industrialization and scientific agriculture to other peoples can be no blessing. But this is a total misunderstanding. It is true that industrialization to date has not realized the spiritual values which city culture makes possible, and for a very good reason. The social order based on the machine is too raw, too immature, and above all has not yet developed the kind of religious faith required to realize its best possibilities. But this has been the theme running throughout this writing and need not here be repeated.

This misunderstanding and disparagement of industrial society in favor of agrarian culture is further augmented by a very com-mon illusion. It is the illusion which so easily arises when we look nostalgically upon the far past. Doubtless there were times and places during the many centuries of agrarian culture which were very pleasant. But the reports we receive from ancient times come almost exclusively from the very limited number of people who were articulate; and the articulate ones were the few who lived off the surplus created by the miserably impoverished millions. These millions had no voice and left no works to commemorate their lives but modern research is discovering how they lived. If we could see the misery, degradation, and alternate animal ferocity and hopeless stupor which prevailed, a view of agrarian culture would emerge very different from what we envision when we read about the noble aristocracies of Egypt, Greece, Rome, the Italian Renaissance, and the Age of the Enlightenment.

The significance of this time in which we live is brought home all the more forcibly when we recognize that industrial civilization and its high promise can never again be recovered if it is destroyed. This, at least, is the argument of Harrison Brown in the book we are reporting. His reasoning seems cogent and is worth examining.

His argument is based on two points: the great difficulty of passing from agrarian to industrial civilization when no outside help is available and the unrepeatable conditions enabling Europe and the United States to industrialize during the last two hundred years.

One of the conditions not likely again to recur which made possible the rise of machine society out of agrarian culture in Europe was the ready accessibility of the required raw materials, notably coal and iron. These remain in great abundance but the problem of mining, transportation, and extracting energy from them at the times and places needed become increasingly difficult. It is not increasingly difficult but rather the reverse, for industry as now developed. But the first stages when industry is getting started might find these difficulties insuperable. The greater depths of the mines, their remoteness from the places needed, the complicated process required to utilize them, will be greater than they were under the conditions when modern industry originated in England.

Another obstacle even more difficult to overcome stands in the way of developing industry out of an agrarian culture when no outside help is available. It is the difficulty of achieving a surplus sufficient to feed the workers when they are not producing food but are getting the raw materials and constructing the machines which industry requires. There is a period during the early stages of industrial development when large numbers of men cannot produce food because engaged in creating equipment which is unproductive for a considerable period of time. During this period so many may starve that the undertaking cannot continue.

A most unusual set of conditions made it possible to circumvent this obstacle when industrialization was getting under way in Europe and America, although great hardship and misery were endured and if certain peculiar social, economic, and political developments had not accidentally occurred at that time, these miseries and difficulties might have blocked the way. What made it possible to overcome this obstacle, in addition to the social developments just mentioned, was the opening up of new lands in America where food could be produced beyond the needs of the resident population and shipped to Europe in exchange for industrial products. Also that part of the population which could not be fed during the early stages of industrialization could emigrate to America and other new lands. Furthermore, colonial empires were established where raw materials could be obtained cheaply. These are some of the conditions and developments which fortuitously combined in a way never to be repeated, making possible the industrialization of the West. Since there is no reason to think that this combination will ever again recur, there is no reason to think that industrial civilization can ever be rebuilt if it should be wiped off the face of the earth.

Brown sees three alternatives open to human kind at this time in which we now live. The most probable of these, he thinks, is the elimination of industrial civilization by war. In that case humanity will revert to food gathering and agrarian culture never again to develop a machine industry comparable in power to what we now have. The second most probable alternative is the preservation of intensive industrialization with coerced collectivism and a regimented life reducing most men to robots and dehumanized automatons.

The least probable but altogether possible alternative of these three is the preservation of the great powers of industry, the elimination of war, the control of population, and the conservation of resources in such a way as to develop the full potentialities of human life.

Nothing in the nature of things other than the mind of man prevents us from following the third alternative. But the mind of man is difficult to persuade. The most urgent task at the present time would seem to be to accomplish this persuasion if it is possible.

To be treated intelligently, the problems of the decade and the century should be seen in relation to that form of human development throughout history which, with all its ups and downs, carries highest promise. Hence the need to unite the problems here discussed with the problem of man's ultimate commitment and the creative transformation of man which history makes possible. Since Brown does not do this we have put his discussion of these problems into this larger frame of reference.

The significance of this time in which we may live may be further exposed and future possibilities unveiled if we examine the contrasting ways in which city culture and sub-city culture have to date prevented the full creation of the human mind, compelling men to live in a sort of twilight zone midway between the consciousness peculiar to lower animals and the consciousness of a fully created human mind.

City culture liberates the individual so that he can live with all sorts of people in all sorts of ways, seek out many kinds of knowledge and entertainment, engage in every kind of occupation for which he can develop the ability. But the human mind cannot be loftily and magnificently structured when it has nothing but these superficial and ever-changing and disconnected experiences. Under such conditions the total self with all its resources and all its experiences cannot be engaged in anything. Rather the individual mind is fragmented, a little of the mind given to this and shaped to meet this situation, another little part of the mind given to something else and shaped to deal with it, and so on indefinitely. This is clutter-minded communication and is not creative. Living in this way the total individuality with all its potentialities is either suppressed and frustrated or else actually broken down into a number of units, so to speak, each unit a false front in the sense that the total integrated individuality is not expressed nor engaged in any of them. Obviously no great depth, richness, and fulness of experience can be developed in this way.

In sub-city culture the mind is confined and impoverished in the opposite way. In primitive society and even in the cultured agrarian society there is lacking that diversity of minds, that wide range of knowledge and the many different kinds of vocation by which the individual might be liberated and enriched. To be sure contact with diversity of minds cannot enrich the individual if each mind is a mere fragment and does not express or communicate the integrated riches of experience gathered through the years by one whose total, unfragmented individuality is engaged in every undertaking. In sub-city culture this total, unfragmented individuality may be engaged more or less completely in all that is said, done, and experienced. Thus integrity may be preserved more or less. But since diversity is lacking, the individual soon exhausts the resources of the community. On that account, also, while there is relative integrity, the scope and richness of mind is lacking which makes interpersonal relations most creative.

Thus in sub-city culture uniformity and narrowness limit the creation of mind even when integrity is preserved. In city culture, on the other hand, the fragmentation of the mind and the superficiality of every engagement limit the creation of mind even when there is great diversity of contacts and wide range of experiences.

While city culture thus corrupts and frustrates, it does at times bring forth magnificent minds, thereby showing its possibilities. Sub-city culture has insuperable limitations which cannot be overcome; but the frustrations and corruptions of city culture can be overcome sufficiently to produce such minds as Jeremiah and Isaiah, Plato and Aristotle, Augustine and Thomas Aquinas, Michelangelo and Leonardo Da Vinci, indeed all the supreme examples of magnificence in human mentality. Again, to prevent misunderstanding, may I repeat that one does not need to live inside the city limits to live in what is here called city culture. City culture can and often does extend into localities far beyond the geographical limits of any city.

The rise of the city six thousand years ago and its increasing dominance ever since, despite many periods of decline, have enabled the creative structuring of the human mind in many times and places to break free of the narrow confines which have held down to low and meager levels the creation of the human spirit during the million years more or less since man first appeared on this planet. To have broken through these limitations is the most promising thing that has ever happened since the origin of human life. This break-through by way of city culture is so recent, this way of living called city culture is so new, the liberation of the individual so strange, that man in city culture is like a chick just out of the egg. But he is unlike the chick in one respect. He lacks the reflexes which show the chick what to do. Consequently, man in city culture has been vastly more self-destructive than ever he was in the sub-city way of living. By means of war and economic oppression and maldistribution of wealth, by means of brutal oppression of the masses and wasteful arrogance of the few, by means of trickery, fraud, and deceit, by way of psychic ill, hypocrisy, and self-deceit, by way of unfaithfulness and treachery in personal relations city culture has recurrently destroyed itself and lapsed back to the sub-city level. But city culture alone opens the way for the unlimited expansion and enrichment of the human mind. The promise of this new freedom and this unconfined creation of the human spirit and its world must be seen and the problem recognized before the possible greatness can be realized.

What is needed first of all is a kind of religion which can guide man's ultimate commitment in a way to realize the potentialities of value in this new way of life. All the religions of the world were shaped in the beginning to meet the needs of human life laboring under limitations which no longer confine it. Christianity arose in the culture of Hellenism which was partially a city culture. But in Hellenism, as elsewhere throughout the entire expanse of human existence until recent date, the city depended upon the productivity of the country for its existence. Today the country is increasingly dependent upon the productivity of the city. This means that the city provides the country with the machines, the science and the technology, the means of transportation, the agencies of distribution, instruction in hygiene and medical care, and almost all the means by which a dense population can escape misery. The city has laced the country with telephone and telegraph and television and radio, with automobiles and railways and all the conveniences of modern living. These are but the physical symbols of something else much more important, namely, the domination of city culture over sub-city and the increasing transformation of agrarian culture into that of the city.

In contrast to all this, the city culture of Hellenism was a thin crust spread over a mass of slaves and laborers whose lives were confined almost as narrowly as sub-city culture confines. Even the minds of those who belonged to the thin crust at the top could not escape the confinement of the sub-city culture which was still largely dominant. Therefore Christianity like the other great religions was shaped to meet the needs of a mentality different from the needs of a mind created in modern city culture and on that account should undergo extensive reinterpretation. It is true that Palestine in Jesus' time was quite cosmopolitan, Paul was a city product, and the development of Christianity in the Roman Empire occurred in the cities. But that is not the point here under consideration. The point is that the cities of that time did not dominate and shape the entire culture as do the modern cities. Therefore the prevailing culture of that time was not city culture in the modern sense because the prevailing culture even in the cities was shaped by agrarian conditions to a much greater degree than it is today.

Prior to the domination of human life by city culture men needed a form of religious commitment which enabled the individual to realize the creative potentialities within the bounds of his own special tradition. Today under the domination of city culture men need a form of religious commitment which enables the individual to realize the creative potentialities of life when lived in a mingling of diverse traditions. There was a mingling of traditions in the society which gave birth to Christianity but not in the form and to the degree now prevalent.

Christianity as currently interpreted and practiced is bound to one single and very special tradition. Not only is it rooted in such a tradition but it is bound to it by the authority of the Bible. The Bible is the expression of this very special and very exclusive tradition. Certainly Christianity has been able to participate in a great diversity of cultures and to take into itself much from all of them. But always it is called back to the "biblical faith" and to the "Judaeo-Christian tradition" for purging and correction.

The conclusion from all this can now be stated. Christianity as currently practiced cannot escape the confines of one particular tradition and so cannot meet the need of man living under conditions of a world-wide city culture. Such a religion has never yet appeared on earth; but it may appear. Out of Christianity and out of other traditional religions may emerge a form of religious commitment able to realize the mind-making potentialities of city culture and able to save from its destructive potentialities. In the city culture of our time man must find a commitment which will enable the individual to attain appreciative understanding of minds shaped by traditions alien to his own. If such a faith should arise, the creativity of history liberated from confinement to sub-city culture might lift the human mind to new heights. At least such a faith could enable the human mind to undergo the creative structuring which city culture makes possible.

If this analysis of our times be correct, the major question stands before us. Will a form of religious commitment emerge which enables the creativity in history to develop the human mind in those dimensions made possible by the liberation and diversity of city culture? The promise of the next fifty years is that such a faith may begin to appear. The peril is that it may not.

Our discussion has reached the point where the significance of history for human living cries for further interpretation. Hence the next chapter will be devoted to this question.

Chapter 13

HISTORY UNDER COMMITMENT

CONCERN about the meaning of history is widespread in our time. Convulsive change in the order and aims of human living is upon us, hence the question about the meaning of history. When new ways of life must be sought men ask: Do any events in history indicate the form and aim which these new ways should assume? Do the constructions and destructions, disappointments and fulfilments, frustrations and illusions of the human past reveal an order and direction which man should follow? Can we find running continuously throughout human history a creativity which calls for the ultimate commitment of man because it creatively transforms the mind in a way to realize the constructive potentialities of human existence, provided required conditions are met?

These several formulations express, as I understand it, the question about history.

Answer to this question may be sought by searching history, but I doubt if any reliable answer can be found in that way. History is too complex with too many conflicts and ambiguities, cross currents and dead ends to yield an answer. Another way to seek an answer is to analyze and interpret human nature. In this way one finds a kind of interchange going on between individuals which creates human language and the human mind and lifts life to the level distinctively human. At this level human history comes into being because history arises when individuals learn from one another. Each adds something to what he gets from the others until a tradition is formed. This tradition with various changes is transmitted through the sequence of genera-tions, shaping the life of man and the course of events. This is history prior to the rise of civilization. Such a tradition with its sentiments, appreciations, habits, knowledge, loves, and loyalties, hates and fears and above all its language distinguishes human life from every other form of existence.

First of all, no doubt, biological drives such as sex and gregari-ousness bound individuals together in such a way that they could learn from one another and gradually create a language and a tradition. During the first half million years of human life before the city arose, tradition dominated and controlled everything else. But with the increase of commercial interchange, division of labor, growth of population within a single society, the mingling of diverse traditions, the forming of a privileged class with eco-nomic surplus and release from manual labor, after all this another agency was required to sustain the social order additional to tra-dition. This other agency was political and economic organiza-tion more or less deliberately devised and planned. This is the beginning of civilization.

All of this development depends upon the kind of interchange by which individuals learn from one another because without this there can be no human mind, no tradition, no history, no political and economic organization.

In primitive society creative transformation of the mind is both sustained and limited by tradition. It is sustained because tradi-tion holds individuals in that relation in which they can learn from one another. It is limited because tradition without more elaborate organization added to it, which primitive society cannot add, is unable to regulate the lives of any great number of indi-viduals. Neither does it permit any great diversity in the minds under its domination. Hence individuals cannot learn so much from one another as they can in a more complex society.

In civilized society political and economic organization is more elaborately developed than in primitive society. In this way a far greater number of individuals are brought together into a single society and a much greater diversity of minds can be associated with one another. This permits each individual to learn far more from others than was possible in primitive society. In the early civilizations this opportunity to learn from others was limited to a small minority because only they enjoyed the eco-. nomic surplus, the leisure, and the diverse contacts required for this more ample learning. However, as society develops under civilized conditions this more ample learning and this higher creative transformation of the mind must spread to increasing numbers, otherwise the society breaks down and civilization declines. This results because increasing social complexity requires increasing numbers able to exercise initiative and responsibility in upholding the social order.

Political and economic organizations have not only sustained, they have also confined and restricted the creative transformation of the mind. They have set the bounds beyond which creative interchange has not been able to pass very far nor very fully. Also they have channeled and confined creative interchange to serve ulterior purposes of the government and of the economy as stated in the chapter on government. But today all men have been brought together into a single society. This requires a far greater extension of creative interchange and appreciative understanding than was ever before demanded. Also leadership in such a society requires a much higher development in the creative transformation of the mind. Consequently we have come to the time when the confinements and obstacles heretofore imposed upon creative interchange must be removed if the human way of life is to continue. This is the meaning of the social turmoil now occurring throughout the world. I shall try to show that this marks a new stage in the creative transformation of the human mind which must be consummated if civilization endures.

So far I have suggested an interpretation of the word "meaning" in the question asked about the meaning of history. Briefly stated the meaning of history is creative transformation of the human mind. But the word "history" also calls for definition. It is used in different senses, three of which will concern us here.

"History" is sometimes used to refer to the totality of the human past. Everything which ever happened in a way to modify human life would be included in history when the word is used with this designation.

The word has also another meaning. In this second sense "history" refers not to the actual events in the total fulness of their actuality, but only to the story about these events as this story is consciously entertained in the present. History in this second sense is not in the past at all. It is what we know in the present, or think we know, about the past.

There is still a third sense in which the word "history" is used and this third sense is what we shall here understand by the word. In this third sense history is the present in so far as it has been shaped by the past. It is the past in so far as it continues to operate in the present. Otherwise expressed, it is the consequences of the past as they continue to shape the present. This includes our present knowledge of the past or what we think we know about the past, but it includes also vastly more. It includes the language we use and this is the most important heritage from the past. No single individual and no single generation could create a language beyond the most meager beginnings. Indeed, it is doubtful if human beings with the kind of organisms they now have could survive at all without a language created by millions of individuals throughout thousands of years.

"History" in this third sense includes the customs, the technology, the modifications of the physical environment produced by the labors of men long dead and forgotten. It includes everything which sustains and shapes our lives in the present which we have received from the past. This includes almost everything by which we live.

"History" in this third sense is the past operative in the present no matter how ignorant and unconscious we may be of those past labors and no matter how inaccessible to research may be the events which created the language we use, the institutions which sustain our society, and all the rest of the products in the present which the past has produced.

These three usages of the word "history" are very different from one another. In the last sense the past is represented by its products in the present. History in the second sense is the past as represented by our imaginative reproduction of it in the present. History in the first sense is the totality of all events which ever happened to human beings and is not in the present at all.

"History" in the sense of past events which are not present in any sense at all cannot play any part in our lives in any way because we are in the present and anything which effects our lives must reach us here where we are. Past events in the form of their original occurrence cannot reach us here in the present; only their consequences can reach us.[1] Furthermore we have every reason to believe that innumerable events occurred in the past which produced no consequences making any difference in our lives at the present time. Doubtless many a man in ages past struggled and died alone in the wilderness or open sea without producing any effects in our lives today. Whole cultures may have arisen and after several hundred years disappeared without a trace beneath the ocean or in desert sands or in the jungle. The past in this sense cannot be our past if "our past" means anything which makes a difference in our lives today.

So we conclude: History in any sense in which it can be of any concern to us must somehow enter into our present lives. This is a tautology but it is a tautology which some thinkers seem to deny.

With this understanding history is the recovery and perpetuation of the products of the past in such a way as to create the present. To repeat, this is not a recovery of the past in the sense of recovering the actual events of the past. Neither is it merely our knowledge of the past, although this is included. But far more important than our knowledge of the past are the products of the past because these include all the resources by which life at the level distinctively human is made possible.

When a child learns to talk and to understand and use the signs and symbols of his society, history in the sense here understood is creating the human mind and the life of the present because these signs and symbols with their meanings are the products of the past. A child learning to talk exemplifies the creativity of history. The child is undergoing creative transformation of his mind by history. We do not know what are the limits of this creative transformation. We do not know how far it can expand the range of what the mind can know; nor how richly it can variegate the qualities which the mind can feel; nor how much it can increase the scope and power of control nor widen and deepen the appreciative understanding of minds for one another. The limits are in part biological, but for the more gifted individuals and perhaps to some degree for all excepting idiots, the ceiling put upon this creative transformation of the mind has been imposed chiefly by the traditions and the social order which provide for creative interchange up to a point but do not allow it to go beyond. The limits thus imposed have often been unnecessary and have caused wars, hates, fears, and great corruption. On the other hand, limitation at some point has always been necessary to protect and sustain the kind of social order without which this creativity could not accomplish as much as it actually has done.

This creativity of history can wax and wane, rise and fall. History becomes more creative when more of the past is recovered and perpetuated and shaped to meet the needs of the present and to widen its vision. The creativity of history sinks to the minimum in most dramatic form when men live almost like the lower animals in the midst of the ruins of a great civilization. Such men may not distinguish the ruins from the raw state of nature. The broken walls, the relics of ancient tools and devices, the fragments of old writing mean less to these men than the nuts and berries they eat and the fish and game they catch. Many obstructions rise up against this creativity of history. Always it has been held down to a low level compared to what it might accomplish.

The small child encounters these obstructions from the very beginning in the minds of his parents and other associates. The parents have learned from their own parents and from others to practice deceptive and manipulative communication and the device of the false front. Consequently, the child must protect itself against these cruel instruments of the human spirit. To protect himself the child adopts the same devices for his own use.

Thus creative communication is cut down to small dimensions compared to what it might be. Obstructed in this way by other kinds of interchange, the creativity of history cannot transform the human mind to the full dimension of its potentialities.

The child becomes involved in conflicts of power which require him to manipulate and be manipulated rather than to understand the true subjectivity of the other person. The frivolities and confusions of life drive him to muddleheaded interchange with others. He encounters in those about him the practice of deception, both self-deception and the deception of others, and is irresistibly drawn into the web of deception by interchange with them.

Evasive and protective kinds of interchange may come to dominate the mind until creative communication ceases to be a matter of concern either to the individual or the group. Attention becomes increasingly focused upon protection and utility. To simplify the complexity of life people reduce it to reiterative communication; and to win approval and social acceptance they practice the device of the false front. The nervous strain of all this calls for relaxation and for this one turns to the anaesthesia of muddleheaded communication. In these ways men forget whatever experience they may have had of the excitement, the ecstasy, and the profound satisfaction of the deepest need of man which can be had only when creative communication dominates over the other kinds.

When deceptive devices are removed individuals can find in themselves many contrary demands and drives which cannot be made to fit into the established order of life. The anxiety, the sense of need, and the suffering generated by these impulses and frustrations cannot be appeased although they can be concealed. But all this can be accepted fully and openly into consciousness when it is seen to be an essential part of man's greatest glory. This condition of man is a necessary part of creative transformation. This condition of the total self is the condition of one whose organization of personality must be continuously reconstructed; whose ideals must be cast off and other ideals accepted as better; whose society must be constantly exposed to reordering, sometimes with great suffering, whose sojourn in any dear and homey place is always brief because he is a pilgrim on his way to ends he cannot know; all this the human being must undergo if he is to be transformed creatively to comprehend a richer abundance of quality and wider scope of knowledge and control, and if he is to have a love which grows in depth and range of appreciation beyond any known limit.

Many claim to have the "Christian interpretation of history." But they do not agree among themselves. Many Christian theologians and authorities on the history of Christian thought have claimed that the Christian view of history is that of progress. William Adams Brown and Kenneth Scott Latourette are examples. But others just as emphatically deny that the Christian interpretation of history shows it to be progressive. Reinhold Niebuhr and Karl Barth are examples. Obviously if there is a Christian revelation which shows the meaning of history, it is not of such a character as to enable the greatest Christian scholars to reach any agreement on what it is.

If the meaning of history was revealed in Jesus Christ, the revelation is not any set of propositions nor any teaching by Jesus or any other, according to the understanding of revelation now set forth by "contemporary theologians." But when this position is taken the question remains unanswered: Just what is revealed about history in Jesus Christ?

Revelation of the meaning of history never could have been correctly interpreted in the form of doctrines at the time the revelation occurred in the lives of the first followers of Jesus. It could not have been correctly interpreted because there could have been no language fit to interpret it. Current usage determines the meaning of words, and since no usage of words could refer to this reality prior to its revelation, no words and no language available to men at the time of the revelation could possibly give expression to it. Therefore it could be transmitted to others only in the form of a transformed life.

This transformed way of life necessarily had its symbols, its myths, its ceremonies and distinctive practices of commitment, and its continuing fellowship. What it did not have and could not have is any set of propositions stating what the revealed reality truly is. But advancing civilization with its increasing self-consciousness, its penetrating analysis, its intermingling of diverse traditions requiring a language able to surmount the barrier between different traditions, the development of the psychological and other social sciences, the development of the arts which seek to interpret experiences not otherwise expressed, notably drama, novel, and short story, and the continuing struggle of men to express to one another what they experience, out of all this after many centuries a language should develop able to state what actually was revealed and is revealed having the character and power to save and transform.

The end of the world is said by some to be a part of the Christian interpretation of history. The teaching about it is called eschatology. Scientific evidence seems to indicate that in time the solar system will come to an end and with it all life. If that is to be the end of all, then human life and human history lose their meaning, say these proponents of the "Christian answer." Only if you believe in a sovereign power able to deliver human life from this final doom can life and history have any meaning.

The answer to this should be obvious. If this is to be the final doom, then no mere belief can make it otherwise. Furthermore, while the physical sciences can predict with various degrees of probability what the physical end may be within the bounds of physical evidence only, they cannot predict what creativity will make of man nor the powers and resources which creativity may develop in man after a few million years, provided that he commits himself to it and shapes his institutions to serve it.

We cannot say with assurance that man with powers and resources developed by the creativity of history will be able to control the sources of cosmic energy in a way to avert the outcome of physical forces as now foreseen by the physical sciences. But on the other hand it must be remembered that this prediction of the physical outcome is based on data which exclude from consideration the creativity mentioned. Therefore it is likewise impossible with such data alone to predict that man will not be able to master the fate foreseen when creativity does not enter into the calculations. If anyone a million years ago with all the equipment of modern science had predicted the future life on this planet, basing his prediction solely on the physical and biological data then available, he could not possibly have foreseen human life, human history, and human civilization brought forth by a creativity producing the human mind.

We cannot predict what creativity will bring forth in the life of man after millions of years, but there is much more reason to believe that creativity will save man at the last than there is reason to believe in divine intervention in any other form. They who believe in divine intervention at the end of history (called eschatology) admit they have no evidence other than a conviction of faith defended on the ground that it saves man from despair on the one hand and from self-destructive pride and cynicism on the other. But when God is identified with the creativity of history we have good reason to believe in a kind of divine intervention, if one wishes to use such words.

In the last resort courage and hope, moral zeal and integrity cannot be sustained by any belief taken by itself alone, no matter how comforting nor inspiring it may seem to be. These qualities of the spirit come by a commitment so complete that one is ready to endure any sacrifice and any danger and final destruction itself for the sake of the best which human life can ever attain. Ultimate peace is attained not by any belief assuring us of final success and glory, whether in history or beyond. Ultimate peace is attained by giving oneself quite completely to the best there is in all being, no matter what hazard of ultimate destruction may be involved. He who cannot do this will never find peace nor the ultimate ecstasy, no matter how comforting his beliefs, if these beliefs cannot endure the tests and categories of reason. Sooner or later the tests of reason will search out these beliefs. Then courage will fail if it depends on those beliefs.

If it is true that the mind of man is created in each individual by the creativity of history, it is nonsense to talk about any kind of human existence beyond history. The human mind and the human way of life come into existence only in history by recovery and perpetuation of the products of the past. Without history life reverts to the biological pure and simple. Therefore to say that the way of man's salvation reaches beyond history is to give the name of salvation to its very opposite, namely, the annihilation of the human mind and everything distinctively human. It is to proclaim the way of man's salvation to be a way of life found only among the lower animals.

The difficulty which has stood in the way of finding a meaning in history to which man can give himself in ultimate commitment has been the complexity, confusion, and ambiguity of all the developments and destructions of the past. But when the problem is approached through an interpretation of the nature of man as we find him in the present an answer can be found to this question about history. With this clue we can trace a thread of meaning through all the confusions and convulsions of time. As we have tried to show, this thread of meaning is the creative transformation of the human mind which does actually occur in the life of every individual. This could never occur except by the creativity of history because this creativity has created the meaning which things convey to the human mind. Pre-eminent among these things which convey meaning as a consequence of the creativity of history are the sounds and marks called language.

The events of history do not fit into a pattern. There is no over-all pattern. But through it all is the creativity of history rearing the human mind in every newborn infant which has normal biological equipment. If the conditions are favorable and the genes are right this creative transformation of the mind by the historic past operative in the present may reach magnificent proportions. This is the promise of history. Most especially it is the promise of this time of peril. It is not only a promise. It has now become an imperative for all mankind, proclaimed by the convulsions of the twentieth century.

This interpretation of history should be distinguished from four other ways of dealing with the problem. It is distinguished from all of these in the first place by its method of inquiry. It seeks the meaning of history not by first searching the events of the historic past but by examining the nature of man. Only when it finds the answer in the nature of man himself does it try to trace the fortunes of creativity throughout the events of history. It differs from the other interpretations also in the answer which it offers to the question about history. The many different theories about history can be classified under four heads.

First is the doctrine which declares that significant events point to a timeless eternity and to this eternity man must give himself in religious faith, thus escaping the turmoil and disasters of time. The significant events pointing to this way of salvation may be certain mystical experiences, or they may be the lives and teachings of certain outstanding individuals, or they may be the apparent futility and meaninglessness which seem to be the outcome of all temporal achievement. All human developments come to nothing in the end, so it is said. Hence the meaning of history points from time into eternity.

The second answer to this question about meaning in history is the claim that an over-all pattern can be found in all human events. This pattern is being worked out by the entire course of history. The gradual fulfillment of the pattern is often called progress. To this progression man must give himself in religious faith and thus find salvation from the apparent futilities and frustrations of life. According to some, however, the pattern is not that of progress but is a pattern of cycles. Still others claim the cycles to be progressive because they form spirals. What is common to all forms of this second answer is the assertion that all events in history fit into some kind of pattern.

The third answer to this question denies progress and denies that there is any over-all pattern in the events of history. But there is a plan and purpose for history in the mind of God, according to this answer. This purpose of God is to be fulfilled at the end of history. This purpose which overrules history cannot be found by any knowledge of temporal events, although certain events in history reveal this purpose to those who have faith. In the Christian tradition the events which carry this revelation are said to be the life and teachings and death and resurrection of Jesus Christ. After this answer has been accepted by faith, so this doctrine declares, it is possible to discover the transcendent meaning of history in many developments occurring now and in the past. But the answer must first come by way of divine revelation accepted by faith.

A fourth answer to the question about history points to the development of some institution, nation, people, or race. For example, the meaning of history may be identified with the development of the economic process or with the destiny of the Aryan race, or with the people of the rising sun who have their home in Japan, or with the institutions of democracy. This view is so much in disrepute at the present time in the Western world that it scarcely needs further comment.

These all should be sharply distinguished from the interpretation of history which is here defended.

History under commitment is intended to suggest that man must now assume responsibility for the creativity of history to a measure never before required of him. Men cannot assume responsibility in the sense of determining the course of future events; but men can, and, if civilization continues, must assume responsibility for maintaining social conditions under which creative transformation of the mind can occur to the measure required to deal constructively with the complexities and problems of a world community.

This responsibility is laid upon man today partly because of his magnified power and knowledge, partly because of the magnified possibilities for creative transformation of the mind, and partly because of the catastrophe which will result if this responsibility is not assumed.

At each higher level in the creative transformation of the mind the individual becomes more conscious of himself in the depth of his own existence. He also becomes more fully aware of the problems and perplexities in the world round about him. Furthermore, the advance of civilizations increases the magnitude of these problems. At the same time, if right social relations are upheld, the creativity of history can magnify the powers of the mind so that the problems are not more difficult relative to these increased powers.

If this increase in the difficulties of human existence is called evil, then evil increases with every advance in the creative trans-formation of man. But if all this is accepted as essential to man's high destiny, and if the individual commits himself completely and ultimately to the creativity which endows him with this destiny, and if he accepts without evasion or concealment these perplexities, these problems and these dangers as essential to the glory of his existence, then he can live in the midst of it all with a peace and joy undiminished by the perplexity and the suffering. This conjunction of joy and suffering is not a contradiction in terms because the joy and suffering pertain to different levels of being. Creativity has found in man the medium of its freedom and its power on condition that man commits himself to it. Therein lies the joy and the greatness of human life for him who dis-covers this level of being and who gives himself over quite com-pletely to the creativity of history.

The years and generations have not yet accumulated the condi-tions under which Western man can feel the need to be creatively transformed by appreciative understanding of the greatness in other peoples, other cultures, and other relations. Even when this need is recognized, it is misinterpreted by those who think the way of salvation is to be found in these other cultures and other religions. That is the mistake which some are making. Neither is the way of salvation to be found in what is common to all the great faiths of mankind. That is another dangerous error. Rather the way of salvation lies in that creative transforma-tion of the mind which results from creative interchange between us all. Out of this interchange will emerge a faith and way of life richer with felt quality, more comprehensive in understanding and more competent to control the movements of life than any of its component parts.

But Western man is not yet ready to engage in this kind of interchange with other peoples. He still has too much feeling of satisfaction in his own achievements for this door to open to him. But in a decade, a half century—how long who knows—the door may open wide by reason of the discovery of his own need. The door will open first not by any change in the great majority. It will open first by the forming of a fellowship of individuals who are so completely committed to the creativity of history that they will find the way of salvation, not merely by intellectual recognition of what is required, but by a change in the organization of the personality of each of them.

This is the predicament of Western man. He is lifted on a pinnacle of power so high that he cannot recognize his own need. His own need is that he be creatively transformed by interchange with other peoples. A swift survey of human history may help us to understand this state of mind which prevails among men of European culture.

As previously stated, the first stage of the creative transformation of the human mind required a span of time measured in hundreds of thousands of years, from the origin of the human species to the beginning of the first cities on the Nile, the Euphrates, the Indus, and Yellow rivers. During this period tradition ruled the life of man, providing the conditions under which the human mind could be created by individuals learning from one another. Within a social order controlled by tradition, signs and symbols and a language were developed with which to communicate from man to man and generation to generation the accumulated resources for human living brought forth by the past.

From eight to five thousand years ago, under the compulsion of climatic changes brought on by the passing of the last ice age, a different kind of social order began to develop in which many more people could live together with minds much more diversified. This enabled certain individuals placed under favorable conditions to learn from others far more than was possible under the domination of a rigid, coercive, and exclusive tradition. When writing and other devices of civilization were added, a much greater accumulation of resources for human living could be gathered from a series of generations.

This greater abundance of resources, both material and spiritual, enabled men to provide conditions for further accumulation and in part were so used. But they could also be used and were used to destroy these conditions, thus preventing any further accumulation and sometimes preventing even the conservation of resources already acquired. When this last happens, the civilization declines, if decline is defined as diminution of material and spiritual resources available for human living. This, I take it, is what is generally meant by decline of a civilization. The greater the accumulation of resources in the form of an economic surplus and productive power, in the form of knowledge, in the form of techniques and methods of all kinds, in the form of loyalties and devotions, sentiments and appreciations, the greater becomes the destructive power of man as also his constructive abilities. Both have been used extensively. Constructive use of power is using it to build, improve, and uphold the conditions under which the creativity of history can rear the human mind to more ample dimensions.

As said before, the chief controlling agency over and above tradition which was used at this second stage in the creative transformation of the human mind was economic and political organization, including the military.

After this second stage, distinguished by the rise of the first civilizations, came a third stage. This can be called civilization at the second level. This second level of civilization is the third stage in the creative transformation of the human mind because the first stage in this transformation of the human mind was primitive society before civilization arose.

The division of history into levels or periods can never be very accurate because developments and societies can always be found which do not fit the divisions. But some such distinctions are necessary to enable the mind to assert anything at all about the vast complexities of history. Also they need not be arbitrary even though the developments of history do not fit into them neatly and completely.

By civilization at the second level is meant those societies which could learn from the products and achievements of the first civilizations. Greece and Rome, Israel, and Persia can be taken as examples. Since I am trying to explain the predicament of Western man by tracing a certain line of development, I shall not refer to China and India except in passing, important as these and other civilizations are in human history.

These civilizations at the second level are distinguished in several respects. The creative transformation of the human mind rose to great heights in a few thinkers and other outstanding figures of Greece, in the Hebrew prophets, in Zoroaster and his followers in Persia and, for the moment to go beyond the bounds of our present discussion, in Gautama the Buddha of India and in Confucius and Laotzu in China. Indeed, all the great religions of the world which to our time provide the faith sustaining and guiding the lives of men in the high civilizations originated at this third stage of creativity in history which is the second level of civilization. For this reason Karl Jaspers calls this the "axial period" in human history.[2]

One outstanding feature of these civilizations at the second level makes them unique in history. The diversity and richness of earlier civilizations to which they had access combining with the integrative coherence of the cultures of these societies at the second level enabled them to absorb and creatively transform what they got from these various sources. A further element of this distinctive feature was a political and economic organization permitting far more diversity in the minds of individuals and far more freedom and fulness of interchange between them than had ever before been possible.

This statement about second level civilization applies most especially to Greece and Israel. The remarkable integrative coherence of their cultures persisted despite devastating internal conflicts between classes and city-states and with other peoples. After Alexander the Great, first, and Rome, second, had conquered Greece along with the rest of the known world, Greek culture spread to all peoples and in so doing preserved some of its identity. On that account the name of Hellenism is given to this period. The same integrative power enabling it to preserve its identity through all acquisitions and through all transformations is seen in the culture of Israel as it was carried by the Jews into all countries and down through the ages to our time. Consequently we find among the ancient Greeks and among the Jews in all ages a creative transformation of the mind scarcely equaled elsewhere.

Diversity of sources, diversity of minds engaged in interchange and freedom of communication have all been equaled and surpassed since the days of Greece and ancient Israel. But what has never been surpassed, it would seem, is the combination of these three with a tradition of such great integrative coherence. There have been many societies with a tradition of equal integrative coherence and there have been many societies with equal diversity and freedom of interchange. But perhaps there has never been a society which combined all these into one. This combination is what seems to have made possible in Greece and Israel the creative transformation of a few individual minds to dimensions never surpassed and perhaps never equaled.

This brings us to the third level of civilization and to the fourth stage in the creative transformation of the human mind. The first stage, it will be recalled, was the enrichment of tradition in primitive society before civilization arose with its cities, its diversities, its great numbers, its rapidity of social change, its complexity, its power of technology, and its high development of political, military, and economic organization. The third level of civilization and this fourth stage in the creative transformation of the human mind is represented by European culture which includes the Americas.

The supreme achievements of European civilization are science, technology, commerce, industrial production, and political organization. No other time and no other society ever approached the magnitude of power achieved by these means at this third level of civilization. Rome in contrast to earlier and other civilizations began to concentrate on the development of these instruments of power. European society has carried its development to inordinate dimensions. Western civilization has contributed notably to the culture of the world in music, painting, architecture, poetry and other forms of literature. But so also have other civilizations. The unique contribution of the West has been its modern science and technology and methods of organizing great numbers of men for collective action. In this respect the West is incomparable.

The instruments of power have value only in so far as they

provide conditions which permit the creative transformation of the human mind to attain those dimensions in which it can attain richest experience of felt qualities and the most complete appreciation of other minds in greatest variety. These two dimensions of human experience can be given the names of beauty and love; but these two words do not cover the scope and depth of experience which is here intended. Ugliness is a form of rich qualitative feeling and hate can enter into the most profound appreciative understanding of another mind.

Now the instrumentalities of power developed by European civilization have not been subordinated to the service of that creative transformation of the mind which attains greatest richness of felt quality and most profound appreciative understanding of other individuals and peoples. These instruments have been used chiefly to control subhuman nature and to dominate other peoples, chiefly the Indians of the Americas, and the peoples of Asia and Africa. But power continually magnified to achieve these ends and only incidentally to enrich the sensitivities and appreciative consciousness becomes highly dangerous.

Power thus developed is dangerous first because the processes of nature brought under control can at last become so enormous that man's control of them becomes destructive of human life itself. We see this occurring today in the explosion of hydrogen bombs.

Power developed in this way is dangerous in the second place because the peoples dominated by such power become resentful and when they acquire these instruments as in time they always do, they turn in hate and destroying wrath upon the people who have humiliated them.

This development of power is dangerous also because people who use great power in this way with impoverishment of the sensitivities and appreciative consciousness cannot detect the harm they do to other people and so unintentionally incite other people to hate them.

This development is dangerous in the fourth place because gigantic power used by minds impoverished in respect to feeling quality and appreciative understanding of other minds makes

them incapable of using the power wisely. Wisdom in this context is the understanding of other minds and of one's own mind
in such a way that one can know what are his own basic needs,
the needs of others, and the most important needs of human
kind. One cannot use his power to serve his own deepest needs
and the needs of others if he does not know what those needs
are. But this is precisely the predicament of Western man. It is
failure to develop wisdom proportionate to power.

A generalization such as the one just made must be qualified
in many ways. Individuals are enormously different in respect
to their wisdom when wisdom is defined as just stated. Doubtless
many individuals in Western culture have had and do have great
wisdom. Perhaps the wisest have been as wise as any in other
cultures. I do not attempt to make any such comparison. But
wisdom must be in proportion to power if power is to be used
wisely. All the evidence seems to indicate that the wisdom of
the majority of people in Western culture has not been increasing
as rapidly as the gigantic increase in power which they have
acquired.

This is the predicament of Western man possessing power such
as no human beings ever before have approached. This reveals
the danger which surrounds him and is now rising up like a
flood to overwhelm him. He can be saved because there is a way
of salvation open to him. This way of salvation has been the
theme of this entire writing. Nothing short of the most complete
commitment to the creativity of history can save him. This, of
course, cannot be a mass movement. It must be led by a dedicated
fellowship. But the way of salvation is there to be followed by
those who will go in that way. Creative transformation of the
mind by commitment to the kind of interchange which produces
appreciative understanding of one another can save us. Nothing else can.

All the power developed by European culture is needed and
more still is needed to provide the conditions under which the
human mind can be creatively transformed to its full potential
dimensions. What Western man has brought forth is not a loss
but a great gain if properly used. If Western man cannot use his

power wisely and if by reason of his lack of wisdom others finally take it from him, these instrumentalities of science, technology, and social organization may yet be one of the greatest contributions ever made to the creativity of history. Such will be the case if these other people and other generations who acquire this power develop the wisdom which our civilization has not developed. This, of course, is on the assumption that civilization survives during the period when this power is passing out of the hands of Western man into other hands. It would be far better for all, however, and far less dangerous, if Western man along with the other members of the world community now emerging would acquire the needed wisdom. This can be acquired by ultimate commitment to creative interchange in every time and place where individuals are associated in a way to make this kind of interchange possible.

Chapter 14

THE DECISION REQUIRED

OF US

I N P A R T O N E the question was asked about man's ultimate commitment and an answer was sought to that question. In Part Two institutions and human history have been studied in their relation to the answer found to the primary question. Now we come to a question about the individual: What can I myself do about it? Suppose there is truth in the answer to the primary question set forth in Part One. I then ask myself: What can this particular individual, my own self, contribute to the vast undertaking involved in our answer to the primary question?

The individual standing in the midst of a history which continues through thousands of years and involves millions of other individuals can be effective in shaping the course of events. Some can do this more powerfully than others, but the apparent disproportion of power exercised by the great man in comparison with you and me is an illusion. The great man is conspicuous, therefore observed, studied, and his influence recognized and described. Individuals who are not conspicuous are not observed and their influence is not recognized and described. Consequently they appear to be nonentities. This is not true. There is every reason to believe that innumerable individuals who have never become conspicuous have influenced the course of history more than many whose names are known and who are called great on that account. Furthermore, the influence of the great man is not other than the reactions of many inconspicuous people to him and the way the many transform his influence by integrating it into their own unique individualities. Hence the difference in power to shape society and history which seems so disproportionate when the great man is compared to the common man is a falsification of what actually occurs. Human history is nothing else than the experience of innumerable individuals and the transmission of this experience in some form to others.

There is another cause of this prevalent illusion that a few conspicuous individuals do the important work of the world while the others are relatively insignificant. The human mind must simplify the complexity of events. It cannot achieve a comprehensive concept which will include all the innumerable individuals and activities which enter into the complex events of human life. It must have symbols which represent this inconceivable complexity. For this reason we seize on the conspicuous figures and attribute to them what happens, thereby obscuring the doings of the many people who actually determine what occurs in human life.

This does not mean, however, that everyone is an effective participant. To be constructive and effective in action one needs to have the right intuitions to guide action. This requires that one recognize his moral predicament. By recognizing it and fully acknowledging it, he is in some measure delivered from it. This enables him to have intuitions which guide action in doing the right thing.

Also to be constructively effective in action requires a unified self under a ruling devotion. This enables him to draw upon all his resources. Otherwise repressions, inhibitions, and inner conflicts obstruct and dissipate his energies and little can be accomplished. This unification of the self under a ruling devotion is attained by practices of personal commitment.

These two conditions required for constructive effective action indicate where to seek an answer to the question: What can the individual do in dealing with the basic problem of human existence? We shall seek the answer by examining first the moral predicament and what can be done about; then examine the practice of personal commitment and how it leads to effective action.

The moral predicament here under consideration has three distinctive features. The first of these results from self-consciousness. One of the supreme endowments of man is that he can be conscious of himself and thus pass judgment on his own worth. But appreciative understanding of unique individuality is at a minimum in most social relations. Hence one is driven to protect his self-esteem against wrong evaluations which others make of the self. I may reject their evaluations, but to protect my own sense of personal worth in the face of them, I am led to judge myself in ways equally mistaken.

It is a vital moral necessity to achieve some degree of correctness in one's evaluation of himself. The common moral predicament is that one cannot do this in the face of all the misunderstandings and wrong judgments about oneself which are encountered. My evaluations of myself become distorted. This leads to false pictures not only of myself but of others, of social conditions and causes, of ideals and standards, of men and deeds, because these all must be fitted into the pattern by which I protect my self-esteem. In this way I am led to judge evil to be good and good to be evil.

Dominated by these distortions, my whole system of values is warped and corrupted. In this condition my intuitions cannot be right. These intuitions can become monstrous errors when I try to judge my enemies or rescue myself from a devastating humiliation, whether the rescue is accomplished by despair of my own worth or an assumed arrogance, vindictive hate or consuming envy. So long as people continue to react to one another with cold indifference or fatuous adulation or cruel prejudice or practice manipulative control or the artifices of domination and subordination in disregard of merit, this predicament of man will continue.

In this condition there is one thing which the individual can do which can deliver him from much of its evil and enable him to have intuitions more nearly right than they otherwise can be.

He can admit freely and fully that he is in this predicament. When one knows that his evaluations are distorted by unconscious processes operating in his own person, he is partially liberated from them. An error which one knows to be an error is already on the way to correction. When one recognizes this moral predicament as his own, he can examine his judgments critically and seek out situations in which more reliable intuitions can break through the "ego system." Thus one can be liberated more or less from this condition and rise toward that reorganization which is endowed with more trustworthy judgments.

The second feature of the moral predicament in which every man stands arises out of his dependence upon one particular social group and culture. Every man judges right and wrong and good and evil from the perspective of the community in which he has been reared. He cannot appreciate the true value of other ways of life and other standards prevailing in communities alien to his own, whether he condemns them as inferior or romantically glorifies them. Neither can he rightly evaluate the partisan prejudice and other evils and limitations in his own culture. He may denounce the ways of his own people or worship them; but to judge them from the standpoint of what is good for man as a creature subject to creative transformation (supposing that to be a valid standard for all humanity) is very difficult.

This distortion of judgment due to my membership in my own community becomes most serious when another community becomes dangerously hostile to my own or mine to the other. The evaluations of one another passed back and forth across the iron curtain are examples.

Here again is a moral predicament from which no man can escape entirely; but one can be liberated to some degree by recognizing that he is in this condition and so discount the validity of judgments made by his own community of the other and also do the same in reverse. If he is profoundly convinced of this fact about human beings, including himself, he can search for evidence with a mind somewhat more open than if he did not know his own condition. In this way he might gradually undergo

creative transformation toward judgments more correct concerning his own people and others.

The third feature of the universal moral predicament arises out
of the unfinished, transitional state of man's present condition.
Human beings are an unfinished lot. They are on the way to
becoming another kind of being, provided that they do not
destroy themselves or regress irreparably before the transition is
consummated. I do not refer to physiological change but to
change in the psychic, social, and cultural conditions. Man is in
a state of acute instability. He must go up or down, indeed rises
to moral grandeur in rare instances and again sinks to degradation and demonry. Not only does this become obvious when we
compare different individuals, peoples, ages, and cultures; it is
also obvious to one who will honestly and correctly appraise his
own states of mind, impulse, and attitude as they change from
one situation to another.

Since man is in transition, not yet the being which he must
become if he continues to exist at all, he does not yet have the
kind of psychic organization which would enable him to judge
what is good for him when "what is good for him" is to undergo
a creative transformation not yet accomplished. A lower level
cannot know with any reliability what is required to reach a level
which has never yet entered the imagination. At the lower
level one will part of the time judge that to be good which
stabilizes his present condition and prevents change. When, however, he succeeds in stabilizing his present condition and making
life easy and comfortable, he finds it boring beyond endurance.
So he seeks excitement either in danger or debauchery or, it may
be, he will turn to wild destruction for excitement and innovation.
This condition of man is set forth by Dostoevsky in his *Notes
from the Underground.*

. . . if you ask me why I tormented myself like that, the
answer is because I was awfully bored.

. . . man will never renounce real suffering, that is to say,
destruction and chaos. . . . Why, it's the sole cause of con-

sciousness! And though at the beginning I did argue that consciousness was the greatest misfortune of man, yet I know that he loves it and will not exchange it for any satisfaction.[1]

Dostoevsky gives three answers to the question, Why do men act this way? One acts in this way when he feels that he is a mouse, lacks personal worth in his present state of being, and so tries to build up the sense of his own importance by acting contrary to all expectation, law, and order. This makes him feel that he is free, can do as he chooses, has importance and power. "It preserves what is most precious and most important to us, namely, our personality and our individuality." Secondly, man acts in this way because he is bored and delights in an intensified consciousness even when suffering is necessary to quicken consciousness to high intensity. In the third place, man acts in this way because he can criticize every goal and every impulse and find that it does not have enough value to outweigh alternative and contrary goals and whims.

This description of the human being, his discontent with changeless comfort, his struggle to attain a significance greater than what he now has, the swarm of contrary impulses which possess him and call for a higher integration with more comprehensive and intensive consciousness, all this is evidence that the self in its wholeness can find satisfaction only in a series of creative transformations.

If this claim is correct, the individual can be partially delivered from the third feature of the moral predicament, namely, the perversity arising from being incompletely created, by recognizing this fact about himself and seeking out those social relations and that kind of work and practicing the kind of commitment next to be described, which will bring creativity to a higher level of dominance in his own person and in social relations.

In addition to recognizing one's moral predicament, there is a second requirement to be met if one is to be an effective participant in what gives to human life its supreme significance. The second requirement is the practice of personal commitment by which the self is unified under a ruling devotion and one's resources most fully brought into action.

Commitment to this end first of all assumes the form of a chosen vocation. That means to seek out a kind of work which has a dual fitness. On the one hand it is fitted to one's own aptitude, thus enabling one to exercise all his powers to the maximum in the doing of it. On the other hand it is a kind of work which enables one to give his strength to providing some of the conditions required for the creative transformation of man.

Obviously it is impossible to state what specific course of action should be undertaken by different individuals. What one person should do is not what another should. What one situation requires is not what is morally and religiously demanded by another. So far as one is creative in his work, the effectiveness of what one does depends on having the right intuitions emerging in each unique situation in answer to the peculiar demands of that time and place. Such intuitions are most likely to arise if one is doing the kind of work which elicits most fully the unique potentialities of his own individuality and is done with devotion and a sense of its profound importance because it contributes to the most important thing going on in human history. Seeking out this kind of work with its dual fitness to self and to the transformation of man is the practice of commitment so far as concerns a chosen vocation.

A second aspect of commitment pertains to the wholeness of self-giving. This means in particular that one gives to the service of creativity his failures, his guilt, his weakness, his shame, his ignominy, as well as his virtues and his strength. If this is not done moral and religious practice makes for spiritual arrogance. The great evil rising out of the deliberate and conscious practice of religion and morality is this arrogance. The way in which morality and religion are practiced seems almost inevitably to make the "good" people feel superior to others who do not engage self-consciously in these practices. This feeling of being morally and religiously superior, when built up in a group of individuals who re-enforce in one another the attitude of arrogance, is one of the major evils issuing from religion and should be classified with those other great evils which bear the evil name because they are not respectable.

Repeatedly in this writing the importance has been emphasized of facing up to the evils in one's self and others. But just now another point is being emphasized. In religious commitment rightly practiced one offers up his weaknesses, his failures, his guilt, his death, his finitude as a part of the precious gift of his total self, given in devotion. His failure and his guilt, so far as he can do nothing more to correct them, are given as part of his service to the creative transformation of man. Often these negative qualities when freely and openly acknowledged and given as a part of his total self in devotion, can render greater service than what one thinks to be his strength and virtue. I am not denying that one has strength and virtue and that it should be given in devoted service also; but when this strong and virtuous side of oneself alone is offered, the inevitable consequence ensues. Spiritual arrogance becomes a ruling trait. More than that, it is literally correct to say that failure, guilt, and shame, after one has done all he can to correct them, and after one has fully acknowledged them and given them in service as a part of his total self, can under some conditions be more creative than what one esteems to be his virtue and his strength. In any case, moral and religious commitment cannot be rightly practiced unless one gives the evil in him as well as the good in him for whatever can be made out of it.

The strain and anxiety, the pretence and self-deception, which result when the individual strives to rectify in himself what cannot be rectified become sources of weakness and corruption. They misdirect action, they waste energy, they confuse thinking, they disintegrate the personality with self-deception and inner conflict. On the other hand, when one not only accepts himself for what he is but gives himself as he is in the wholeness of his finitude with a devotion not diminished but magnified by failure, guilt, and error, one lives with a magnified power of action, with a more reliably discriminating judgment concerning good and evil.

It is pride which makes it painful to acknowledge the evils in onself. It is complacency which acknowledges these evils without serious concern. It is joy and triumph to commit these evils to creativity to be transformed if they can be and if not, to give them for whatever can be made out of them in the free and open interchange between man and man and in the work of the world. Even though the outcome of one's life is apparently ruin and failure, this kind of commitment has its own triumph. It is the triumph of devotion unabated by the struggles and failures of life. To have this kind of devotion, however, the practices of commitment must be as persistent and intense as, say, the practices by which one masters jiujitsu or the satori of Zen Buddhism.

This brings us to the last aspect of commitment here to be considered. It is persistence and intensity in the practice of commitment.

The practice of commitment is a kind of autosuggestion. It is autosuggestion in the sense that it is designed to organize and unify the total self under the dominant control of what can transform and save man as he cannot do for himself. Therefore to call it autosuggestion is not to imply that the commitment is to oneself. Rather the autosuggestion is the way one commits himself to what is beyond himself, namely, to what transforms man creatively. Any practice by which the individual tries to commit himself to anything involves autosuggestion. Any current of life which draws all the resources of the individual most fully into sweeping power will involve autosuggestion, whether practiced deliberately and consciously or spontaneously and automatically.

This is not the place to describe the practices of religious commitment. There are manuals upon the subject although I have not derived much help from any of them. For myself I have found it necessary to develop my own practices and these might not be suitable for any other. Perhaps to be effective these practices should not be taken secondhand from any other person but developed by each to fit his own need. In any case, the rule can be affirmed that enduring and profound commitment is possible only by diligent and intensive practices of commitment, whether or not these are called prayer or worship or religious ritual or meditation or given some other name.

The goal of this commitment is to unify the self for action, to attain that reorganization which will have right intuitions, and to join oneself with the most important reality there is. The most important reality is the creative transformation of man which is going on in human history.

That man can undergo creative transformation is demonstrated by the fact that it has actually occurred to various degrees in many cases. It is described at length by D. T. Suzuki in his account of Zen Buddhism. St. Paul in his epistles tells of this transformation which occurred in his own person. William Blake proclaims it as an experience of his own. In our present time Martin Buber and Karl Jaspers are telling about it. Many mystics have had the breakdown of the conventional mind and become possessed of this more inclusive and powerfully integrative capacity.

Albert Camus has said, "man has not been endowed with a definitive nature . . . is not a finished creation but an experiment of which he can be partly the creator." [2] The same idea has been expressed by Nietzsche, Paul Sartre, G. B. Shaw, Hegel, Karl Marx, Arnold Toynbee, and others. When Paul Tillich talks about the "New Being" he seems to be referring to something like this. These men do not agree on the kind of transformation which will bring man to the kind of being which he must become if he is to be saved from degradation or destruction; nor do they agree on the procedures to be followed to this end. But that man is not complete, that he is in process of being created, that he must be further transformed before he can attain his definitive nature, on this crucial issue they are all agreed.

The transformation under consideration is a reorganization of the unconscious structures of the mind such that sources of experience can reach awareness which are profoundly satisfying even though they are integrated with what causes dread and acute anxiety when this integration is lacking. The wholeness of this experience neutralizes what was previously not endurable. "The Whole Idea" is the term used by Hocking to designate this wholeness of experience. [3] Karl Jaspers calls it "The Comprehensive." Martin Buber describes it as the I-Thou experience. Zen Buddhism gives it the name of *satori*. Many Western mystics simply call it "God" in human experience.

This reorganization of the conscious and unconscious levels of the human being is the greatest good to be sought because [1] it is triumphant over the dark realities, [2] it enables one to act effectively under the guidance of reliable intuitions, [3] it unifies the self so that all the resources of his life can be brought into action, [4] it satisfies the wholeness of his being as nothing else can do.

The goal of personal commitment is to bring about this creative transformation of the self and like transformation in others. This way of dealing with dark realities, including death, is interpreted by a dream which was related to me. A woman in close and loving attachment to her husband comes to understand him intuitively in ways she cannot describe. The understanding may be so profound that it cannot come clearly to consciousness but may manifest itself in a dream. So it was in this case. The dream she related was this. She dreamed that her husband was about to die. When he was to die he was somehow put into a boat and drifted out to sea. Later, after he died, the boat drifted back with his body. When she found him lying dead in the boat she began to grieve that she had not gone with him so that they might have been together at the last. But then in her dream she seemed to remember that he had a way of meeting things like that alone. Immediately she ceased to grieve over his loneliness when he died. She kissed him many times and found that his lips were still a little warm. But she did not sorrow any more. For she knew that he had a way of meeting things like that alone.

This dream is a symbolic representation of a way of life wherein the ultimate situations no longer devastate. Some evils can be corrected and controlled by human effort. But death, inescapable guilt, unforeseen catastrophe, and some forms of failure, in sum, our finitude, cannot be corrected by human effort. These must be surmounted by a reorganization of the human psyche. They are not surmounted in the sense of being eliminated or avoided but in the sense of being integrated into the rest of all that human beings can experience when deceptive and evasive devices no longer restrict and distort the fulness of what can reach the conscious and unconscious levels of response. The blessedness of this way of life is such that one can welcome the dark realities in their capacity of bringing about this reorganization of the total psyche. These dark realities are not good in themselves; but when the full recognition of them leads men to the more abundant and masterful life wherein creativity dominates over counter processes, then these dark realities in this relation and when serving this function take on a positive value of their own.

The dark realities do not necessarily bring about the transformation. They will not unless in such a time of darkness one casts himself by practices of religious commitment into the depth and keeping of whatever in reality sustains, transforms, and renews. This must be done, however, without illusion. One must recognize that he is casting himself in the wholeness of his being into the power and into the keeping of what not only sustains and creatively transforms but which also destroys. That to which he thus gives himself in loving and unqualified devotion produces the suffering of Job, the dread of Kierkegaard, and the transvaluation of all values announced by Nietzsche. But in this way all the resources of the total self are released for constructive action; all the depth and fulness of experience to the limit of human capacity is apprehended, integrated, and endowed with meaning. The consequent richness and depth of appreciative awareness satisfies more completely than anything else can do. Prior to this reorganization and restored wholeness, enjoyments, no matter how intense, could satisfy only parts of the total self while other parts were suppressed and frustrated.

This reorganization and unification of the total self, involving a prior breakdown of the conventional mind, may be illuminated by a quotation from Karl Jaspers.

> Crucial for man is his attitude toward failure: Whether it remains hidden from him and overwhelms him only objectively at the end or whether he perceives it unobscured as the constant limit of his existence; whether he snatches at fantastic solutions and consolations or faces it honestly, in silence before the unfathomable. The way in which man approaches

his failure determines what he will become. In ultimate situations man either perceives nothingness or senses true being in spite of and above all ephemeral worldly existence.[4]

Another quotation from Jaspers may further develop his meaning.

When we face only concrete situations and master them for our profit, we react to them by planning and acting in the world, under the impulsion of our practical interests. But to ultimate situations we react either by obfuscation or, if we really apprehend them, by despair and rebirth; we become ourselves by a change in our consciousness of being.[5]

The "despair" mentioned by Jaspers is the breakdown of the conventional mind; the "rebirth" is the reorganization and unification of the total self, which we have been describing. We "become ourselves," i.e., attain wholeness of the self, by "a change in our consciousness of being" because we no longer exclude from consciousness nor distort with phantasy the most important realities with which we deal.

This completes what answer we are able to offer to the question: What can the individual do to identify himself with the most important reality which touches the life of man, namely the creative transformation which works through history and which enters the life of every individual to be accepted or rejected, to be served or ignored, to become the passion of one's life or a theory rumored? To accept and serve it and be caught into the keeping of its power two things can be done: Recognize the moral predicament of man which is my own predicament; practice personal commitment by choosing a kind of work that can be a vocation, by committing to this creativity my guilt and failures as well as my virtue and success, by persistent and intensive practice of the methods of commitment, by understanding what calls for this ultimate commitment and what is involved in it.

AFTER THIS account of what the individual can do for himself and for humanity, we turn again to a brief study of history. What the individual can do attains its full significance only when seen in the context of history; his action takes on full magnitude of meaning when it is caught up into a movement continuous with the major creative transformations of human existence occurring in the past and pointing to the possibility of higher levels of creativity in the future. The study of history begun in the last chapter is here continued to see if action by the individual of the sort we have been describing can have this connection with the past and with the future of human life.

The meaning of history as here interpreted can be briefly stated. It is the creation of man by way of a series of transformations which are not yet complete. A series of new creations, the first occurring long before civilization arose, reveals the significance of the time in which we live and the task demanded of us if a culminating outcome of these earlier developments is to occur. The decision required of us is to undertake this task by way of the procedures described in recognizing our moral predicament and in practice of personal commitment.

Man is a creature and creator of history because of his unique capacity to undergo transformation, psychological, social, cultural, and historical, by the sharing, the accumulation, the integration, and the expanding of all the dimensions of meaning which signs can carry. These dimensions can be variously analyzed and classified. The following classification of the dimensions of meaning which signs can carry is neither exhaustive nor are the divisions mutually exclusive. But the list serves to indicate the scope and variety of human experience which can come under the head of "meaning" as the term is here used. Indeed there is no experience distinctively human which is not the meaning of signs in some one or more of these dimensions of meaning.

There is a cognitive dimension of meaning called knowledge. There is the technological dimension by which men exercise power of control. In the aesthetic dimension we experience diversity of qualities in vivifying contrast, both of sense and of feeling; but the most compelling are those of feeling. The formal dimension appears in logic, mathematics, and the syntax of language. The interpersonal dimension of meaning enables us to understand evaluatively the unique individuality of the experience of associates. The adumbrative dimension is our awareness of the possibility of meaning in some area where creativity has not yet produced a structure sufficiently defined to apprehend it, but where some meaning is foreshadowed by intimations. Myth and some other symbols convey this adumbrative dimension. It is of utmost importance since it is sometimes the growing edge where wider dimensions of meaning are being created in the life of the individual and in the developments of human history.

Finally there is the dimension of meaning which yields self-consciousness and self-knowledge. In this dimension the individual turns the meaning of signs he uses back upon himself to search the structure and quality of his own selfhood.

History is the creation through a sequence of generations of these dimensions of meaning, namely, the cognitive, the technological, the aesthetic, the formal, the interpersonal, the adumbrative, and the self-conscious. Obstructions to this creation of meaning are institutional, interpersonal, and also internal to the individual in forms we have been examining. These obstructions can become so obdurate that the meaning created in history through a series of generations may become less and less, leading into a period of cultural decline. Nevertheless, no matter how great the obstructions, there is always creation of meaning in the several dimensions. Otherwise the newborn infant could never become a bearer of history and culture and life at the level distinctively human would cease altogether, even though an anthropoid animal continued to exist, supposing that possible. Without creation of meaning in each generation, history and culture would come to an end. All the institutions, customs, traditions, and technology, not to speak of the language and the religion which make up a culture, are sustained by signs which convey meaning to the people who live by them. Apart from such signs and their meanings there is no institution, no custom, no tradition, no technology, no language, morals, religion, or art. Therefore history can be defined as the creation, accumulation, and integration of meanings in all their dimensions. More simply stated history is the process which makes human life meaningful to whatsoever measure it can have meaning. When required conditions are present, history makes human life progressively meaningful. Individuals through interchange with one another in a sequence of generations and through internal, unconscious integration within each individual of what he gets from others, acquire a language and other products of the past by which they are able to find in what they do a more comprehensive purpose; are able to find in what they think a more inclusive understanding; are able to find in what they feel more abundance of aesthetic quality; are able to find in what they love more appreciative understanding of diverse individuals and peoples; are able to find in the exercise of their freedom more control over the conditions of existence.

Obstruction to creation of meaning and destruction to created meaning without service to further creation are developments which occur more or less continuously throughout history. To the measure that such obstruction and destruction prevail, they destroy history. That is to say, history occurs only because meanings have been created and accumulated in such a way that people now living are sustained, empowered, and enriched by what the past has done. Therefore everything which obstructs and reduces this endowment of the present by the past does at the same time obstruct and reduce the very thing which sustains history in being. If such obstructions and destructions should prevail, there would be no history. Consequently, everything in history which obstructs and destroys the creation and accumulation and integration of meanings from one generation to another can be described as that in history which tends to destroy history itself. So we reach the conclusion: If "meaning of history" refers to what creates and sustains history in being, then the meaning of history is the progressive creation and integration of meanings in all the dimensions of meaning. More briefly stated, the meaning of history is the creation of meaning; and this is identical with the creation of man, as yet incomplete.

If this is a true interpretation of history, there is a task to be done in our time more imperative than any other. It could not be done until a series of creative transformations occurring in past ages had established the required conditions. Now it can be done. More than that it must be done, because the past has reared, so to speak, an arch lacking only the keystone at the top. If this keystone is not put in, the entire structure will fall.

Most simply stated this task is to bring creativity to a level of dominance in the institutional and everyday affairs of life in a way never before attained. This does not mean utopia. It does not mean that creativity will dominate in every life nor in all areas of life. It does not mean to deny that some individuals in the past may have undergone more radical transformation than can occur today. It does not mean that great individual achievements of creative power in other times will be surpassed. All this may or may not happen. But all this is not the claim here made. The claim is that civilization cannot continue, that degeneration or destruction will set in, if creative interchange and individual integration of meanings are not sustained in wide areas of life by appropriate modification of institutions and appropriate practice of commitment on the part of individuals, even though these individuals be a minority, as perhaps will always be the case. This is the peculiar vocation of our time, given to it by the developments of the past.

We have reached a point in human history where interdependence has become so intimate and so coercive between different regions, social levels, and areas of experience that interchange and integration of meanings must occur more pervasively throughout the expanse of human life if the story of man is to continue. This vocation and imperative of our time will be more clearly manifest if we trace the four great creative transformations which have occurred in human life, with a fifth now imminent. The fifth is imminent not in the sense that it will inevitably occur but in the sense that it is more imperatively needed than ever before and in the further sense that the prevailing state of human society makes it possible of attainment as it was not in other times.

The first of the five transformations occurred prior to the rise of the first civilization. It was brought about during the million of years more or less when men lived in what is called primitive society. It was the creation of the kind of organism peculiar to homo sapiens, which is the only kind on this planet capable of extensive creative interchange and integration of meanings. Not only was the required kind of organism brought into existence during this period but also language and other symbols which are the necessary media in which the life distinctively human can be sustained and progressively created.

The second innovation which established a further condition necessary for the indefinite creation of meaning and the progressive creation of man was civilization. With civilization came writing which extends the range of time and space over which interchange and accumulation of meaning can occur. Human memory is limited but the writing on tablets, parchments, and pages is not. Also with civilization came that kind of social organization which can increase indefinitely the diversity of individuals and peoples engaged in interchange with one another. These two conjointly were brought into human life ،with civilization. Writing opened the way for the indefinite increase, accumulation, and integration of meanings. Social organization centered in the city opened the way for indefinite increase in the diversity of participants contributing to the creativity of history by interchange with one another.

A third condition necessary for the creative transformation of man toward the level of being which he may become emerged in what Karl Jaspers calls the axial period between 800 B.C. and 200 B.C.[6]

Groups of individuals widely scattered over the planet during this period underwent a creative transformation of the psyche which made them aware of man's capacity for transformation beyond any known limit, both toward greater good and toward greater evil. Man can become better and he can become worse beyond what any person at any one time can imagine except by way of the adumbrative dimension of meaning. This is to say, one can know that there are possibilities for good and evil, the specific form of which he cannot know; and he can know that they reach into depths of horror and heights of blessedness, although he cannot imagine the specific form and content which these experiences might take. The discovery that human life has this reach into infinity in the form of these unexplored and un-actualized possibilities is what occurred in the axial period.

In Israel the Hebrew prophets, in Persia Zoroaster and his followers, in Greece the tragedians and philosophers, in India Buddha and his followers, in China Confucius and Laotzu, opened up to human life what has been called the "vertical dimension" involved in our existence. It has also been called the transcendent or transcendental realm of being or the "all Encompassing" or "Being as such" or "the Absolute." It has been mythically repre-sented as the supernatural. It has been called "the Infinite" and "the Comprehensive."

All the great religions which seek to be universal and infinite in their outreach originated at this time, if we recognize that Chris-tianity and Mohammedanism were outgrowths of what the He-brew prophets accomplished.

The axial period, including whatever has come from Jesus Christ and the early Christians, did not complete the work of establishing the conditions which must be present for creativity to operate widely and securely throughout human life. Two other conditions must be added. One of these is now being produced by the twentieth century. A technology must be created capable of providing all men with the utilities and environmental condi-tions needed to undergo creative transformation indefinitely be-yond the present state of human existence. Such a technology carries with it a system of communication and interdependence reaching all people on the planet. This magnified power of con-trol and this world wide interdependence can bring on great evils and can reduce creativity to a minimum. In many cases such has been the consequence and it will continue to be so, with greater evils yet to come, unless a fifth condition is added to this fourth. On the other hand this magnified power to produce goods, to organize, to administer, and to communicate, are indispensable to the end of enabling all people to contribute to, and to par-ticipate in, the creative transformation of human life.

This brings us to the fifth condition. This is what our period during the next two or three hundred years must bring forth.

Without this further condition the four we have mentioned will not issue in man's creative transformation to any high degree but will rather bring on his degradation if not his annihilation. Every one of the four conditions mentioned has increased the evils of life enormously while at the same time opening the way to a great increase in human good. In some cases this increase has been attained but the fullest attainment of human good can never be reached and secured until the fifth condition has been established.

The fifth condition is what we have been describing throughout this writing. It is change of institutions and action of individuals resulting from recognition of the moral predicament of man and from practice of personal commitment. It is a change in institutions and action of individuals which will bring into the lives of many people that higher dominance of creativity which in the past has occurred only in the lives of a few. This is not only our vocation and opportunity. It is a demand forced by a peril hanging over us more deadly than ever before threatened the whole of humanity at once. This peril may never cease to threaten so long as civilization continues. But it may be mastered by turning it into a servant of man's creative transformation. The stick and the carrot have always been necessary for any marked change for the better in human life. The devil and the angel, the peril and the hope, we must have them both if life is ever to rise to greatness.

Repeatedly we have pointed to the dark realities without which human life sinks to a low level of triviality and perversity. When wrongly treated they drive men to greater evil. When rightly treated they drive him to creative transformation. The peril which hangs over us now is another example of the same. We may never master it by making it a servant of creative transformation. Rather it will master us unless we change our institutions and act under the guidance of those intuitions which arise when we recognize our moral predicament and rightly practice religious commitment. It should be further added that the peril peculiar to our time is common to all humanity, not limited to one region or class or people or particular individuals.

We are all equally threatened by it and it requires the united action of all to deal with it effectively. In time this should draw all men into closer bonds of fellowship. Common danger seems to have more uniting power than common good.

The secure establishment of all five of the over-all conditions needed for the fullest measure of creative interchange and integration of meanings will not bring man's work and responsibility to an end. Exactly the opposite is true. Only after these conditions have been established will men be able to provide the ever-changing, detailed and local conditions required for this creativity in the family, in the neighborhood, between members in the industrial plant and in the classroom, between the various specialized kinds of work and research, between political units and cultures, and elsewhere throughout the multiform existence of humanity. Men may not live up to this responsibility. Certainly they will not do it perfectly. But after the five conditions prevail, men will have this responsibility because they will then have the power to meet the demands of creativity as they could not previous to the establishment of these over-all conditions.

Human history has scarcely yet begun. Millions of years have yet to run. Man is yet to be created in the fulness of his being. No form of life, so far as we know, has ever been the carrier of this creativity of history. Surely this is a destiny immeasurably beyond any other in the grandeur and tragedy of what has happened and in the glory of its possibilities. Each individual by proper action can become a participant in this grandeur, in this tragedy, and in this glory. To undertake such action is the decision required of us.

I HAVE explained what I mean by creative and transforming power. I mean two things: [1] interchange which creates appreciative understanding of unique individuality; [2] integration within each individual of what he gets from others in this way, thus progressively creating his own personality in power, knowledge, and capacity to appreciate more profoundly diverse individuals, peoples, and things.

I know that I cannot be in error in holding the belief that I am

at least partially in error concerning the character of the reality
to which I am ultimately committed. Hence I know with certainty that I am ultimately given to what is more than, and in
some respects different from, everything affirmed in this book.
With this triumph over error I make my last commitment: I cast
my error, my failure, and my guilt into the keeping of creative and
transforming power.

CHAPTER ONE

1. Harry Stack Sullivan, *The Interpersonal Theory of Psychiatry* (New York: Norton, 1953), pp. 261–62 and 290–91.

2. David Riesman, Nathan Glazer, and Reuel Denny, *The Lonely Crowd* (New York: Doubleday Anchor Book, 1953).

3. Many Christians and great theologians have claimed that the child at birth is infected with sin. Examination of the situation out of which this claim arises shows that it is unwarranted. In comparison with other animals the child of human parents is prematurely born. It is not yet distinctively human. But the influence of the parents and other nurturing adults begins to influence the development of the child from the very beginning. Since these adults are themselves infected with sin they transmit it to the child by shaping the course of the child's development while the infant is still entirely helpless under their manipulation. As the child develops, the adults find the consequences of their own sin transmitted to the child. When the adults deny their responsibility in this by insisting that the child was infected with sin at birth, they are themselves revealing their own sin in this most vicious form is in that part of oneself which one will not admit is a part of himself because it is so humiliating or otherwise unacceptable to his own idea of himself. This deepest and darkest level of sin is expressing itself when parents say that the sin they find in the child is born in him rather than being transmitted to him by the parents themselves.

CHAPTER TWO

1. Virgil Jordan, *Manifesto for the Atomic Age* (New Brunswick, N.J.: Rutgers University Press, 1946), pp. 42–44.

2. David Riesman, *et al., op cit.*

3. Robert Jungk, *Tomorrow Is Already Here* (New York: Simon and Schuster, 1954).

4. *Ibid.*

CHAPTER THREE

1. Henry N. Wieman, *The Source of Human Good* (Chicago: The University of Chicago Press, 1946).

CHAPTER FIVE

1. Harry Stack Sullivan, *op. cit.*

2. See George Caspar Homans, *The Human Group* (New York: Harcourt, 1950). This is only one of many studies which support the claim here made.

3. See Paul Tillich, *The Courage To Be* (New Haven, Conn.: Yale University Press, 1952) and other writings by him.

4. Harry Stack Sullivan, *op. cit., passim.*

5. E. A. Burtt, "The Value Presuppositions of Science," *The Bulletin of the Atomic Scientists,* XIII (1957), 99–106.

CHAPTER SIX

1. The word "favor" covers "approve," but "approve" emphasizes one's judgment on the interests of other people and is added for the sake of this emphasis.

2. Ralph Barton Perry, *General Theory of Value* (New York: Longmans, 1926) and *Realms of Value* (Cambridge, Mass.: Harvard University Press, 1954).

3. Ian McGreal, *The Art of Making Choices* (Dallas, Tex.: Southern Methodist University Press, 1953).

4. *Ibid.,* p. 37.

5. Paul Tillich, *Love, Power and Justice* (London and New York: Oxford, 1954); see also his *Systematic Theology* in which both the existence and the personality of God are denied although God defined

as "being-as-such" is affirmed (2 vols.; Chicago: The University of Chicago Press, 1951), I, 204–89. The last chapter of Tillich's *The Courage To Be* contains the same denial and the same affirmation about God.

6.   Paul Tillich, *Love, Power and Justice.*

7.   *Ibid.*, p. 23.

8.   *Ibid.*, pp. 38–39.

9.   Tillich insists that power of being participates more fully in man than in dogs and trees. He cannot consistently say this because he defines power of being as the common ground which sustains every existing thing. Therefore power of being cannot be identified with any one form of existence more than another. He says that power of being is love. But he defines love as striving to reunite over a separation and denies that union without separation is love. In power of being there is no separation to be overcome. To be sure, Tillich says that power of being is love only in a symbolic sense and so can be denied even when affirmed. But this makes power of being a grab bag out of which you can get anything you like combined with its contradictory. To dignify this by calling it a mystery hardly helps at all. Rather it makes this mystery seem like a magician's trick.

10.   Paul Tillich, *Love, Power and Justice,* p. 76.

11.   For a penetrating criticism of this defect in the teaching of the existentialists, combined with profound appreciation of the value of their teaching, see John Wild, *The Challenge of Existentialism* (Bloomington, Ind.: Indiana University Press, 1955).

CHAPTER SEVEN

1.   This lecture has been published in *Man's Right to Knowledge, First Series: Tradition and Change* (New York: Columbia University Press, 1954).

2.   *Ibid.*, p. 13.

3.   Raphael Demos and C. J. Ducasse, "Are Religious Dogmas Cognitive and Meaningful?" in *Academic Freedom, Logic and Religion,* ed. Morton White (London: Oxford, 1954), pp. 95–96.

4.   *Ibid.*, p. 96.

5.   Reinhold Niebuhr, *The Nature and Destiny of Man: A Christian Interpretation* (2 vols.; New York: Scribner, 1947), I, 165–66.

6.   See E. A. Burtt, *op. cit.*

CHAPTER EIGHT

1. Martin Niemoeller, "The Impossible Existence," *The Divinity School News* (Chicago: The Divinity School of The University of Chicago, 1957), XXIV, 2–5 *passim.*

CHAPTER NINE

1. See Educational Policies Commission, *Moral and Spiritual Values in the Public Schools* (Washington, D.C.: National Education Association of the United States, 1951)

CHAPTER TEN

1. Peter Drucker, *The Practice of Management* (New York: Harper, 1954); also, by the same author, *The New Society* (New York: Harper, 1950). Adolf A. Berle is saying the same thing as well as other experts in the field.
2. See books above cited by Peter Drucker and books by Adolf A. Berle.
3. See *The New Society* and *The Practice of Management* both by Peter Drucker.

CHAPTER ELEVEN

1. See Ernst Cassirer, *The Myth of the State* (New Haven, Conn.: Yale University Press, 1946).
2. See Hans Kohn, *The Idea of Nationalism, A Study in Its Origin and Background* (New York: Macmillan, 1944); also Fredrick L. Schumann, *International Politics, The Western State System in Mid-Century* (New York: McGraw, 1953) and the book by Cassirer named above.
3. See the last two chapters of this book.
4. Barbara Ward, "One Answer to the Challenge of Africa," *New York Times Magazine*, October 31, 1954, p. 57.
5. Richard McKeon (ed.), *Democracy in a World of Tensions: A Symposium Prepared by UNESCO* (Paris, 1951), p. 527.
6. See M. L. Barron, "Society is the Delinquent," *The Nation*, CLXXVIII (1954), 482–84; also Mr. Barron's *The Juvenile in Delinquent Society* (New York: Knopf, 1954), and a report of the subcommittee headed by Senator Robert C. Hendrickson, *Juvenile Delin-*

quency (83d Cong., 1st sess.; Senate Report 170. [Washington, D.C.: Government Printing Office, 1953]).

CHAPTER TWELVE

1.   The theme of Seidenberg's book is that organization demands more organization with the consequence that organization will become so comprehensive and restrictive as to reduce the significance of individual personality toward the vanishing point. *Posthistoric Man* (Chapel Hill, N.C.: University of North Carolina Press, 1950), pp. 234–38.

2.   Lawrence S. Kubie, M.D., "The Forgotten Man of Education," *Harvard Alumni Bulletin,* February 6, 1954.

3.   Harrison Brown, *The Challenge of Man's Future: An Inquiry Concerning the Condition of Man During the Years That Lie Ahead* (New York: Viking Press, Inc., 1954). In writing this book, Mr. Brown has had the advice and co-operation of many specialists of high competence in the several fields discussed. So far as I have been able to discover, his treatment of these problems is considered by reliable critics to be as authoritative as anything in this area of inquiry can be. All statements made by the author are guarded, cautious, and documented and have been subjected to critical review by several highly trained men in specialized fields. However, we are using the book not as a final authority but as a device for looking into the future as far as we are able with the help of competent persons.

4.   *Ibid.,* pp. 220–21.

5.   *Ibid.,* pp. 246–47.

CHAPTER THIRTEEN

1.   See Chapter 4 for interpretation of past and present in human experience.

2.   Karl Jaspers, *The Origin and Goal of History* (New Haven, Conn.: Yale University Press, 1953).

CHAPTER FOURTEEN

1.   Fëdor Dostoevsky, *The Best Short Stories of Dostoevsky,* trans. David Magarshack ("The Modern Library"—New York: Random House, Inc., 1955), pp. 121 and 140.

2.   Albert Camus, *The Rebel* (New York: Knopf, 1954), p. 106.

3. William Ernest Hocking, *The Meaning of God in Human Experience* (New Haven, Conn.: Yale University Press, 1912), *passim*.
4. Karl Jaspers, *The Way to Wisdom* (New Haven, Conn.: Yale University Press, 1954), p. 23.
5. *Ibid.*, p. 20.
6. Karl Jaspers, *The Origin and Goal of History*.

INDEX

INDEX

315